Employment Law in the UK
A Practical Guide for Managers and Supervisors

GW00601809

Employment Law in the UK

A Practical Guide for Managers and Supervisors

LYNDA MACDONALD

BLACKHALL
Publishing

This book was typeset by Gough Typesetting Services for
Blackhall Publishing
26 Eustace Street
Dublin 2
Ireland
e-mail: blackhall@tinet.ie

ISBN: 1 901657 62 0

A catalogue record for this book is available from the British Library.

Printed in Ireland by
Betaprint Ltd.

ABOUT THE AUTHOR

Lynda A C Macdonald is a self-employed, freelance employment law specialist, management trainer and writer. For fifteen years, prior to setting up her own consultancy business, she gained substantial practical experience of employee relations, recruitment and selection, dismissal procedures, employment law and other aspects of human resource management through working in industry. With this solid background in human resource management, she successfully established, and currently runs, her own business in management training, and employment law/human resource management consultancy. She is also appointed as a panel member of the Employment Tribunal service in Aberdeen, where she lives.

Lynda is a university graduate in language and a Fellow of the Institute of Personnel and Development, as well as having a post-graduate qualification in employment law and practice.

Lynda can be contacted at:

1 Whitelands Road
Newtonhill
Aberdeen
AB39 3TR
Scotland

Tel./Fax: 01569 730277

TABLE OF CONTENTS

CHAPTER ONE

CONTRACTS OF EMPLOYMENT

The relationship between an employer and an employee is governed by the terms and conditions contained within their contract of employment. A contract of employment comes into existence as soon as a firm offer of employment has been made and the individual has accepted it. Thus a contract of employment can exist whether or not anything has been put in writing and the absence of any written documentation does not mean that the employee has no employment rights. The law does stipulate, however, that certain terms of employment must be put in writing, and this is known as a 'written statement of particulars of employment' (see later in this chapter under 'Terms of the Contract which must be in Writing').

For a contract of employment to exist, there must be an agreement between the employer and the employee and once agreement has been reached on the terms they are legally binding on both parties.

FORMS OF CONTRACT

An individual may be engaged on a full-time permanent contract or on the basis of some other arrangement. The following sections aim to provide an overview of the different forms of contract which may exist and the key features of each.

Open-ended (Permanent) Employment Contracts

The so-called 'permanent' contract is the traditional form of employment and is still the most common type of working arrangement in most organisations. Permanent contracts are of no fixed duration, and both parties may expect the engagement to last for an indefinite period of time until one or other of the parties gives notice to terminate.

Part-time Workers

Employees who are engaged on a part-time basis have the same statutory rights as full-time workers. This is the case irrespective of the number of hours the person works in a week or month. This has been the case since the implementation of the Employment Protection (Part-time Employees)

Regulations 1995. Statutory rights which part-timers enjoy include (for example) maternity rights, the right to claim unfair dismissal, the right to a redundancy payment and the right to statutory holidays.

Furthermore, since in the UK the majority of part-time employees are women, it can be discriminatory to treat part-timers less favourably than full-time employees in relation to pay and other contractual terms of employment. It is, therefore, advisable to ensure that part-time employees are afforded equal pay (on a pro rata basis), equal pension rights, equal entitlement to company sick pay, etc.

Additionally, there are proposals in the pipeline based on an EC Directive, the aim of which is to provide equal contractual rights to part-time employees, in terms of pay and benefits and to encourage a positive attitude towards part-time working. It is likely that this Directive will be implemented in the UK in the year 2000.

Temporary Employment Contracts

Many employers like to engage workers on temporary contracts because they offer a number of advantages.

1. They allow the employer considerable flexibility which can be important where uncertainty exists as to whether there is a longer term need for a particular job.

2. The allow the employer to assess an employee's suitability and competence in the job, before making a longer term commitment.

3. They allow the company to employ people for one-off tasks or projects.

4. They are useful to cater for seasonal fluctuations in a company's workload.

5. Their use may achieve a reduction in overtime at premium rates.

6. They can be used for holiday and sickness absence cover.

The significance of a temporary employment contract is that many employment rights depend on a minimum period of continuous service. For example the right to claim unfair dismissal at an employment tribunal depends on the individual having a minimum of two years' continuous service, the right to statutory maternity pay requires the individual to have six months' service and the right to paid statutory holidays clicks in after three months' service. Thus, temporary employees engaged on a single contract may not gain sufficient length of service to receive certain statutory entitlements.

Other rights, however, such as the right not to be discriminated against on the grounds of sex, race or disability, and health and safety rights, exist from the employee's first day of employment.

It is important to note that an employee engaged on a temporary or fixed-term contract (or a series of temporary contracts which run consecutively) may, depending on the length of their continuous employment, still gain certain statutory employment rights. The fact that a person is engaged on a series of short-term contracts does not deprive him of such rights provided the contracts run consecutively thus allowing him to accrue continuous service.

Temporary workers engaged from an employment agency are dealt with separately below under 'Employing Agency Workers'.

Fixed-term Contracts

A fixed-term contract is a temporary contract in which there is a specified start date and a defined termination date on which the contract will expire automatically. It is the existence of a defined termination date which makes the contract fixed-term. A fixed-term contract can be of any duration agreed between the employer and the employee and can be extended or renewed upon expiry of the fixed-term, if both parties agree.

A fixed-term contract would normally give the employee the right to continued employment for the whole of the fixed-term and thus create an obligation on the employer to continue to employ the person until the expiry date defined in the contract. Early termination would constitute a breach of contract entitling the employee to raise a claim for damages in a court or employment tribunal. This could be a key disadvantage from the employer's point of view in that there is no opportunity to terminate the contract prior to the expiry date (unless the employee commits an act of gross misconduct).

This disadvantage can be eliminated, however, by inserting notice clauses into the fixed-term contract. It may seem inconsistent to describe a contract as being of a defined term and, at the same time, structure it so that it can be terminated early, but there is nothing unlawful in such a course of action and the notice clauses would provide the employer with additional flexibility.

Despite the agreement at the outset that a fixed-term contract will expire automatically on the nominated date, the expiry of a fixed-term contract without renewal constitutes a dismissal in law. In all likelihood the dismissal would be fair, unless the employer acted in some way unreasonably in refusing to renew the contract. To guard against this, the employer should seek, before the contract expires, to identify whether there is any alternative work available which the employee could be offered either on the basis of another fixed-term contract or on a permanent basis.

Waiver Clauses in Fixed-term Contracts

One feature which distinguishes a fixed-term contract from any other form of contract is the ability of the employer to introduce 'waiver clauses' into the contract. A waiver clause is designed to exclude the employee from unfair

dismissal or redundancy pay rights on expiry of the contract on the date specified without renewal. However, strict rules are in place governing the legiti-
macy of waiver clauses, and these rules differ according to whether the waiver
clause is intended to exclude unfair dismissal rights or redundancy pay rights.

In order for a waiver clause exempting the employee from the right to
claim unfair dismissal to be valid, the fixed-term contract must be for at least
one year, whilst for a redundancy pay waiver clause to be enforceable, the
fixed-term must be for at least two years. Thus fixed-term contracts for a short
period, for example six months, cannot contain waiver clauses and if waiver
clauses are nevertheless incorporated in the contracts, they will be unenforceable. It is important also to note that waiver clauses are valid only on expiry of
the contract on the due date and not on the occasion of the early termination
of the contract.

When a fixed-term contract (which was for a year or more and which
contained a valid waiver clause excluding the employee from claiming unfair
dismissal) is extended, the waiver clause may be extended along with the
contract. For this to be valid, there must be a clear written agreement to this
effect. If, however, the renewal of the contract in reality constitutes a completely new contract on different terms and conditions (as opposed to an extension of the original contract), then the new contract itself must be for at
least one year if the unfair dismissal waiver clause is to be valid.

For redundancy pay waiver clauses, any extension or renewal of the fixed-
term contract can contain a valid waiver clause, provided the original contract
was for at least two years, and provided it contained a waiver clause excluding the employee from claiming redundancy pay on the expiry of the contract.

Further information relevant to employees' rights when they are engaged
on a series of fixed-term contracts, is contained in Chapter 2 'Continuity of
Service'.

Employing Agency Workers

Where a manager engages workers via an employment agency, the workers
would not normally be deemed to be employed by the client company on a
contract of employment. The client company's contract is with the agency
rather than with the worker.

The employment agency itself, however, may be deemed to be the person's employer for the purposes of statutory employment rights, and the law
in this area is still developing.

Although employment agencies are required, in law, to deduct income
tax and national insurance payments from their workers' earnings, that, in
itself, does not support the contention that the worker is employed by the
agency for the purpose of statutory rights. Often the contracts of individuals
working through an employment agency are not typical of traditional contracts of employment. For example, the agency would not normally control

the day to day duties and activities of the workers nor adopt responsibility for supplying them with the tools and equipment (for example a computer) to do the job.

Nevertheless in 1998 the Court of Appeal held (in the case of *McMeechan v. Secretary of State for Employment* [1997] I.R.L.R. 353) that two separate relationships existed between the worker and the agency. The first of these was the relationship which existed as a result of the worker simply being registered on the agency's books without actually being engaged on a specific contract with a client. During such times no contract of employment existed because there was no obligation on the agency to offer work, nor was there any obligation on the part of the worker to accept work if it was offered.

By contrast, however, the Court of Appeal found that, despite the absence of a 'global' or 'umbrella' employment contract, there could be a contract of employment in place for the duration of a specific engagement with a client company. In *McMeechan*, there were specific terms which indicated the existence of a contract of employment between the worker and the agency during periods when the individual was working.

This does not mean that an agency worker will always be the employee of the agency through whom they work, but rather that they may be deemed to be employed under a contract of employment, depending on the terms of the specific engagement. It is therefore in the interests of the agency to ensure that the contractual agreements they put in place, governing the relationship with their workers, are clearly drafted and that they reflect accurately the working relationship between them. In particular, to ensure protection from claims of employment status, it should be stated that there is no obligation on the agency to provide work, nor on the individual to accept, work where it is offered.

Employing Casual Workers

A casual worker is normally someone who is called in to work for an employer on an as required or intermittent basis and who is paid only for the hours worked. Casual workers are usually not entitled to any company benefits beyond a basic hourly rate of pay.

Casual workers may be used by a company for a variety of reasons:

(a) to cover fluctuating or unpredictable levels of work, for example in industries where the work is seasonal;

(b) to meet unexpected work demands;

(c) to perform short-term work, for example as waiting staff at functions held in a hotel;

(d) to avoid the commitments and obligations inherent in employment contracts.

The legal status of casual workers is presently unclear and whilst it was traditionally held that casual workers did not enjoy status as employees, and hence had no statutory employment rights, this notion has been cast into doubt in recent years.

The key factor in determining the status of a casual worker is whether or not there is a mutuality of obligation between the parties, i.e. whether the employer is obliged to provide a reasonable amount of work to the person, and whether the worker is obliged to accept work when it is offered by the employer. This mutuality of obligation is often completely absent in the working arrangements between a casual worker and an employer.

However, where it can be shown from the history of the working relationship that there is a reasonable degree of obligation on both parties to provide and accept work, then it could be argued that a contract of employment exists, thus entitling the worker to a wide range of employment rights and benefits. Where an individual challenges their employment status at tribunal, the tribunal would examine the actual working relationship between the parties (rather than the label the employer had put on the arrangements).

Case Study

Two workers were hired by the company, to conduct guided tours around power stations. The terms of their engagement stated that they were "employed on a casual, as required basis". The two worked part-time when work was offered to them, and were paid an hourly rate for hours worked only.

When the two challenged their employment status, the Court of Appeal held that there was an implied term in their contracts that the employer was obliged to give them a reasonable amount of work and that they were obliged to accept a reasonable amount of work. The Court of Appeal took the view that it was necessary to read this term into the contracts in order to make them workable.

Carmichael and Leese v. National Power plc, The Times, 2 April 1998.

Like the *McMeechan* case referred to in the previous section, *Carmichael* turned on whether there was a sufficient degree of mutuality of obligation between the parties for a contract of employment to exist. Clearly it is possible for a casual worker successfully to argue employment status if it can be shown that there is an obligation to provide, and accept, a reasonable amount of work. The argument that an employment contract exists would be even stronger if the casual worker was engaged on a regular pattern of hours, if the employer relied on the casual worker to work at specific times or if the worker had come to expect to attend work at predetermined times.

It is advisable for employers who regularly engage casual workers to:

(a) refrain from assuming that their casual workers are not employees;

(b) put a clearly worded written agreement in place defining the employment status of the casual workers;

(c) clarify to what extent, if any, there is an obligation on the employer to offer work and an obligation on the worker to accept work;

(d) keep detailed records of who is engaged, the dates of 'employment' and the occasions when work was offered but refused by the casual worker.

Zero-hours Contracts

A standard zero-hours (or 'nil-hours') contract is one whereby the employer does not guarantee to provide any minimum amount of work to the employee, but where the employee has agreed to undertake all work offered. With this type of contract, the employee is paid only for actual hours worked, hence it is akin to a situation in which casual workers are engaged on a regular basis.

Another type of zero-hours contract could be one under which the employer guaranteed to provide, and the employee agreed to accept, a minimum amount or a reasonable amount of work.

A zero-hours working arrangement does constitute a contract of employment in law because the contract is deemed to continue in force even when no work is available for the employee to do.

Zero-hours contracts are, in practice, very one-sided arrangements with all the control, and the flexibility benefits, accruing to the employer whilst the unfortunate employee lacks any guaranteed level of work or pay but remains bound to make themselves available to come to work, usually at short notice. This is, perhaps, not the most shrewd or rational way for an employer to encourage motivation or loyalty from his workers.

Homeworkers' Contracts

Individuals who work for an employer at home may be classed as either employed or self-employed in law. In one case (*Nethermere (St Neots) Ltd v. Gardiner and Another* [1984] I.R.L.R. 240), a court held that a long-standing relationship between homeworkers and the company for whom they worked had developed into a global contract of employment. This was because it was custom and practice for the company to provide work on a regular basis and for the workers to accept it, which had created a mutuality of obligation between the parties.

It is likely that a homeworker would be classed as an employee (and consequently entitled to the full range of statutory employment rights) where:

(a) there is mutuality of obligation regarding the offering and acceptance of a reasonable amount of work;

(b) the employer exercises close control and direction over the work, how it is done and the time-scales within which it must be done;

(c) the employer provides the necessary tools and/or equipment for the job;

(d) the worker works exclusively for one employer.

On the other hand a homeworker would be likely to be classed as self-employed where they:

(a) are in business on their own account;

(b) have freedom to turn down any work offered;

(c) carry out work for several different companies;

(d) own and use their own tools/equipment;

(e) are able to exercise a considerable degree of freedom as regards how the work should be carried out and how much work is done.

When setting out homeworking arrangements, the manager responsible should consider the following matters:

(a) how the work is to be managed and co-ordinated;

(b) how to manage the health and safety of the worker;

(c) what insurance needs to be taken out to cover the worker working from home;

(d) how quality standards will be monitored;

(e) how training requirements will be met;

(f) whether a minimum amount of work is, or set working hours are, to be prescribed;

(g) how work performance will be appraised;

(h) how communication links will be established and maintained, e.g. whether the homeworker should be obliged to attend the office at predetermined intervals.

Trainees and Apprentices

Although apprenticeship contracts have diminished in number over recent years, some companies are once again recognising the value of training young people in specialist skills leading to time-served tradesman status.

A contract of apprenticeship represents a different type of contract to a contract of employment in that it is a contract, often in the form of a deed, which:

(a) stipulates that training will be provided to the individual over a specified period of time;

(b) cannot contain notice clauses;

(c) cannot be lawfully terminated before the training has been completed;

(d) must be in writing.

If the employer terminates an apprenticeship contract before the training has been completed, this will constitute a breach of contract unless the termination is due to one of the following:

(a) an act of gross misconduct on the part of the apprentice;

(b) unreasonable refusal of the apprentice to fulfil their training or duties;

(c) inability of the apprentice to continue the training as result of illness/accident;

(d) the employer no longer being in a position to teach the apprentice the trade in question, for example if the business closes down.

In the event of a dismissal of an apprentice in breach of contract, it is likely that the apprentice would be able to claim compensation in respect of the unexpired portion of the apprenticeship contract and also potentially in respect of subsequent loss of wages.

Once the contract of apprenticeship is complete, the employer is not obliged to offer employment to the individual. Furthermore, the individual is not entitled to a statutory redundancy payment on termination of the apprenticeship contract.

Another type of contract for training is one through which an individual is taken on as part of a government-sponsored training scheme. This type of training contract is not regarded as a contract of employment, as the trainee is neither an employee of the training body nor of the company to which they are assigned. The only possibility of their being classed as an employee of the company would be if they performed paid duties in addition to, and outside the scope of, their training contract. The key feature of a contract for training is that it is established to provide the individual with training, whilst the provision of work for the employer is a secondary feature.

SOURCES OF A CONTRACT OF EMPLOYMENT

The terms in a contract of employment will derive from a number of sources. Over and above the many terms which are expressly agreed between employer and employee, there may be other terms which are implied into the contract.

An employee's entitlements under his contract of employment also derive from statutory provisions, whether or not reference is made to these within the contract itself. Employment rights which have been created by the passing of legislation, both in the UK and, where relevant, in the EU, are automatically incorporated into every individual employment contract. If there should be any inconsistency between the entitlements conferred on the employee by statute and the express terms of the contract, then the statutory terms will always take precedence. Thus employers cannot 'contract away' the rights of employees, which have been bestowed by legislation.

Express Terms

The express terms of the contract are those which are specifically agreed between the employer and the employee. Express terms may have been agreed verbally or in writing and, provided agreement has been reached, all express terms are legally binding. Since it is not a legal requirement for a contract of employment to be in writing, terms of the contract can exist as a result of a verbal agreement.

There must, however, be actual agreement between the parties in order for the terms of the contract to be enforceable. Terms or conditions which are imposed unilaterally by the employer will not be legally binding, unless the employee has accepted them.

Although it is not a legal requirement for a contract of employment to be in writing, certain terms must be put in writing. This is generally referred to as a 'written statement of particulars of employment' (see 'Terms of the Contract which must be in Writing'). The difference between a contract of employment and a written statement is essentially that the contract consists of *all* the terms which have been *agreed* between the parties (whether verbally or in writing), plus any implied terms, whereas the written statement is a summary of the key terms of employment which the employer believes form part of the contract, and which are *issued by the employer* with or without the express consent of the employee. The terms in the written statement are, in most instances, a true representation of the key terms of the contract, but unless the employee has agreed to them, they are not legally binding.

Implied Terms

Implied terms in a contract are terms about which there has been no express agreement but which, if challenged, would be presumed to have been the intention of the parties to the contract. If no express term exists to define a particular issue, and if an employee launches a challenge at tribunal, the tribunal may imply a term into the contract.

To do this, the tribunal will first examine the available evidence in order to establish whether they can make a finding of fact as to what terms were agreed between the parties. Then, if there is no evidence of any express term having been agreed, the tribunal will deal with the matter by implying a term into the contract according to what they believe the parties would have agreed if they had addressed the issue themselves.

Terms can be implied into a contract by various methods, namely:

(a) because they are necessary due to 'business efficacy' (this means that without the term the contract would be unworkable);

(b) as a result of the conduct of the parties (i.e. both employer and employee act as if the term was agreed);

(c) through custom and practice over a period of time;

(d) through common law (i.e. as a result of decisions made by senior courts or tribunals).

The main implied duties which have been implied into contracts of employment over the years as a result of common law are as follows.

1. **The duty to maintain trust and confidence within the employment relationship.** This means that the employer must not treat the employee in such a way as to make their continuing employment intolerable. Examples of a breach of the duty of trust and confidence could include severe bullying, victimisation, humiliating treatment, lack of support, enforcing discretionary policies in a high-handed, irrational or unreasonable manner, etc;

2. **The duty to provide reasonable support to employees to enable them to carry out their duties.** This would include the duty of the employer to take appropriate and reasonable steps to protect an employee who is being subjected to bullying or harassment.

3. **The duty to allow employees the opportunity to obtain redress for any grievance they may have in connection with their employment.** Employers should have in place a clear grievance procedure and afford the right to all employees to use it.

4. **The duty to provide a working environment which is reasonably suitable for employees to perform their work.** This term was implied by a tribunal in relation to an employee's right to work in a smoke-free environment.

5. **The duty to provide work.** This duty applies only in very limited circumstances, namely in cases where:

   (a) pay depends on the amount of work provided, for example 'piece work' and commission-only based employment;

   (b) lack of work could affect the competence or reputation of the individual, for example an actor;

    (c) lack of work over a period of time could lead to a deterioration of the employee's skills.

6.   **The duty to pay agreed wages.** The actual amount of wages to be paid is a matter for the contract itself to determine, subject to any minimum wage provisions laid down in statute.

7.   **The duty to compensate or reimburse employees for expenses and liabilities incurred in the course of their employment.**

8.   **The duty to take reasonable care of employees' health and safety.** In practice, this common law duty has been largely superseded by health and safety legislation. Managers may wish to note that this common law duty incorporates the duty to take care of employees' mental health – a factor becoming more prevalent in modern times as a result of workplace stress.

Terms will not be implied into a contract where a clearly defined express term exists covering the matter in question. This is because courts and employment tribunals are generally reluctant to interfere with contractual terms which have been freely agreed between the employer and the employee. Under normal circumstances, therefore, the express terms of a contract of employment take priority over implied terms.

It can happen, however, that a court or tribunal may impose an implied term to qualify or restrict how an express term should be applied by the employer.

Case Study

An example of this occurred in a case where the employer instructed an employee to move from Leeds to Birmingham under the terms of an express mobility clause in his contract. However, the employee was given less than a week's notice to relocate and was not offered any financial assistance under the company's discretionary relocation scheme. Even when he requested a 3-month postponement on account of his wife's illness, and to give him time to sell his house, the employer refused to co-operate. The employee resigned as a result of this intolerable situation and took a case to the employment appeal tribunal.

The EAT implied a term into the employee's contract that the employer should not exercise their express contractual right to relocate the employee to a different place of work in such a manner as to make it impossible for him to comply with their instructions. The way the employer had acted was judged to be a breach of the duty to maintain trust and confidence in the employment relationship.

United Bank v. Akhtar [1989] I.R.L.R. 507.

TERMS OF THE CONTRACT WHICH MUST BE IN WRITING

All employees are entitled to receive a written statement of the key terms and conditions of their employment within two months of starting work. This right applies to both full and part-time employees, provided the contract is to last more than one month. The information may be provided in instalments, provided all the particulars required by statute are given within two months.

This written statement of particulars of employment does not have to be presented in any predefined format or sequence, nor is it necessary for all the terms to be contained in the same document (although certain terms must be written into a single document known as a 'principal statement' – see below).

The terms which must be in writing are listed below.

1. **The names of the employer and the employee.**

2. **The date employment began, and whether any previous employment counts towards the employee's continuous service.** Previous employment may count towards continuous service where there has been a transfer of the business in which the employee works to another employer (see Chapter 12) or where the employee has moved from one company to an associated company.

3. **The scale or rate of pay and the pay intervals (e.g. weekly, monthly).**

4. **Any terms and conditions relating to hours of work.** This should include terms relating to normal working hours and any overtime requirements. There is, however, no need to specify exact hours of work (for example 9.00 am to 5.00 pm Monday to Friday) so long as the written statement makes it clear what the employee's obligations are. The clause governing hours may stipulate that the employee must be available to work any reasonable hours required for the performance of the job (subject to the working time restrictions laid down in the Working Time Regulations 1998 (see Chapter 5).

5. **Entitlement to holidays, including public holidays, and holiday pay.** This should include clarification of employees' entitlement to be paid for holidays accrued but not taken on termination of employment.

6. **Any terms and conditions relating to sickness absence, including any provision for sick pay.** This provision relates to the provision of company sick pay, i.e. continuation of the employee's wage or salary during periods of sickness absence. The provision of statutory sick pay is an entirely different concept (dealt with in Chapter 10).

7. **Any terms and conditions relating to pensions and pension schemes.** The written statement should say whether or not a company pension scheme is in operation and, if so, whether a contracting-out certificate is in force.

8. **The length of notice which the employee is entitled to receive, and is obliged to give, to terminate the contract of employment.** Minimum notice periods are prescribed in law, but the written statement may impose longer periods on one or both parties. Fuller information about notice periods is available in Chapter 16.

9. **The job title.** Either the job title or a brief description of the work must be provided. There is no obligation in law on employers to provide a job description (although to do so represents good management practice).

10. **The likely duration of a period of temporary employment.** If the temporary contract is for a fixed-term, the precise finish date must be stated. Alternatively, if the contract is to come to an end on the occurrence of a particular event, for example the return to work of another employee who is absent from work on maternity leave, this should be clearly notified to the temporary employee.

11. **The place of work.** The employee's normal place of work, including the employer's address, should be stated. If there is a requirement for the employee to work at different places, this must also be specified.

12. **Details of any relevant collective agreements which directly affect the employee's terms and conditions of employment.** This must specify the persons who are party to the collective agreement.

13. **Details of overseas assignments.** Where an employee is to be assigned to work overseas for a period of more than one month, they must be provided with written information on the duration of the assignment, the currency in which their salary will be paid, details of any special terms, conditions and perks relevant to the assignment and terms governing the employee's return to the UK.

14. **The name or designation of the person to whom the employee should apply if they have a work-related grievance.**

15. **Disciplinary rules.** The requirement to provide written disciplinary rules applies only to employers who have twenty or more employees.

The Principal Statement

Although there is no prescribed format for the provision of this information, the Employment Rights Act 1996 specifies that there should be a 'principal statement', i.e. a single statement which includes details of: the names of the parties, the date when employment began and whether any previous employment counts towards continuous service, rates of pay and pay intervals, hours of work, entitlement to holidays and holiday pay, job title and place of work.

Flexibility Clauses

When preparing a written statement outlining the key terms of an individual's employment, a far-sighted employer will write some flexibility into the terms of the contract in order to meet business requirements not only in the present but also for the future.

Flexibility clauses are particularly useful in relation to hours of work, job duties, if these are specified along with the job title or designation, and the employee's place of work.

When drafting the written statement, it may be prudent to build in to the clause covering working hours, a requirement that the employee must be available to work variable hours or additional hours beyond the stated normal working hours. Similarly, a flexibility clause authorising the employer to move the employee to different standard hours, or a different shift pattern, where the needs of the business demanded it, could be useful. Without such flexibility, the employer could be severely restricted in terms of covering their business needs and the changing demands of their customers or the market place.

The same principle applies to job duties if these are defined in a job description. It makes sound sense for the job description to include an 'any other duties' clause. So long as the 'other duties', which are subsequently expected from the employee, are compatible with the employee's capabilities and level of seniority. This type of clause would entitle the employer to require the employee to be reasonably flexible in terms of taking different duties on board, adjusting priorities within the job duties or introducing new methods of working.

In terms of place of work, if there is any possibility that the employee may be required to move to a different place of work at any time during their employment, either temporarily or permanently, a mobility clause should be incorporated into the written statement. Without a mobility clause, the employer would be prevented from moving employees to a different workplace, unless their express consent was obtained at the time.

There may be many reasons why an employer may wish to move an employee to a different workplace, for example the nature of the work may demand a degree of mobility, the employee, may have specialist skills which the employer wishes to use at different company locations, the company may expand and need to move to larger premises or a lease may expire without renewal.

A mobility clause should be drafted so that it is quite clear as to the geographical boundaries of the employee's mobility, e.g. it may require an employee to move to another place of work within a range of (for example) 50 miles or alternatively provide for a move anywhere in the UK (or the world). It is advisable also that the mobility clause should provide for both temporary postings and permanent transfers.

When drafting flexibility clauses, the manager should bear in mind that a flexibility clause will authorise the employer to alter only the term which is specified in the clause. For example, a flexibility clause entitling the employer to move employees from day to night shift (or vice versa) would not give authority for the employer to increase or reduce the number of working hours. For a change to the number of hours worked to be lawful, this specific point would also have to be covered in the clause. This is because the wording of flexibility clauses tends to be interpreted strictly by courts and tribunals and managers cannot expect to be able to vary terms and conditions in any way they please.

FORMING THE CONTRACT

As stated earlier in this chapter, a contract of employment may be formed as a result of either a verbal or a written agreement (or a combination of both). In law, there are three requirements for the formation of a contract.

1. There must be an agreement between the parties following an offer of work by the employer and acceptance of the offer by the employee.

2. The agreement must be made with the intention that the agreement is to be legally binding on the parties.

3. The agreement must be supported by 'consideration'. This means that each party must promise to give the other something of value. Generally the consideration is the employee's promise to do the work and the employer's promise to pay a wage or salary. Without consideration, a contract of employment cannot be formed.

In drafting contracts of employment, employers should pay heed to the following key points.

1. All the important terms of the contract should be put in writing, including, but not necessarily restricted to, those which statute prescribes should be in writing (see above).

2. The wording of the contract should be clear, accurate, concise and certain.

3. The status of all documents given to employees should be made clear (e.g. 'this letter forms part of your legally binding contract of employment', 'this handbook contains policies which do not form part of your contract of employment but are for guidance only').

4. It should be fundamentally clear which terms and rules are prescriptive (e.g. 'you *will* receive four weeks holiday per year'; 'you *must not* engage in outside employment') and which are discretionary (e.g. 'continuation of salary during periods of sickness is at the manager's *discretion*').

5. If a perk is to be non-contractual, the wording should make this absolutely clear (e.g. 'payment of an annual bonus is not a contractual right, but may be made at the company's discretion depending on the company's financial position').

6. Any right for the employer to vary or modify the terms of the contract should be clearly and precisely stated, together with the scope of the flexibility (see above).

7. Reference should be made to any documents which are to be incorporated into the contract (e.g. disciplinary procedure, pension scheme booklet). It is important to state clearly whether these documents form part of the contract or whether they are for guidance or information only.

8. Where a collective agreement is in force, which is incorporated into an individual's contract of employment, this fact should be clearly stated, together with a clear indication of which employment terms are governed by the collective agreement.

9. The employee's signature should be obtained to indicate receipt of all contractual documents.

The Implications of Withdrawing a Job Offer

Because a contract of employment can be created as a result of a verbal promise to provide work combined with a verbal agreement to accept it, a job offer made verbally at interview and accepted by the applicant constitutes a binding contract. This will be the case even though, at that stage, the precise terms of the contract may not have been fully discussed or agreed.

Managers should therefore avoid making offers to candidates at interview but should instead take a more reasoned and structured approach to recruitment.

Case Study

A job applicant was offered, and accepted, a post with a Health Authority. She received a letter confirming the offer and a second letter confirming the terms of her employment and start date. However, because of a subsequent disagreement, the Health Authority withdrew its offer of employment before the start date, following which the individual brought a complaint to an employment tribunal for breach of contract, wrongful dismissal and unfair dismissal on the grounds of asserting a statutory right (see 'Automatically Unfair Dismissals', Chapter 17).

The EAT held that, although the individual had not started work, a contract of employment had existed, and the individual's complaints were sustainable.

This case thus established the principle that, where an offer to employ (which has been accepted) is withdrawn, this constitutes not only a breach of contract, but also a dismissal in law, even though the person has not started work.

Sarker v. South Tees Acute Hospitals NHS Trust [1997] I.R.L.R. 328.

CHAPTER TWO

CONTINUITY OF SERVICE

The length of an employee's continuous service is important because it forms the basic qualification for the majority of statutory employment rights.

Continuity will normally be broken if there is a period of one week (or more) during which the individual's contract of employment is not in force. It should be noted that, for this purpose, a week is defined in statute as a period running from a Sunday to a Saturday. Thus a break in employment from the Wednesday of one week until the Friday of the following week would not amount to a break in continuity, because it does not include a period from a Sunday to a Saturday.

RIGHTS DEPENDENT ON LENGTH OF SERVICE

A summary of statutory employment rights which are dependent on length of service appears below.

Statutory Employment Right	Length of Service Required to Qualify for the Right
The right to guaranteed pay where an employee is laid off.	One month.
The right to a written statement of the key terms and conditions of employment.	Two months.
The right to a minimum of three weeks paid holiday per annum.	Thirteen weeks.
The right to statutory maternity pay.	Six months, calculated as at fifteeen weeks before the employee's baby is due.
The right to statutory maternity leave.	None.
The right to extended maternity absence.	Two years, calculated as at eleven weeks before the employee's baby is due. To be reduced to one year in the near future.
The right not to be unfairly dismissed.	Two years, but to be reduced to one year in the near future.

Statutory Employment Right	Length of Service Required to Qualify for the Right
The right to a written statement detailing reasons for dismissal.	Two years.
The right to redundancy pay.	Two years.

Employment rights to which an employee is entitled from day one of employment include:

(a) the right to an itemised pay statement;

(b) the right to a minimum wage;

(c) the right not to have unauthorised deductions made from pay;

(d) the right to statutory sick pay during periods of absence from work due to personal incapacity;

(e) the right to equal pay (for men and women) for work that is judged to be 'like work', work rated as equivalent under a job evaluation scheme or for work of equal value;

(f) the right not to be discriminated against on the grounds of sex, race or disability;

(g) the right to limit working hours to an average of no more than 48 hours per week;

(h) the right for employees to belong, or not to belong, to a trade union of their choice and to take part in trade union activities at an appropriate time;

(i) the right to time off work for public duties and certain other purposes;

(j) the right to statutory minimum periods of notice upon termination of employment;

(k) the right to claim automatically unfair dismissal in certain defined circumstances (see 'Automatically Unfair Dismissals', Chapter 17);

(l) the right to a safe workplace and a safe system of work.

PERIODS WHICH COUNT TOWARDS CONTINUOUS EMPLOYMENT

Clearly, so long as the employee's contract of employment remains in force, continuity will be preserved whether or not the employee is at work. Where, however, the contract is suspended for a temporary period of time and later renewed, it is possible for the employee to assert that the weeks during which the contract did not subsist nevertheless count towards continuous employment. Thus an employee's length of continuous employment does not always equate with the period during which their contract of employment is in force.

A period of time during which the contract of employment is suspended will count towards a period of continuous employment in the following defined circumstances.

1. When an employee is incapable of work due to sickness or injury and the contract of employment has terminated. Up to 26 weeks of sickness absence falling between periods of normal employment can be counted for this purpose. Obviously, where the contract of employment continues in force during sickness absence, continuity is automatically preserved.

2. When an employee is absent from work on maternity leave. During any period of maternity leave, in which the employee's contract of employment does not subsist, employment is nevertheless counted towards the employee's long-term continuous service (provided the employee returns to work following maternity leave).

3. If an employee who has been dismissed is subsequently reinstated or re-engaged as a consequence of a successful unfair dismissal claim, or following conciliation through ACAS, all the intervening weeks count towards continuous service.

4. If the employee is laid off due to a temporary cessation of work (see below).

5. If the employee is absent from work as a result of an arrangement or in accordance with a custom in the particular industry.

BREAKS BETWEEN PERIODS OF EMPLOYMENT AND THEIR EFFECTS ON CONTINUITY OF SERVICE

As explained in the previous section, certain breaks falling between periods of employment may count towards the individual's continuous service once the person has resumed work. Two slightly unusual situations are where the employee's absence is due to a temporary cessation of work and where the employee's absence has occurred as a result of an 'arrangement' or a 'custom'. These are explained further in the following sections so that managers may be aware of their obligations in law towards employees who have had a break in their service due to one of these situations.

Temporary Cessation of Work

The set of circumstances most likely to motivate an employee to claim that a temporary cessation of work did not break their continuity of service, is when the individual has been engaged on a series of temporary or fixed-term contracts and they wish to demonstrate that they have sufficient continuous service to assert one or other of their employment rights.

Case Study

A teacher had been employed for eight years on a series of fixed-term contracts, each of which lasted for the duration of the academic year and expired at the start of the summer holiday period. When eventually her contract was not renewed, she took a claim to employment tribunal and the issue of continuity of employment had to be resolved before her rights could be determined.

The House of Lords analysed the reason for the gaps between the fixed-term contracts and held that these were due to the fact that there was no work available for the employee to do during the summer months. Thus they held that the gaps between employment contracts each constituted a 'temporary cessation of work'. It was irrelevant that the absences from work were regular, predictable and agreed in advance between the employer and the employee.

In determining whether gaps between contracts can be counted as temporary cessations of work, the House of Lords stated that the factors which would need to be taken into account would include the individual's total length of service, the regularity of their employment and the duration of the periods of absence compared with the periods of employment on either side of the gaps.

Ford v. Warwickshire County Council [1983] I.C.R. 273.

Where a fixed-term contract expires without renewal, this can give rise to a redundancy since the implication would be that the employee's dismissal was due to the requirements of the business for employees to carry out work of a particular kind having ceased or diminished. This leads to the contention that an employee engaged on a series of fixed-term contracts is entitled, in principle, to a statutory redundancy payment on the expiry of any one contract, provided they have accrued two years' continuous service at that point in time, (and provided the contract is not renewed within four weeks of the date of the contract ending). Gaps between the contracts which are due to a temporary cessation of work would not break continuity for the purposes of calculating overall length of service for this purpose.

Case Study

The above dilemma faced the EAT when a part-time lecturer, who had been employed for thirteen years on the basis of a series of fixed-term contracts, each of which had lasted for one term of the academic year, was told that the next renewal of her contract would be on the basis of a 29 per cent reduction in pay. The employee took a claim for constructive dismissal and a statutory redundancy payment.

The EAT upheld the principles of the *Ford* case (see page 22) and decided that the gaps between each contract amounted to temporary cessations of work and that the employee therefore had continuity of employment throughout. Furthermore, the EAT held that the termination of each contract constituted a redundancy because the college's need for part-time lecturers had ceased or diminished for the duration of the vacation.

Pfaffinger v. City of Liverpool Community College [1996] I.R.L.R. 508.

The principle emerging from the above case is that an employee, who is engaged on a series of temporary or fixed-term contracts, will be entitled to a statutory redundancy payment on the first occasion that a contract expires without immediate renewal following the accrual of two years' continuous service and then another redundancy payment following another two years' continuous service whenever there is a cessation of work causing the contract not to be renewed immediately. Service may be continuous despite the occurrence of gaps between each contract, provided the gaps are due to a temporary cessation of work. In theory, therefore, an employee engaged on this basis could put in a claim for a statutory redundancy payment every two years. This would be the case unless the employee was offered a renewal of the contract before the due expiry date and the renewal commenced within four weeks of the termination of the original contract.

Statutory redundancy pay cannot be paid twice for the same period of service, however it is significant that the payment of a statutory redundancy payment does not affect the employee's right to make a claim for unfair dismissal on the expiry of a contract without renewal. Receipt of a statutory redundancy payment breaks the employee's continuity of service only in relation to the calculation of future qualifying service for redundancy pay purposes. Thus, when an employee is made redundant again on the expiry of another fixed-term contract, an earlier redundancy payment would have no effect on any other employment rights, including the employee's right to claim unfair dismissal. In other words, all other employment rights would still be based on the employee's total period of service.

These principles would potentially apply to any employment where employees are regularly employed then laid off from time to time as result of a downturn in trade during certain times of the year, for example, in businesses whose trade varies according to the seasons of the year.

Provided a cessation of work is genuinely temporary, there is no limit to the number of weeks of absence which can count towards an employee's continuous service.

Managers should be wary, therefore, of assuming that, just because there has been a gap(s) between two (or more) fixed-term contracts, the individual has not accrued sufficient service to become eligible for certain statutory rights.

Absence by Arrangement or Custom

It is stated, in the Employment Rights Act 1996, that if an employee is absent from work by arrangement or custom, their continuity of service will be preserved. Courts and tribunals have thus dealt with cases challenging the meaning of 'arrangement' and 'custom' in this context.

Potentially any agreement between the employer and the employee would be valid to qualify under this heading, provided the agreement was entered into before the contract was suspended, and not at a later date. Equally, if there was an agreement between management and a recognised trade union that employment was to be regarded as continuous in certain defined circumstances, this could constitute an 'arrangement' in law.

Continuity can also be preserved as a result of a custom, provided that custom is consistently adopted in a particular employment or industry. The logic in this is that the custom has evolved into a term which is implied into employees' employment contracts.

There is no maximum period of time when an employee may be absent by arrangement or custom and still maintain continuity of employment.

PROBATIONARY PERIODS

It is common practice for managers to place new employees on probation for a temporary period in order to assess their suitability for the job. This is sound management policy because it allows both parties to evaluate whether there is a 'fit' between the person and the job, and encourages the manager to give the new employee feedback on their performance and any areas where improvement is needed. The period of probation has no effect, however, on the employee's statutory rights, as these come into force when employment begins. Thus continuity of service is unaffected by a period of probation, whatever its length.

CHAPTER THREE

BREACH OF CONTRACT

Once the terms of a contract of employment have been agreed between employer and employee, they can only be altered with the consent of both parties. This is because the terms of a contract of employment, like those of any other type of contract, are legally binding on the parties.

It follows that any attempt on the part of the employer to alter one or other of the key terms of an employee's contract unilaterally, will constitute a breach of contract, unless the employee's agreement has first been obtained. Furthermore, a change, which is unilaterally imposed, will not be contractually binding on the employee.

Agreement can be secured in three ways.

1. By inserting a flexibility clause into the contract at the start giving the employer authority to vary a particular term of the contract. The existence of a flexibility clause means, in effect, that the employee has agreed, in advance, that the employer may alter a specific term of the employment contract, as defined in the flexibility clause. It should be noted, however, that a universal flexibility clause, purporting to give the employer the right to alter any of the terms of the contract at any time, is unlikely to be enforceable. Further information about flexibility clauses appears in 'Flexibility Clauses', Chapter 1.

2. By means of a clause in a collective agreement with a recognised trade union, the terms of which are binding on individual employees.

3. By securing the employee's agreement to the change at the time it is proposed.

Clearly employers will wish, from time to time, to introduce changes to the way they work, and consequently changes to the terms of employees' contracts may become necessary from a business point of view. There may, for example, be a need to alter working hours to fit in with customer demands or a need to introduce new working methods or procedures.

Where the change to the contract is significant, with the result that it goes to the very root of the contractual relationship, then its imposition without the employee's agreement will be regarded as a fundamental breach of contract in law, thus entitling the employee to regard the contract as at an end. The practical effect of a fundamental breach of contract is that it releases the employee from all further obligations under the contract. Employees' possible remedies for a breach of contract are discussed in 'Remedies Open to Employees if the Employer alters the Terms of the Contract of Employment without Agreement', Chapter 4.

Not every breach of contract, however, will be serious enough to allow the employee to succeed with legal action. Whether or not a breach is fundamental will depend on a number of factors. These will include:

(a) the nature of the change;

(b) the size of the change in relative terms, for example the effect of a £10 per week pay cut would be a substantial change for someone earning £80 per week, whilst the same reduction would (arguably) be insignificant to an employee whose take-home pay was £800 per week;

(c) the impact the change has on the employee, for example a change of hours may be acceptable, or even welcome, to one employee, whilst making life impossible for another employee who might have family responsibilities which would preclude him from working the new hours;

(d) the reason for the change, e.g. whether there is a sound business reason necessitating the change or whether it is introduced to accord with administrative convenience or the whim of a particular manager;

(e) the manner in which the employer proceeds to introduce the change (see Chapter 4).

Where employment rules, conditions or benefits are clearly non-contractual, then management may, of course, alter them, provided they do so in a manner which is reasonable. Work rules, for example, are sometimes non-contractual and, where this is the case, such rules may be altered by management without securing the agreement of employees. Care should be exercised, however, and unilateral changes should be made only where there is an unequivocal written statement that the particular rule or term is, in fact, not a contractual right for the employees affected.

ACTIONS WHICH MAY CONSTITUTE BREACH OF CONTRACT ON THE PART OF THE EMPLOYER

There are many different actions which may give rise to a breach of contract. A breach may arise as a result of either a breach of one of the express terms of the contract of employment or one of the implied terms. These are examined further in the following sections.

Breach of Express Terms

A fundamental change to any one of the express terms of an employee's contract, which is imposed without the employee's agreement and has an adverse effect on the employee, may give rise to a breach of contract. The most common scenarios are examined below.

Pay

Since an employee's pay is central to the whole contractual relationship, any action on the part of the employer to alter the amount of an employee's pay would affect the whole essence of the contract. A breach of contract may arise where the employer alters any of the following (without the employee's agreement):

(a) the amount of pay;

(b) the formula for calculating pay;

(c) the basis on which an employee earns commission or rules for eligibility for a bonus;

(d) the timing of pay, in particular late payment of wages or salary would give rise to a breach of contract.

There is no legal obligation on employers to increase pay on an annual basis, unless, of course, such an obligation had been written into the contract of employment or a collective agreement incorporates a term whereby wages are to be increased in line with a national or industry-wide agreement.

Fringe Benefits

Most employees receive fringe benefits as a contractual right, i.e. they form part of the terms and conditions of their employment, rather than being subject to the employer's discretion. Consequently, any reduction or removal of these benefits, without the employee's consent, would amount to a breach of contract. Examples include:

(a) removal of an employee's entitlement to a company car;

(b) reduction of the contribution an employer makes towards an employee's telephone bill;

(c) withdrawal of a petrol allowance;

(d) a requirement that employees should contribute towards the cost of insurance provided by a company scheme (for example private medical insurance) where such benefits were previously funded wholly by the company.

Working Hours

Unless there is a flexibility clause in the employee's contract governing working hours, a unilaterally imposed change to working hours would, unless it was minor, constitute a fundamental breach of contract. This could be:

(a) an alteration to working patterns or shift systems;

(b) a demand that the employee works longer hours;

(c) a reduction in hours of work;

(d) a change to the start and finish times of the working day;

(e) a move to a different shift;

(f) a change to the days of the week on which a part-time employee is required to work;

(g) a reduction in the number or length of rest breaks during the working day.

Holidays

Any attempt to shorten holiday, or other time off, entitlements could amount to a fundamental breach of contract if the change was significant.

Job Content

A breach of contract under this heading could include:

(a) imposition of new duties outside the scope of the existing job description;

(b) removal of job duties;

(c) transfer to another job;

(d) demotion or transfer to less skilled work;

(e) a diminishing of an employee's status, for example if an important element of the employee's work was removed.

Any of these actions on the part of the employer could constitute breach of contract if the change had been imposed on the employee without their agreement, unless either, or both, of the following was in place:

(a) a flexibility clause in the written terms of employment authorising the employer to transfer the employee to different work;

(b) a clause in the job description entitling the employer to alter the employee's job duties.

Prudent employers will ensure that all job descriptions contain a clause to the effect that their job includes 'any other duties within their capabilities which they are reasonably requested to carry out'. The employer may also wish to include a flexibility clause in the contract entitling them to move employees to different work if the needs of the business demand such a move.

Altering the method of doing a job, however, is not likely to be a breach of contract providing the change is not so radical as to completely redefine the employee's job. Employees are expected to adapt to new methods and techniques of performing their jobs and to be willing to co-operate with their employer in learning new technology. The employer, for their part, is obliged to provide adequate training in new methods of working.

Place of Work

Place of work is as much a fundamental term of an employment contract as any other term. It follows that if the employer was to attempt to enforce a move to a different workplace on an employee whose contract did not contain a mobility clause, this would, in all likelihood, constitute a breach of contract. Such a breach, however, may or may not be fundamental depending on the relative distance of the new workplace from the old. Arguably, if the new premises were located within easy distance of the old workplace and the employee was not disadvantaged in any way, the breach would not be fundamental. If, however, a move involving a short distance involved a major change of some kind and thus disadvantaged the employee, this could in theory still constitute a breach of contract, depending on the circumstances. Similarly it would be a breach of contract to attempt to move an employee to a location which was outside the geographical scope of a mobility clause.

Company Procedures

The imposition of a new policy or procedure without the employee's agreement could give rise to a fundamental breach of contract, depending on the effect the procedure had on the employee. For example, the introduction of a no smoking policy or a drugs testing policy would be a breach if the policy was introduced arbitrarily without consultation or agreement. In the case of a drugs screening policy introduced without agreement, the first time the employer insisted that a particular employee should undergo a drugs test would render the employer in breach of that employee's contract.

Once policies and procedures are in place, any failure on the employer's part to follow the terms of the policy or procedure could, if the policy or procedure was incorporated into the employee's contract, lead to a breach of contract. This would not be the case, however, if the policy or procedure was simply a statement of management's overall approach or a statement defined as being for guidance only, for example, a general statement outlining the employer's approach to equal opportunities.

Normally a disciplinary procedure forms part of employees' contracts of employment. Thus any failure on the employer's part to follow the procedure, could be a breach of contract. Failure to follow properly the disciplinary procedure prior to dismissing an employee for misconduct, can also lead to a finding of unfair dismissal in an employment tribunal (see 'Wrongful Dismissal' below and Chapter 17 for full details of unfair dismissal).

Breach of Implied Terms

A fundamental breach of contract may also occur as a result of a breach of one of the implied terms in an employee's contract. Examples include a breach of the duty:

(a) of trust and confidence;

(b) to provide reasonable support to employees to perform their duties;

(c) to afford employees a reasonable opportunity to obtain redress for a grievance;

(d) to provide and monitor a working environment for employees which is reasonably suitable for the performance of their duties;

Examples of these are provided below.

Trust and confidence is regarded as a key element in all employment relationships, and any breach of this duty is likely to amount to a fundamental breach of contract. A breach of contract may occur as a consequence of a single incident or as a result of a series of incidents which, when considered together, have the effect of destroying trust and confidence. Breach of trust and confidence may result (for example) from:

(a) bullying, victimisation or harassment;

(b) constant unfair criticism;

(c) placing unreasonable requirements on an employee in terms of workload, deadlines, etc.;

(d) seeking to apply a contractual term in a manner which makes it impossible for the employee to comply;

(e) humiliating or degrading treatment;

(f) falsely accusing the employee of misconduct or unsatisfactory job performance;

(g) unfair or discriminatory application of any discretionary policy;

(h) treating the employee in any way calculated to force them to resign.

Case Study

An employee who had worked for over thirteen years as a hotel telephone supervisor was subjected to a very severe and humiliating reprimand by her manager following an incident when she had taken time off work to attend a dental appointment without first obtaining permission. The reason for the unauthorised absence was that the employee had severe toothache. Following the reprimand, the employee resigned from the company and claimed constructive dismissal based on the premise that the manager's behaviour constituted a fundamental breach of contract.

The EAT held that the rebuke had been officious and insensitive and the employee had not deserved that sort of treatment. She had been humiliated, intimidated and degraded to such an extent that there was a breach of trust going to the root of the contract.

Hilton International Hotels (UK) Ltd v. Protopapa [1990] I.R.L.R. 316.

Breach of the duty to provide reasonable support to employees may also amount to a breach of contract. This could involve a range of possible omissions on the part of the employer, for example, a failure to:

(a) take appropriate and reasonable steps to support or protect an employee who is the victim of bullying or harassment;

(b) provide the basic or necessary training to enable an employee to perform their job to an adequate standard;

(c) support a manager or supervisor in dealing with staff problems;

(d) provide a manager with the resources needed to perform their job to a satisfactory standard. See the case study below for an example of this.

Case Study

The employee, who was a branch manager in an off licence, was asked to take on the management of a larger branch which had experienced staff and operational problems. She accepted the transfer with misgivings on the understanding that, if she so requested, she would be moved again to another branch.

The employee experienced considerable difficulties in the new post, in particular because of a lack of support from management in terms of employee resourcing, as a result of which she, herself, had to work inordinately long hours. When she returned from a holiday, she discovered that the area manager had transferred two of her most experienced staff to other branches without consulting her. She subsequently found she could not cope with the job and requested a transfer to another branch. This was refused. The employee resigned and brought a complaint to tribunal alleging unfair constructive dismissal on account of the employer's behaviour, which, she claimed, constituted a fundamental breach of contract.

The EAT upheld her case and found that she had not received the support and assistance necessary for her to perform her contract. Because the employer had known that she had insufficient experience for the job, and had failed to provide the necessary back up, this had prevented her from performing her contract to an acceptable standard.

Whitbread plc t/a Thresher v. Gullyes [1994] E.A.T. 478/92.

An employer's failure or refusal to provide an employee with a proper method of dealing with a work-related grievance can amount to a fundamental breach of contract.

Case Study

Two employees who worked as jewellery salesmen were paid on a salary plus commission basis. However, when the employer introduced a change to the methods of selling, their commission dropped substantially. As a result of this, they raised a complaint with their manager, but nothing was done. They made two further attempts to raise their grievance, first with the managing director and subsequently with the company chairman, but no action was taken to deal with the grievance. Both employees subsequently resigned and claimed constructive dismissal.

The EAT, on examining the case, implied a term into the employees' contracts that the employer should "reasonably and promptly afford a reasonable opportunity to their employees to obtain redress of any grievance they may have". In this case, the employer's failure to provide the employees with a proper method of dealing with a work-related grievance amounted to a fundamental breach of contract.

W A Goold (Pearmak) Ltd v. McConnell and Another EAT [1995] I.R.L.R. 516.

To avoid this type of situation, managers should ensure that, whenever an employee raises a grievance, whether formally or informally, they should be prepared to:

(a) listen to the grievance;

(b) take the employee's complaint seriously – even if it appears trivial to the manager, it may not be trivial to the employee;

(c) give the matter fair consideration;

(d) take reasonable steps to find a solution.

Another situation in which an employer may find that they are in breach of an implied term in an employee's contract, could be where *the employer neglects to provide employees with a working environment which is reasonably tolerable and suitable for them to work in.* This implied term could relate (for example) to noise levels, excessive smells and, as in the case study below, the presence of cigarette smoke in the working environment.

Case Study

A long-standing employee in a firm of solicitors, who was a non-smoker, was, following a move to a different part of the office, caused discomfort by the air quality due to the fact that colleagues, who worked nearby, smoked heavily. Following various complaints to management, she was ultimately told that she would just have to put up with it. Shortly after that, she resigned and claimed constructive dismissal.

The outcome of the case was a finding that the air quality had been intolerable for a non-smoker and the employer was in breach of an implied term to provide the employee with a reasonably suitable working environment. Moreover, the EAT held that the employer had also been in breach of the implied term to provide a reasonable opportunity to the employee to obtain redress for a grievance. Thus the employee succeeded in her case.

Waltons & Morse v. Dorrington [1997] I.R.L.R. 488.

As a result of the above case, managers should ensure that appropriate steps are taken to ensure that all employees who wish it, are accommodated in a smoke-free working environment. Failure to take the appropriate steps to ensure this requirement is granted, may constitute a breach of contract entitling employees to resign and claim constructive dismissal. Additionally there is the possibility of claims for injury to health caused by passive smoking.

THE CONCEPT OF WRONGFUL DISMISSAL

Where an employee is dismissed in breach of contract, this will amount to a 'wrongful dismissal' in law. The most common examples of wrongful dismissal are:

(a) dismissal without proper notice under the contract;

(b) dismissal with no notice, where there are no grounds for summary dismissal;

(c) dismissal in breach of a contractual disciplinary procedure;

(d) dismissal in breach of a contractual redundancy procedure;

(e) the termination of a fixed-term contract before the agreed expiry date;

(f) the termination of a temporary contract for a specific task, before the task has been completed.

Case Study

A woman who worked as a social worker was summarily dismissed (i.e. without notice) following an enquiry by her employer, a Local Authority, into her alleged negligence in carrying out her duties.

The employer's disciplinary procedure, which was incorporated into the employee's contract, provided for an entitlement of eight weeks' contractual notice on dismissal except in cases of gross misconduct when no notice would be given. There was also a rule that employees should be granted a hearing prior to any decision to dismiss, but the employee in this case was not offered any opportunity to put forward her version of events.

The employee succeeded in a claim for breach of contract against her employer. In the court's view, the employee's conduct did not amount to gross misconduct, as defined in her employer's disciplinary rules, and she should, therefore, have been given eight weeks' notice on dismissal. Furthermore the employer was in breach of contract in denying the employee a disciplinary hearing. She received damages totalling sixteen weeks' net pay, this being the period of time the court estimated would have been required for the employer to follow their disciplinary procedure properly.

Dietmann v. London Borough of Brent [1987] I.R.L.R. 259.

An employee who has been dismissed wrongfully, may take a claim for wrongful dismissal either to an employment tribunal or to an ordinary civil court.

Where claims for both wrongful and unfair dismissal are being taken, it is usual for both to be brought together to an employment tribunal. There is no minimum length of service requirement for an employee to bring a claim for wrongful dismissal.

Compensation for a wrongful dismissal will be assessed according to the actual financial losses which the employee has suffered as a result of the breach of contract. The aim of damages for wrongful dismissal is to put the employee back in the financial position they would have been in had the contract been terminated lawfully. No compensation can therefore be awarded for loss of job security or on account of an employer's unreasonable behaviour towards the employee.

Enforcement of Outstanding Contractual Terms in the Event of Dismissal without Proper Notice

If there has been a fundamental breach of contract in the manner in which the contract is terminated, then the employer cannot rely on any provisions within the contract which were designed to come into effect after termination. This is because, in the event of a breach of contract by the employer, the employee is immediately freed from all outstanding contractual obligations.

Post-termination provisions may include a restrictive covenant (see the next section) or a clause rooted in a contractual agreement that the employee should, in the event of termination of employment, repay to the employer part or all of any training or relocation expenses granted to them in the course of their employment.

Case Study

The employee's contract contained a term stating that relocation expenses would be repayable to the company if he left before completing twelve months' service following relocation. Nine months later the employee was dismissed but he was not given proper notice of termination under his contract of employment. When he subsequently claimed at tribunal that he had been wrongfully dismissed, the employer made a counter-claim for repayment of the relocation expenses, which amounted to £5,000.

The decision was that the employee had indeed been wrongfully dismissed and that, as a result, the employer's breach of contract had the effect of releasing the employee from any further obligations under the contract. It was therefore ruled that the employee could not be obliged to repay the relocation expenses.

Pearce v. Roy T Ward (Consultants) Ltd [1996] E.A.T. 180/96.

RESTRICTIVE COVENANTS

The aim of a restrictive covenant in a contract of employment is to restrain an employee, who has left the company, from undertaking certain activities which may damage the employer's business interests. The underlying objective is to enable the employer to protect their legitimate business interests. A restrictive covenant cannot be designed to prevent any competition whatsoever from ex-employees, nor to prevent an ex-employee from earning a living elsewhere. Unless a restrictive covenant is necessary for the employer's protection, and reasonable in its scope, it will be void on the grounds that it is in restraint of trade and contrary to public policy.

Examples of the legitimate business interests which an employer may seek to protect by using restrictive covenants include:

(a) trade secrets;

(b) other confidential information, for example names and details of customers;

(c) trade connections, i.e. the employer's relationships with their customers, clients (and possibly suppliers);

(d) the stability of the workforce.

Restrictive covenants, generally, are designed to prevent the departing employee from doing one, or more, of the following.

1. Working for a competitor.

2. Setting up their own business in competition with the employer.

3. Doing business with, or soliciting, the employer's past or present customers (or suppliers).

4. Enticing other employees to leave the company in order to join the ex-employee in another business.

5. Using confidential information gained during the course of employment.

In order to be enforceable in a court of law, a restrictive covenant must be reasonable in its scope and must not go beyond what is required to protect the employer's legitimate business interests. Thus the limits of the covenant must be specified in terms of time-frame and geographical location. A typical example might be a clause which states that, if an employee's employment is terminated for any reason, the person must not work for a competitor company or set up a competing business within a distance of 50 miles of the employer's business for a period of six months following the date of termination of their employment.

The law on restrictive covenants is complex and detailed and any employer who wishes to draft restraint clauses to protect their interests should seek the services of a qualified lawyer.

CHAPTER FOUR

ALTERING EMPLOYEES' TERMS OF EMPLOYMENT

As explained in the previous chapter, once the terms of a contract of employment have been agreed between the employer and the employee, they are legally binding and, therefore, cannot be unilaterally altered by the employer. Nevertheless, the need will inevitably arise from time to time to make changes to employees' contracts in order for the company to meet its business objectives.

HOW THE EMPLOYER CAN ALTER THE TERMS OF AN EMPLOYEE'S CONTRACT LAWFULLY

Where the employer wishes to alter one or more of the terms of employees' contracts, and where there is no authority contained within the contract itself for such a change, the employer must embark on a process of consultation aimed at securing the employees' agreement to the proposed change. If the employer proceeds to implement the change without such a course of action, employees are likely to have a valid claim for breach of contract.

It may be that once the proposed change is explained fully to employees, they will be prepared to agree to it, thus removing the need for any further action, other than to provide written confirmation of the change. There is no requirement in law to re-issue the complete contract of employment, but notification of the terms which have changed must be provided to each employee in writing within four weeks of the date the change was implemented.

If, however, it is clear that there will be no general acceptance of the change, the procedure outlined below should be adopted. This overall approach is appropriate whether it is one employee whose terms the employer wishes to change, or whether a proposed change will affect a large number of employees.

Act Reasonably

Approach the issue in a rational, fair and patient manner and treat employees reasonably. Changes to contractual terms should not be introduced over-hastily.

Sound Business Reasons

Examine the reasons behind the proposal to make a change, and whether these reasons are genuinely related to the needs of the business. A change which is rooted in administrative convenience or personal preference is unlikely to amount to a sound business reason.

Consultation

The employer should embark upon a process of full consultation in relation to the proposed changes. Consultation may be with the representative of a recognised trade union (if there is one), a staff committee or with individuals directly. Meetings should be held so that proposals can be put forward, the reasons for the proposals can be fully explained and so that questions can be answered. Employees should be given the opportunity to put forward their views, suggestions and objections to the proposed changes. The employer should be willing to consider these views, suggestions and objections, and subsequently to amend the proposals to accommodate them where it is practicable and reasonable to do so. For example, if there is a proposal to alter hours of work so that employees occasionally work until 10.00 pm and there is an objection to this, on the basis that some employees have no access to public transport at that time of the evening, the problem could be overcome by the employer offering to provide transport, perhaps by arranging for a taxi to take the employees home.

Offer to Vary the Contract

Once the proposals have been modified in the light of consultation, the employer should write to every employee who will be affected by the change, fully explaining the proposed changes and offering to alter the particular terms of their contracts of employment. At this stage the change should still be in the form of a *proposal* and not a decision which management has already taken. If necessary, further consultation should be undertaken.

Keep Records

Full, written records should be kept of each part of the consultation process. Such records should document the proposals put forward, any particular suggestions or objections, and any other options which have been suggested, or which might be explored.

Confirm the Position in Writing

Following consultations, the employer should send a letter to each employee, confirming the position so far and putting forward any revised proposals. If employees agree to the proposals at this stage, then the remaining steps detailed below will not be required.

Warning

If some, or all, employees continue to refuse to accept the changes, they should be warned in writing that the consequence of their continuing refusal could be termination of their existing contract of employment (i.e. dismissal) and an offer of re-employment on revised terms. This should be communicated to each individual by letter, and, at the same time, they should be offered one more opportunity to confirm their acceptance of the proposed changes by a date specified in the letter.

Terminate Existing Contracts and Offer to Re-employ on the Revised Terms

In the event that employees continue to refuse to accept the proposed changes, despite full consultation, the employer may proceed to introduce the changes by giving employees notice of termination of their current employment contract and contemporaneously offering re-employment on the new terms. Employees who accept the offer of re-employment maintain their continuity of service, whilst those who do not are effectively dismissed. Clearly this approach is not risk-free, since those with the necessary qualifying service will have the right to take a claim of unfair dismissal to an employment tribunal. If, however, the employer has followed the procedure outlined above, it is likely that any dismissals would be found to be fair under the heading of 'some other substantial reason', especially if the majority of employees had been prepared to accept the new terms. The advantage of this approach is that there can be no breach of contract claims from employees, provided, of course, that the notice given to terminate the contracts complies with employees' contractual notice entitlements.

Introducing the Change without Termination and Re-employment

The alternative course of action is for the employer to give employees notice that they intend to introduce the change from a stated future date. This would allow the employees to claim breach of contract irrespective of the employer's efforts to act reasonably and engage in the consultation process (see 'An Employee's Claim for Breach of Contract – Claims for Damages', below). Thus it is important, if breach of contract claims are to be avoided, that the notice given must be to *terminate* the contract and not to *vary* its terms.

Introducing New Policies/Procedures

In instances where the proposed change involves the introduction of a new policy or procedure, for example a no smoking policy, termination of employees' contracts, combined with an offer of re-engagement, would not normally be appropriate. Here, the employer should follow a process of consultation as outlined above, ensuring that:

(a) the proposed new policy/procedure is fully explained to employees;

(b) employees are given full opportunity to put forward their views, suggestions and objections to the new policy/procedure;

(c) management takes those views into account.

Once consultation has been carried out, the employer may notify employees of their intention to introduce the policy or procedure at a stated future date, giving reasonable notice. Further considerations would include the need to:

(a) ensure the policy/procedure was communicated in writing to all employees individually prior to its implementation;

(b) post the policy/procedure on staff notice boards;

(c) in the case of the introduction of a no smoking policy, consider offering employees counselling or professional help to give up smoking;

(d) state clearly the consequences of any breaches of the new policy/procedure, i.e. whether a breach will constitute misconduct under the company's disciplinary procedure, and the penalties for such a breach. It is important that employees are fully informed of the likely penalties for refusing to comply with the new policy/procedure after its introduction, especially if they may be liable to be dismissed;

(e) following introduction, ensure the policy/procedure is enforced consistently throughout the company.

REMEDIES OPEN TO EMPLOYEES IF THE EMPLOYER ALTERS THE TERMS OF THE CONTRACT OF EMPLOYMENT WITHOUT AGREEMENT

Where the employer imposes a change to an employee's terms or conditions of employment without the person's agreement, the employee has a choice of courses of action:

(a) to signify acceptance of the change by signing to indicate agreement;

(b) to do nothing and continue working under the contract;

(c) to refuse to work under the new terms if, for example, they involve a change in duties;

(d) to continue working under protest but sue the employer for damages for breach of contract. No minimum period of service is required;

(e) if the breach involves a pay cut, to make a claim for unlawful deduction of wages under the Employment Rights Act 1996. No minimum period of service is required;

(f) to resign and claim constructive dismissal. For this to succeed, the breach must be fundamental and go to the very root of the contract of employment. Employees need a minimum of two years' continuous service to take this course of action.

These courses of action are explored in the following sections.

The Effect of the Employee Doing Nothing

If, following a change to the terms of the contract, the employee carries on working normally and takes no action to indicate their objection to the change, they will be taken to have accepted the new terms after a relatively short period of time. This implied acceptance does not depend on the passage of a defined period of time but rather on the employee's conduct. If it can be argued that the employee's actions are consistent with them having accepted the change, then they will lose any right to claim breach of contract or constructive dismissal at a later date.

An example could be in the event of a pay cut. If the employee continued to work normally and accepted their weekly pay cheque, taking no action to express any formal objections to the change, it could be argued that this behaviour constituted an acceptance of the pay cut after only a week or two.

The employee may, however, reserve their position, in other words keep their options open to take a claim for breach of contract or constructive dismissal at a later date by communicating their objection to the change to the employer in writing and stating that they are continuing to work under protest. They may also reserve their position and buy time by invoking the company's grievance procedure.

Where a change does not immediately affect the employee, for example the introduction of a mobility clause into the contract which may or may not be activated at some future date, the employee would not be deemed to have accepted the change simply by carrying on working normally. The same principal would apply upon the introduction of a new policy, for example, a drugs-screening policy. Acceptance would only be implied if and when the employee subsequently went along with the procedure, i.e. consented to be screened.

Lack of action on the part of an employee is often explained by the fact that most employees are anxious not to lose their jobs, are unaware of their rights or are reluctant to resign on account of the change. They may also fear the repercussions if they object, or may prefer to maintain harmonious working relationships rather than complain.

Even if there are no legal repercussions following a change, which is imposed on employees without their agreement, managers may wish to consider the impact on morale and motivation created by unwelcome changes to working terms or conditions. These can be considerable, long-term and can have damaging effects on the company, for example a lower productivity, higher labour turnover, higher rates of sickness absence, etc.

Clearly, it is in the interests of the company to ensure that signed acceptance of any change is received from all employees who are affected, as this removes any doubt over whether or not the employees have expressly agreed to the change. However, the absence of an employee's signature indicating acceptance of the change will be inconsequential if the employee continues to work normally without expressing any formal objections, as this conduct will constitute an implied agreement to the change which, ultimately, has the same effect as an express agreement.

An Employee's Refusal to Work under the New Terms

A refusal on the employee's part to work under the new terms would effectively put the ball back into the employer's court to decide what, if any, action to take. This could occur where an employee refused to work different hours or declined to take on board additional or different job duties outside the scope of their existing job description.

If the employer was to dismiss an employee for such a refusal, it would be likely that the dismissal would be judged unfair by an employment tribunal, unless either there was a flexibility clause in the contract authorising the change, or the employer had gone through a full process of consultation prior to the dismissal (see above). Conversely, the employee would probably fail in a claim for unfair dismissal if:

(a) the employer had a sound business reason for the change;

(b) consultation had been carried out prior to the change being introduced;

(c) the employer had acted reasonably in attempting to introduce the new terms;

(d) the employee has no justifiable reason for refusing to agree to the change;

(e) the employer had properly followed their disciplinary procedure prior to dismissing the employee.

The outcome, of course, would depend on all the circumstances of the individual case.

An Employee's Claim for Breach of Contract – Claims for Damages

Where a change to an employee's terms and conditions results in some tangible loss, a claim for damages may be brought to an ordinary court (not an employment tribunal). The employee can remain at work whilst following this course of action, provided they make it clear to the employer that they are continuing to work under protest, in other words write a letter to their manager stating that they object to the change and regard it as a breach of contract. It is significant to note that, in order to sue for breach of contract, the employee does not require any minimum period of qualifying service.

When a court is assessing a claim for breach of contract, it will not be concerned with the reasonableness or otherwise of the employer's actions. They will be interested only in establishing the terms of the contract, whether these have been altered without agreement and whether the employee has suffered any monetary loss as a result.

Case Study

A Local Authority announced a series of amendments to the employment terms of dinner ladies, which had the effect of reducing their take-home pay. A group of the dinner ladies, whilst continuing in their jobs, made it clear that they objected to the change and that they were continuing to work under protest. At the same time they brought a High Court action for damages for breach of contract.

The Court decided that the change to the dinner ladies' terms of employment did constitute a breach of contract because the Council had introduced the change unilaterally and the dinner ladies had not agreed to it. They awarded arrears of wages and a declaration that the Council was not entitled to vary the employees' contracts in this way.

Burdett-Coutts and Others v. Hertfordshire County Council [1984] I.R.L.R. 91.

The aim of a court in determining a claim for damages for breach of contract is to put the employee back into the position they would have been in if the employer had not breached the contract, in other words to restore the status quo. There will be no compensation for unreasonable treatment or hurt feelings.

Pay-cut Claims

If an employer imposes a unilateral pay cut on one or more employees without first obtaining their agreement in writing to the change, the employees concerned would have a high chance of success with a claim for unlawful deduction of wages under the Employment Rights Act 1996 (provisions formerly contained in the Wages Act 1986). There is no minimum period of service required for an employee to bring a claim of this kind to an employment tribunal.

Case Study

In order to boost productivity, the employer had paid double the previous overtime rate for night-shift workers over a period of four years. When they cut the overtime rate back to its previous level without agreement from the union or the employees, the employees, whilst continuing to work under protest, brought a claim to an employment tribunal for unlawful deductions to their wages.

The EAT ruled that, since there had been no agreement to the reduction in overtime rates, the reduction constituted an unauthorised deduction from the amount properly payable to the employees. The employees were entitled to receive the higher rate of overtime.

Bruce and Others v. Wiggins Teape (Stationery) Ltd [1994] I.R.L.R. 536.

Essentially a case can be brought under this heading because of the contention that a *reduction* in wages imposed without agreement is no different from an unlawful *deduction* to wages which the Employment Rights Act 1996 is designed to prevent. The end result is the same, i.e. the employee suffers an unauthorised net loss in pay.

Full details of the provisions concerning unlawful deductions from pay are in 'Deductions from Pay – When they are Lawful and When they are Unlawful' in Chapter 6.

Claims for Constructive Dismissal

If there has been a fundamental breach of contract on the part of the employer, and provided the employee has at least two years' continuous service, the employee may resign and bring a claim for constructive dismissal to an employment tribunal.

To succeed in a claim for constructive dismissal, the employee would have to prove that:

(a) the employer's actions were significant enough to constitute a fundamental breach of the employee's contract; *and*

(b) the employee resigned, with or without notice, as a direct result of that breach; *and*

(c) the employee did not wait too long before resigning in response to the employer's breach.

To succeed in a claim for constructive dismissal, an employee must be able to demonstrate to an employment tribunal that the contractual change imposed by the employer made the prospect of them continuing in employment intolerable to the extent that there was no alternative but to resign. Minor changes to terms and conditions would not justify a constructive dismissal claim. To claim constructive dismissal, the employee must actually have resigned from employment, in contrast to a claim for damages which can be pursued whilst the person is still in employment.

CHAPTER FIVE

WORKING HOURS, HOLIDAYS AND TIME OFF

THE WORKING TIME REGULATIONS 1998

The Working Time Regulations 1998, which took effect on 1 October 1998, apply to all employers in the UK, regardless of size or industry sector. This legislation emanated from Europe with the Working Time Directive. The Regulations give entitlements not only to employees, but also to agency staff, temporary employees, those on fixed-term contracts, home-workers, casuals and other atypical workers. The main provisions of the Regulations cover:

- working hours;
- rest breaks;
- night shift working;
- holiday entitlements (covered in the section titled 'Holiday Entitlements' below).

Working Hours

The most far-reaching provision in the Regulations is that employees have the right, if they wish, to restrict their working hours to a maximum average of 48 hours per week (including overtime). The reference period for averaging is seventeen weeks (and may be longer in certain circumstances). When calculating working hours, any periods when the employee was absent from work due to sickness, holiday or maternity leave must be excluded.

The detail of what does and does not constitute 'working time' is not made entirely clear in the Regulations, and several areas remain to be interpreted by employment tribunals when specific claims come before them. However, there is nothing in the Regulations which states that working time equates with time spent at the employee's normal workplace, so it follows that time spent working at home (or in any other place) may count towards working time, as would time spent at a training course. Uncertainty appears to exist, however, in relation to time an employee is required to be on call, lunch breaks and time spent travelling on company business. Another undefined area is the question as to how statutory time off should be dealt with (statutory time off is explained below 'Time Off for Public Duties and Other Functions').

Rest Breaks

Under the Regulations, employees are entitled to several types of rest break. Firstly, where the working day exceeds six hours, employees are entitled to a break of at least twenty minutes during the working day. This rest break cannot be taken at the beginning or end of the employee's working day, but rather must be taken as a break from work *during* the working day. The worker must be permitted to leave their workplace during this break. This provision would affect all but part-time workers.

Secondly, there is a compulsory daily rest period of at least eleven consecutive hours, i.e. the time interval between finishing work one day and starting the next day must be at least eleven continuous hours. No averaging is allowed in this calculation.

Thirdly, there is a compulsory weekly rest period of at least 24 hours, which may be averaged over two weeks. Employers should, wherever possible, allow employees to take the weekly rest break along with the eleven hour daily break, in order to give them a break each week of at least 35 consecutive hours.

There are a number of permitted derogations (exemptions) from the rest break provisions (see 'Permitted Exemptions from the Working Time Regulations' below).

Night Working

The Regulations state that employees working at night should not have a contractual night shift of longer than eight hours on average. The reference period for averaging is a period of seventeen weeks (and may be longer in certain circumstances, subject to agreement). However, if the employee's work is hazardous or if it involves heavy physical or mental strain, no averaging is allowed and the limit of eight hours must therefore be applied rigidly. It is up to employers to agree with their unions or the workforce what constitutes 'heavy physical or mental strain'.

'Night-time' is defined in the Regulations as a period which lasts from 11.00 pm until 6.00 am, although this may be varied by a relevant agreement (see below). A night worker is defined as someone who works at least three hours during night-time. It is important to note, however, that individuals may be regarded as night workers even if they work only some of their time at night, so long as they work a material proportion of their working time during night-time 'as a normal course'.

The provisions on night working exist independently from the requirement to limit the working week to an average of 48 hours. In other words, the restrictions on night working must be applied irrespective of whether the total number of hours an employee works in a week is more or less than 48.

There are a number of permitted derogations from the night working provisions (see the next section).

Permitted Exemptions from the Working Time Regulations

There are certain exclusions and exemptions from some aspects of the Regulations as follows.

Excluded Jobs

There are certain categories of workers which are excluded altogether from the Regulations. These are medical doctors under training, armed forces personnel, police officers, transport workers (e.g. drivers), sea fishing workers and those who are engaged in 'other work at sea'. This latter definition includes personnel working on ships and those employed on offshore oil and gas installations.

At the time of writing, a draft EC Directive is being considered which contains provisions to introduce working time restrictions for some of the categories of personnel who are exempted from the current Working Time Regulations. It is therefore likely that, at some time in the future, new legislation on working time and rest breaks will be introduced for junior doctors, sea fishing workers and offshore workers.

Exemptions

Managing executives and other people who have autonomy over their working time, or whose working time is unmeasured, are excluded from the provisions of the Working Time Regulations covering working hours, rest breaks and night working. The theory is that, where an individual is genuinely in control of their own working time, there is no need for them to be protected by statute.

Apart from senior executives, this exemption may extend (for example) to some salespeople and homeworkers. Such people will, however, be entitled to the minimum holiday entitlement laid down in the Regulations (see 'Holiday Entitlements' below).

Permitted Derogations from the Rest Periods and Night Working Provisions

Certain workers may be exempted from the provisions relating to rest periods, length of night work and the reference periods (for averaging) *but not from the 48-hour week*. Furthermore, where an employee is not granted a statutory rest period, he must be given an equivalent period of compensatory rest. This derogation is, therefore, considerably diluted in terms of granting freedom to employers to disapply the Regulations.

The categories of worker to whom this derogation may apply include:

(a) workers who have to travel some distance to get to work or who travel extensively between different work places. A typical example would be a construction worker who has to travel a considerable distance and live away from home whilst working at a remote construction site;

(b) security and surveillance workers where there is a requirement for a continuous presence throughout the day and night. This would include security guards, caretakers, etc.;

(c) workers involved in a business where 24-hour continuity of service or production is required. This is based on a provision contained within the Working Time Directive which states that this derogation can apply whenever work cannot be interrupted on technical grounds. The Regulations give a number of examples, including those working in hospitals, docks, airports, press, radio, television and film production, postal and telecommunications services, civil protection services, including ambulance and fire services, gas, water and electricity production, transmission and distribution, household refuse collection and incineration, research and development activities and agriculture;

(d) workers involved in peak periods of work, e.g. work with seasonal highs, for example work in agriculture and tourism or post office workers in the period running up to Christmas;

(e) workers involved in unusual and unforeseeable circumstances or where there has been a major incident.

There are also special rules relating to shift changes which have the effect of excluding daily and weekly rest periods for:

(a) shift workers during the changeover from day to night shift (or vice versa) if they are unable on that occasion to take their daily and/or weekly rest period between the end of one shift and the start of the next one;

(b) workers who work split shifts, i.e. work split up over the day.

It is important to note that for these categories of workers, there is still an obligation to restrict the average working week to a maximum of 48 hours.

Voluntary Agreement to Work Longer Hours

Individual employees are permitted to volunteer to work longer than 48 hours if they wish but no employee can be compelled or coerced into agreeing to do so by the employer. This provision is strictly controlled as follows:

(a) contracts of employment may not impose a working week of longer than 48 hours;

(b) exceptions to the 48-hour working limit cannot be imposed on individuals by collective agreement;

(c) workers must not be compelled by their manager to work more than an average of 48 hours per week;

(d) workers must not be subjected to any detriment for refusing to agree to work more than 48 hours per week;

(e) any agreement for an individual to work more than an average of 48 hours per week must be in writing;

(f) where an individual has agreed in writing to work more than an average of 48 hours per week, they may terminate the agreement at any time by giving notice (seven days' notice, unless a relevant agreement provides for a longer notice period).

Where an employer permits employees to work more than an average of 48 hours per week, they are creating a weighty administrative burden for themselves. This is because employers must keep accurate, up to date and detailed records of every occasion when an employee works over 48 hours per week and these records must be made available for inspection on demand by the Health and Safety Executive.

It is important to note also that this derogation applies only to the maximum weekly hours provision and not to any of the other aspects of the Regulations. There is no facility for employees to volunteer to give up their rest periods, work night shifts of more than eight hours on average or forfeit statutory holiday entitlement.

Interestingly, the UK is the EU Member State to have taken advantage of the derogation that employees may volunteer to work longer than 48 hours per week on average. This provision will, in any event, be subject to a future European Commission review, and it is highly likely that following this review an absolute ban on working more than an average of 48 hours per week may be imposed. This is likely to happen in the year 2003.

Agreements

There are a number of provisions within the Working Time Regulations which can be modified by employers by setting up an agreement with the workforce. The practical effect of this is that employers may modify the way in which the Working Time Regulations apply to them in certain defined areas.

There are three types of possible agreement.

1. A collective agreement.

2. A workforce agreement.

3. A relevant agreement.

Collective Agreements

A collective agreement is an agreement made with a recognised independent trade union.

Workforce Agreements

As an alternative to a collective agreement, an employer may set up a workforce agreement in one of two ways:

(a) through elected workplace representatives; *or*

(b) by obtaining the signature of the majority of the workforce as individuals (where there are twenty or fewer workers).

All employees covered by a workforce agreement have the right to receive a copy of the workforce agreement and appropriate guidance notes to enable them to understand it fully.

Relevant Agreements

This type of agreement is a 'catch-all' category, and the term 'relevant agreement' includes collective agreements, workforce agreements and individual agreements with the workers. The key features are that:

(a) the agreement must be in writing;

(b) it must genuinely be an agreement, as opposed to a written document which is simply issued by the employer to the workers.

A new employee's (written) contract of employment would be valid as a 'relevant agreement' in this context for that individual.

The areas, in which an employer can vary the application of the Regulations through a relevant agreement, include matters such as:

(a) modification or exclusion of the provisions covering length of rest periods and length of night work;

(b) the start dates for the reference periods for calculating average working hours. If no agreement is in place, a rolling reference period will apply;

(c) extension of the reference period for averaging working hours for certain categories of worker;

(d) the length of notice an employee must give in order to cancel a voluntary agreement that they will work longer than 48 hours per week. The default notice period is seven days (i.e. if no agreement is in place covering this issue) but an agreement can impose a longer period of up to three months;

(e) the length of the rest break during the day for workers whose working day exceeds six hours. The default length is twenty minutes;

(f) the day of the week on which a 'week' starts for the purpose of calculating weekly rest periods. The default is Sunday at midnight;

(g) when 'night-time' starts and ends. The default period is from 11.00 pm until 6.00 am;

(h) the type of night work which the company regards as hazardous or as involving heavy physical or mental strain;

(i) rules regarding the timing of annual leave and notice periods required prior to an individual's holiday dates being agreed;

(j) the start and end of the holiday year.

PART-TIMERS' RIGHTS

Part-time employees enjoy the same statutory rights as full-time workers. Previous rules which conferred different entitlements on part-time staff with regard to certain statutory rights were abolished in 1995. Part-time employees, therefore, have equal rights to redundancy entitlements, maternity benefits, statutory sick pay, trade union rights, protection against unfair dismissal, and a range of other statutory entitlements.

Technically this does not mean that employers need to offer equal *contractual* benefits to part-time staff compared to full-time staff. However, because in most instances the majority of part-time staff within an organisation are women, the application of less favourable terms and conditions of employment to part-timers could indirectly discriminate against them on the grounds of sex. An example of this would be an occupational pension scheme which excluded part-timers from membership. This would be unlawful unless the employer could justify the less favourable treatment on objective job-based grounds. The subject of indirect sex discrimination is dealt with fully in Chapter 7.

Essentially, employers should make no distinction between the terms, conditions and benefits offered to their full-time and part-time employees. In any event, provisions are to be introduced in the Employment Relations Act to equalise the contractual rights of part-time staff so that it will become expressly unlawful to treat part-timers differently from full-timers in the provision of pay, benefits and other terms and conditions of employment. This is likely to be introduced in the year 2000.

HOLIDAY ENTITLEMENTS

Prior to the introduction of the Working Time Regulations in October 1998, there was no law in the UK compelling employers to grant their employees any holiday entitlement, whether paid or unpaid. It was customary, however, for employers to do so as part of employees' contractual terms but typically workers such as temps, casuals, and agency staff, were not granted holidays.

The Working Time Regulations provides statutory holiday entitlement for all workers, including agency staff, casuals, homeworkers and temporary staff who are engaged on a contract for thirteen weeks or more. The minimum length of holiday entitlement is four weeks per annum, although initially, up until November 1999, it is three weeks per annum. Public holidays may be treated as counting towards employees' statutory holiday entitlement, if the employer wishes.

The aim of the Regulations is to ensure that workers receive a proper break from work from a health and safety perspective. The Regulations, therefore, state that there can be no cash substitutes for holiday not taken, except on termination of employment. This means that it is unlawful for employers to permit employees to forgo their annual holiday entitlement and receive pay in lieu. There is also a ruling that holidays must be taken during the year in which they are due, and so carrying over holidays to the next holiday year is not permissible. Equally it is no longer lawful for an employer to require an employee to work a full year before becoming entitled to take paid holidays.

One note of consolation for employers is that the restrictions on carry over and pay in lieu apply only to the period of statutory leave imposed by the Regulations. It follows, therefore, that where an employer grants annual leave in excess of the statutory minimum, they are free to make their own rules and arrangements regarding carry over and pay in lieu in relation to the portion of the leave which is in excess of the statutory minimum.

There are special provisions in the Regulations relating to the timing of holidays, which give employers certain powers to regulate when workers take their statutory leave. An employer may set up an agreement with the workforce whereby they are empowered:

(a) to require employees to give notice of the dates of any proposed holiday. The notice required cannot be longer than twice the amount of leave the employee is proposing to take (e.g. if the employee is applying for one week's leave, they can be compelled to give at least two weeks' notice);

(b) to nominate specified dates on which employees must take some or all of their statutory leave, in which case employees must be given written notice of the relevant dates. Once again this notice must be at least twice the length of the period of leave being imposed;

(c) to refuse to accept an employee's proposed leave dates by notifying the employee that authorisation for the dates requested will not be granted.

Such notification must be at least as long as the period of leave the employee was proposing to take (e.g. if the employee applies for one week's leave, notice of the employer's refusal must be at least one week);

(d) to decide whether statutory holiday entitlement must be taken all at once, or whether it may be taken in instalments.

Under the Working Time Regulations, when an employee leaves the company, they are entitled to receive pay in lieu of statutory holidays which have been earned but not taken. Furthermore, the Regulations allow employers (if they wish) to claw back an amount of money equivalent to holiday entitlement taken in excess of the statutory entitlement earned, provided such action is authorised in a written agreement.

Public Holidays

Most employers grant their employees paid time off on public holidays, such as Christmas day, Spring bank holiday, etc. Contrary to general belief, however, there is no statutory obligation on employers to observe public holidays or bank holidays. Employees have no general right in law to be granted time off on public holidays, nor to be paid at an enhanced rate of pay if they work on a public holiday. Employers are free to decide which public holidays, if any, are recognised, whether or not the business should close and whether or not employees should be granted time off with pay on the nominated days.

It is a legal requirement that the written terms of an employee's contract should specify the amount of holiday entitlement, including public holidays, the employee is entitled to, and whether such time off is paid or unpaid. It is therefore important to ensure that employees' written terms make the following matters clear:

(a) how many public holidays are to be granted as days off;

(b) which days are nominated as public holidays or whether they are variable at the employer's discretion;

(c) whether employees may be required by the employer to work on a public holiday in line with operational demands;

(d) what (if any) extra entitlements will accrue to employees if they work on a public holiday, e.g. whether they will be paid at an enhanced rate of pay, or receive a day's holiday in lieu or both;

(e) whether paid public holidays constitute part of employees' statutory entitlement to paid leave under the Working Time Regulations.

It is also worth noting that public holidays differ in the various constituent countries within the UK, and in Scotland traditionally some public holidays vary from region to region.

SUNDAY WORKING

Special provisions are in place (contained within the Employment Rights Act 1996) which give retail and betting workers the right to opt out of working on Sundays. It is unlawful to dismiss or victimise a shop or betting employee on account of their decision not to work on Sundays, whether or not the refusal is for religious reasons. Employers must therefore respect their employees' right to choose whether or not to consent to work on Sundays, or on a particular Sunday. These rights apply to all shop workers, except those who have been recruited specifically to work only on Sundays.

An employee may opt out of Sunday working at any time by giving their employer three months' notice. Employees may also opt back in again if they change their mind about Sunday working.

The law does not prevent employers of shop workers from paying enhanced rates of pay for Sunday working. The choice lies with the employer who may elect to offer financial incentives for Sunday working or simply pay the same rates as for weekday working.

The term 'shop' specifically includes any premises where any retail trade or business is carried on including:

- shops;
- hairdressers and barbers;
- betting shops;
- a business where goods may be hired by members of the public;
- retail sales by auction.

Catering businesses, e.g. restaurants, cafes, takeaway establishments and bars are not covered.

'Betting work' includes:

- work at a licensed betting office;
- work at a track for a bookmaker where the employee is dealing with betting transactions.

All employees who work in shops are covered by these provisions, i.e. not only sales staff who deal directly with customers on the shop floor. The Act applies equally to cleaners, shelf-fillers, administrative workers, canteen staff managers/supervisors and all others based at the shop.

If an employee is dismissed, threatened with dismissal or selected for redundancy on account of a refusal to work on Sundays, they may bring a claim to an employment tribunal irrespective of their age, number of hours worked per week or length of service. If the dismissal is found to have been caused by the person's refusal to work on Sundays, it will be automatically unfair.

It is a legal requirement for the employers of shop and betting workers to provide all employees with a statement explaining their rights to opt out of Sunday working and the consequences of such action. This must be done within two months of an employee starting work.

These Sunday working provisions apply only to shop and betting work ers and not to employees engaged in other types of work.

PARENTAL LEAVE

One of the many recent imports from Europe is the Parental Leave Directive. The government announced proposals for the implementation of the terms of the Directive in its Employment Relations Bill, published in early 1999. It is likely that the provisions of the Directive will be introduced during the latter part of 1999.

The objectives of the Parental Leave Directive are to:

(a) reconcile the parental and professional responsibilities of working parents;

(b) promote equal opportunities and treatment between men and women.

Once implemented, all employees, both men and women, will have the right, if they wish, to take parental leave of up to three months on the birth or adoption of a child. The option to take parental leave will be available (for both full-time and part-time employees) at any time up to the child's 8th birthday. Parental leave, however, will not require to be paid, although employers may, if they wish, continue to pay full or part of the employee's salary during periods of parental leave.

There will be a one year qualifying period of service before employees become eligible for parental leave.

A further aspect of the Parental Leave Directive is that it will confer on employees the right to take time off work for urgent family reasons. 'Urgent family reasons' in this context is defined as reasons of family 'sickness or accident making the immediate presence of the worker indispensable'. This will compel employers to allow employees time off in the event of the serious illness or accident of a family member or other critical family situation. There is to be no minimum period of qualifying service required for employees to be entitled to this benefit.

The introduction of provisions for parental leave will not alter the range of maternity rights to which female employees are entitled (see Chapter 8).

The parental leave provisions will introduce, for the first time, statutory time off for male employees who become parents. Although many employers do offer paternity leave as a contractual benefit (usually a few days or a week's paid time off), there have never previously been any statutory provisions in the UK entitling male employees to take paternity leave.

TIME OFF FOR PUBLIC DUTIES AND OTHER FUNCTIONS

Employees are entitled in law to take time off work for certain defined purposes. In some, but not all cases, the time off must be paid. Where an entitlement to time off exists, and an employee is refused such time off, the employee can take a complaint to an employment tribunal. The same principal applies to a situation where an employer refuses to pay the employee for time off taken and the employee is entitled in law to be paid for such time off. Unfortunately, there is no indication in statute as to how much time off should be granted, only the stipulation that the amount of time off given should be "reasonable".

The functions for which time off must be granted include the following.

1. **Time off for public duties.** Time off from work must be granted for those who fulfil any one of a range of public positions, such as Justice of the Peace, members of a statutory tribunal, etc. Such time off need not be paid.

    Strangely, there is no statutory obligation on employers to grant time off for employees to attend jury service. However, in practice, refusal to grant time off would place the employer in contempt of court, so the effect is the same.

2. **Time off for ante-natal care for pregnant employees.** An employee who is pregnant is automatically entitled to reasonable paid time off during working hours for ante-natal care. This right does not depend on any minimum length of service.

    It is worth noting that pregnant employees cannot be compelled to arrange medical appointments outside working hours or to make up for lost time by working extra hours in lieu of time spent at appointments.

3. **Time off to take part in trade union activities (other than industrial action).** Employees who are members of an independent trade union, which is recognised by their employer, have the right to take reasonable time off work during working hours so that they may take part in the activities of the union. The type of trade union activity envisaged would include time off for representation and time off to attend meetings, including those called for the purpose of considering industrial action. Employers are not obliged to pay employees for such time off.

4. **Time off for officials of an independent trade union recognised by the employer to carry out trade union duties or undergo relevant training.** Where the employer recognises a particular trade union, employees who are officials of the union are entitled to reasonable, paid time off during working hours to carry out the duties associated with the position and to attend relevant training. There is, however, no right for a trade union official to claim additional pay where they have undertaken

trade union duties during hours which fall outside their normal working hours.

5. **Time off for appointed safety representatives to allow them to perform safety functions or undergo relevant training.** A trade union which is recognised by an employer is entitled to appoint safety representatives. Such elected safety representatives are entitled to paid time off to carry out the duties associated with the position, including time off to attend relevant training.

5. **Time off for those under notice of redundancy to look for a new job.** Where employees have been given notice of redundancy, they have the right to take reasonable time off work with pay to look for new employment. To qualify for this right, the employee should have at least two years' continuous service.

    Time off, under this heading, could include time spent attending interviews, visiting job centres or making arrangements for training and travel time associated with these purposes.

CHAPTER SIX

PAY

THE MINIMUM WAGE

The National Minimum Wage Act came into effect in April 1999. The scope of the Act is wide in that the right to receive the national minimum wage applies to all 'workers' over compulsory school age (rather than only 'employees' which is a narrower definition). The Act expressly includes agency workers within its scope, whilst homeworkers, part-timers and even some self-employed people are also covered. The only specific exceptions are prisoners, share fishermen and voluntary workers, who work for no remuneration.

The government has set the minimum wage initially at £3.60 per hour with a lower rate of £3.00 per hour for young people between the ages of eighteen and 21. Those aged sixteen to seventeen are exempt, as are apprentices under the age of 26 during the first year of their apprenticeship. There is also a special rate for trainees (of any age) who are undertaking a recognised accredited training programme. This rate, which has been set at £3.20 per hour, may be paid to the worker for the first six months in a new job with a new employer. Rates of pay may be averaged out over a reference period of up to one month in order to calculate whether, on average, the worker has received at least the minimum wage to which they are entitled.

The minimum wage is one single national rate. There is no differentiation on the basis of different regions, different industry sectors, different sizes of employers or different occupations. These provisions mean that all employers are equally obliged to operate the minimum wage, regardless of their size, the nature of their business or where in the country they are based.

The minimum wage of £3.60 per hour includes certain elements of pay, which the employee receives over and above basic pay. The elements of pay which count towards the minimum wage are bonuses, incentive payments, performance pay, profit-related pay and tips which are pooled and paid by the employer through payroll. Conversely, shift and overtime premium payments, stand-by and on-call payments, allowances, and tips paid directly to the worker by a customer do not go towards discharging an employer's responsibility to pay the national minimum wage.

The National Minimum Wage Act imposes specific record-keeping responsibilities on employers. For workers who earn less than £1,000 per month, employers must keep specific detailed records, whilst for workers who earn more than £1,000 per month, the records need only show that that they are being paid at least at the level of the minimum wage.

It was the enforcement provisions of this law which excited the most interest when they were announced. There are three separate measures designed to ensure enforcement. These are described below.

Contractual Rights and Tribunal Claims

Individual employees can enforce their right to the national minimum wage by taking a claim to either an employment tribunal (for unlawful deduction from wages) or a county court (for breach of contract).

Employees also have the right not to suffer a detriment or be dismissed on account of bringing or being involved in proceedings related to the enforcement of the national minimum wage.

Enforcement Officers and Penalty Notices

The Act introduces a power to appoint officers to carry out enforcement of the national minimum wage. Officers have the authority to enter employers' premises and demand access to wage records. Where an officer believes that workers are being paid less than the national minimum wage, the officer has authority to issue an enforcement notice on the employer requiring them to pay the worker(s) at a rate at least equivalent to the national minimum wage and to make up the balance of pay for past periods in which the minimum wage was not paid.

If an employer fails to comply with an enforcement notice, the officer may take proceedings on behalf of the relevant workers in order to recover the amounts due.

There may also be financial penalties for non-payment of the national minimum wage following an enforcement notice. The penalty consists of twice the hourly rate set for the national minimum wage for each day of non-compliance and these penalty amounts will be payable to the Secretary of State.

Criminal Sanctions

The third enforcement strategy involves the creation of a new criminal offence. Specifically it is an offence to do any of the following.

1.   Refuse or wilfully neglect to pay a worker at a rate not less than the national minimum wage.

2.   Fail to keep records in accordance with the regulations.

3.   Knowingly keep false records.

4.   Knowingly produce or furnish false records or other information.

5.   Intentionally delay or obstruct an officer appointed under the legislation,

or refuse to answer a question, furnish information or produce a document when required to do so by an officer.

If found guilty of this criminal offence, employers would face prosecution and a fine of up to £5,000.

CONTRACTUAL AND NON-CONTRACTUAL PAY

An employee's pay may consist of one or more of a number of different elements, for example:

- basic wage or salary;
- overtime earnings;
- regional allowance;
- shift allowance;
- allowances for petrol, telephone, etc.;
- statutory maternity pay;
- statutory sick pay;
- contractual sick pay (i.e. continuation of salary during periods of sickness absence);
- bonus;
- commission;
- outstanding holiday pay on termination of employment, etc.

Clearly, basic pay will always be contractual whilst certain other payments (namely statutory sick pay and statutory maternity pay) are statutory requirements and therefore *must* be paid to employees who qualify for them.

Other elements of pay are often discretionary, but may alternatively be contractual, depending on the wording of the employee's contract. Where bonuses, allowances, etc. are contractual, the employer would not be entitled to remove or reduce them, otherwise this would be a breach of contract. Where, however, it is clearly stated in writing that a particular payment is non-contractual, or discretionary, the employer would be entitled to exercise his discretion not to pay it. All rules and conditions relating to pay should, therefore, be clearly set out in writing and a consistent approach taken. Information can appear either in individuals' contracts of employment, in a separate policy booklet, or staff handbook, so long as it is made clear which elements of pay are contractual entitlements, and which are at the discretion of management. Clear written documents (signed and dated), will ensure that the employer will not have to face breach of contract claims from employees in the event that, for example, an annual bonus is not paid in a particular year due to a downturn in business.

It is in both the employer's and the employee's interests to ensure that terms of employment related to pay are clearly stated so as to avoid misunderstanding, misinterpretation or argument at a later time over what entitlements are applicable.

Managing Overtime

Different employers take different approaches to overtime working. Typically employees engaged in manual work, support staff and more junior employees are paid enhanced rates of pay for overtime working, whilst those in senior or professional jobs are expected to work variable hours without additional remuneration. Some employers discourage overtime working, whilst others insist that employees must gain the approval of their manager prior to working overtime.

Employers are obliged in law to provide written details to each employee of their normal rate of pay and normal working hours (see 'Terms of the Contract which Must be in Writing' in Chapter 1). The written statement should include details of any contractual requirement to work overtime (subject to the working time restrictions laid down in the Working Time Regulations 1998). It should also include information clarifying whether or not overtime hours are paid or unpaid and, if they are paid, whether the rate of pay is the employee's normal rate of pay or a higher rate (for example time-and-a-half or double-time).

It is always advisable to have a clear term in employees' contracts stating that they must be available to work additional hours outside their normal working hours (including evenings and weekends) at the request of their manager. Without such a flexibility clause, the employee could legitimately refuse to work overtime.

Excessive overtime working can be expensive for employers and managers should therefore exercise sensible control over employees' hours of work by operating a system of hours recording and monitoring. Records of working hours in excess of 48 hours per week are, in any event, required under the Working Time Regulations 1998 (see 'The Law on Working Hours', Chapter 5). It may even be advisable for managers to implement a rule that overtime will only be paid for if the line manager's express written permission has first been obtained. In this way employees will be less inclined to slack during the week and then argue that they had to work on a Sunday (and thus earn double-pay) to complete their week's work.

There is no obligation on employers to pay premium rates for overtime worked and the level of pay applicable is entirely a contractual matter. The employer may pay overtime at single-time (i.e. the employee's normal rate of pay), time-and-a-half or double-time. Similarly, time off in lieu for periods of overtime worked may, or may not, be offered to employees, depending on the employer's rules.

The important point is that these matters should be clear as part of employees' contracts of employment and apart from the restrictions imposed by the Working Time Regulations 1998 (see Chapter 5) on the number of hours employees work, the employer is free to decide what overtime requirements and terms are appropriate.

DEDUCTIONS FROM PAY: WHEN THEY ARE LAWFUL AND WHEN THEY ARE UNLAWFUL

Employers are severely restricted in law as to what deductions they may make from their employees' pay. In order for a deduction from pay to be lawful, it must meet one of the following criteria:

(a) that the deduction is required by statute (income tax and national insurance payments are the most usual elements in this category);

(b) that the deduction must be made because it is authorised by a court (for example an attachment of earnings order on account of the employee's failure to pay child support, council tax, etc.);

(c) that the employee's contract contains a statement that a particular type of deduction may be made from the employee's pay. For this to be enforceable, the employee must have received a copy of the appropriate clause before any deduction from pay is made;

(d) that the employee has signed a written agreement in advance stating that they agree to a deduction being made for a specific purpose.

It follows that, apart from statutory deductions, such as income tax and national insurance, it is unlawful to deduct money from an employee's pay without the employee's specific written agreement obtained in advance.

Case Study

A nurse who left her employment just two days after commencing her job was refused any wages for the days she had worked. This was in accordance with a term in the contract of employment which expressly provided for forfeiture of pay in the event of the employee leaving without proper notice.

The employee applied to an employment tribunal claiming that the refusal to pay her wages for the two days worked constituted an unlawful deduction from her pay. Her claim succeeded because, although she had been verbally informed when she started work of the terms and conditions of her employment, she had not received a written copy of the contract nor had she

---

> been given a written copy of the relevant term governing forfei-
> ture of pay. She was therefore awarded a sum of money equiva-
> lent to two days' wages.
>
> *Bird t/a Mayfair Nursing Home v. Honey* [1993] E.A.T. 14/93.

There is also a clause in the Employment Rights Act which effectively prevents employers from making deductions from pay following a written agreement made after the event which gave rise to the deduction. What this means
is that, retrospective consent to a deduction from pay will not entitle the employer to make a deduction. This effectively prevents employers from exert-
ing pressure on employees to consent to a deduction from pay in respect of
past events or conduct which has already taken place.

As a result of the provisions governing deductions from wages, employers
are not allowed to deduct money from employees' pay for misconduct, lateness,
poor job performance, damage to company property, etc. unless either there is
an express term in the contract authorising such deductions or the employee
has agreed in writing in advance that a deduction from pay may be made in
the specific circumstances.

Case Study

The employee was the manager of a retail outlet where, on several occasions between December 1988 and May 1989, stock
checks revealed deficiencies in stock levels when compared to
the amount of money which had been taken by the shop. The
employee had signed a statement on 14 March 1989 consenting
to deductions to make up for the shortfall in the shop's takings.
When he was dismissed shortly afterwards, the employer refused to pay his outstanding wages because the remaining shortfall was still in excess of the amount of wages due to him on
termination.

When the employee brought a claim for unlawful deduction of
wages to a tribunal, the decision was that the deduction from
pay was not validly authorised by dint of the employee's signed
statement because this had been signed *after* the stock deficiencies had been discovered.

Discount Tobacco & Confectionery Ltd v. Williamson [1993] I.C.R.
371.

If money is deducted from an employee's pay without authority, the employee
can take a case to an employment tribunal claiming that there has been an
unlawful deduction made from their wages and the result would be that the

employer would be ordered to repay the money to the employee. There is no minimum length of service required for an employee to take a claim to an employment tribunal for unlawful deduction of pay.

There are some exceptions to the law covering deductions from pay which apply in the following circumstances.

1. Where there has been an accidental overpayment of wages or expenses made to the employee (see below).

2. Where there is a court or tribunal order requiring the employee to make a specific payment to the employer, and the employee has given their prior written consent to this.

3. Where there are disciplinary proceedings provided for in legislation, e.g. police disciplinary proceedings.

4. Where the deduction from pay is made because the employee was absent from work whilst participating in a strike or other industrial action.

Retail Employees

Special provisions exist in relation to retail employees. These provide that any contractual term authorising deductions from pay in relation to cash or stock shortages must not involve a deduction in excess of 10 per cent of the employee's gross wage for a particular pay period.

Overpayment of Wages

Normally, an employer may proceed to recover any amounts of wages or expenses accidentally overpaid to an employee. This should, however, be done in a reasonable fashion so that the employee is not left short of cash as a result of a huge deduction from a single pay cheque. Agreement should be sought to fix deductions over a number of pay periods so that the employer may recoup their money without impoverishing the employee.

In certain, limited circumstances, even an accidental overpayment of wages can be irrecoverable. Recovery could be unlawful if:

(a) the employer had misled the employee into believing they were entitled to the money; *and*

(b) the employee was genuinely unaware that the employer was likely to reclaim the money; *and*

(c) the employee had already spent the money or made a commitment to spend it; *and*

(d) the overpayment was not the employee's fault.

PAY CUTS

Any attempt on an employer's part to reduce an employee's pay is likely to
constitute a fundamental breach of contract (this subject is covered fully in
Chapters 3 and 4). An employee's pay is central to the whole employment
relationship and, therefore, any action on the part of the employer to alter it
would affect the whole essence of the contract. A pay cut implemented without the employee's consent could, therefore, entitle the afflicted employee to
take any one of a number of courses of action.

1. To indicate to their employer that they object to the change and are con-
    tinuing to work under protest, and sue the employer for damages for breach
    of contract. No minimum period of service is required.

2. To make a claim for an unlawful deduction of wages under the Employ-
    ment Rights Act 1996. It has been established that, for the purposes of the
    Act, a *reduction in* pay is the same as a *deduction from* pay because the
    end result is the same, i.e. the employee suffers an unauthorised net loss
    in pay. No minimum period of service is required to bring this type of
    claim to a tribunal.

3. Subject to the employee having the minimum qualifying service, to re-
    sign and claim constructive dismissal.

EMPLOYEES' RIGHT TO AN ITEMISED PAY STATEMENT

All employees have the right to receive an itemised pay statement each time
they receive pay from the employer. The statement must include:

(a) the gross amount of their pay;

(b) the amounts of all fixed deductions and the purposes for which they are
    made (although it is permissible to provide a separate statement covering
    fixed deductions which need not then be reissued for every pay period);

(c) the amounts of all variable deductions and the purposes for which they
    are made, e.g. income tax;

(d) the net amount of pay payable to the employee.

If different elements of net pay are paid in different ways, e.g. part by direct
credit transfer and part by cheque, the statement must also show the amount
and method of each part-payment.

CHAPTER SEVEN

SEX AND RACE DISCRIMINATION

Although the laws banning sex and race discrimination have been with us for many years, employees continue to suffer discrimination and victimisation on the grounds of gender and race in their employment. Much of the discrimination which takes place is unconscious, i.e. the manager is unaware that their actions are potentially discriminatory. Often traditional, entrenched attitudes are to blame or there may be prejudice based on past experiences. Nevertheless, motives are largely irrelevant in determining whether or not unlawful discrimination has occurred. An employment tribunal will be concerned with what actually happened to the employee, not their manager's intentions.

THE CONCEPTS OF DIRECT AND INDIRECT DISCRIMINATION

Discrimination, on the grounds of sex and race, may be *direct* or *indirect*. Direct discrimination is a straightforward concept: it occurs where an individual is treated less favourably than another individual of the opposite sex or a different racial group was treated, or would have been treated, and that this less favourable treatment was on the grounds of their sex or race.

In order to succeed in a claim for direct sex or race discrimination, the individual only has to show that, had they been a member of the opposite sex, or of a different racial group, then they would have been more favourably treated than they were, in fact, treated. This is known as the 'but for' test, e.g. 'I would have gained the promotion, but for the fact that I am a woman'. UK discrimination law is based on the notion of comparisons.

Case Study

In one important case, a male employee took a case of alleged direct discrimination against his employer, the Ministry of Defence, on account of different working practices between men and women. It was the employer's practice not to require female employees to carry out certain dirty work, as this entailed the need to take showers afterwards, which the women did not wish to have to do. Male employees who did the work received extra pay to compensate them for the fact that the work was dirty.

The Court of Appeal addressed whether this practice was

---

discriminatory against men despite the extra premium paid to them when they performed the dirty work. They concluded that employers cannot buy the right to discriminate. The outcome was therefore that the practice was held to be discriminatory against the male employees.

Jeremiah v. Ministry of Defence [1979] I.R.L.R. 436

Indirect discrimination occurs where the following conditions are met:

- the employer applies a rule, condition or requirement to the job, which on the face of it applies to everyone, *but*

- because of the nature of the condition or requirement, a considerably smaller proportion of women than men (or vice versa) or fewer people from a minority racial group than British people can comply with it, *and*

- as a result of the condition or requirement, a particular individual suffers a disadvantage, *and*

- the employer is unable to justify the rule, condition or requirement on objective, job-based grounds.

Thus, indirect discrimination involves a rule, requirement, policy or condition which has a greater adverse impact on one sex or race group than on another. Examples could include:

(a) a requirement at the recruitment stage that the person selected for the job must be physically strong enough to lift heavy objects, where physical lifting is not a necessary component of the job (this would discriminate indirectly against women);

(b) a requirement that candidates for a promotion must speak fluent English where the job does not involve face to face contact with the public (which would discriminate indirectly against those of foreign nationality whose first language was not English).

It can be seen in these examples, that it is not the requirement itself which is inherently discriminatory, but rather its effect on a particular group. If, however, the employer can justify the rule, requirement or condition on objective grounds, then it will not be unlawful. This could be the case, for instance, in the first example above, if lifting heavy weights constituted a major part of the job or, in the second example, if the job did involve regular face to face contact with customers. If a case of indirect discrimination is taken to an employment tribunal, it is up to the employer to prove that the requirement or condition was justifiable. It is not enough merely to show that the rule or condition was introduced as a matter of convenience, but instead the employer will have to demonstrate that the condition was appropriate and necessary to achieve a real business need, in which case it will not be unlawful.

Good practice for managers to ensure avoidance of sex and race discrimination, would include the following.

1. Developing an understanding of the legal principles and the scope of the Sex Discrimination Act 1975, the Equal Pay Act 1970 and the Race Relations Act 1976.

2. Ensuring all staff, especially managers and supervisors, receive some form of equal opportunities awareness training.

3. Reviewing policies, procedures and practices carefully to ensure that they do not impose any rules, conditions or requirements which could be indirectly discriminatory and which cannot be justified on objective grounds.

4. Carrying out a review of employees' pay to ensure there is no inequality as between male and female employees.

5. Adopting a positive approach to equal opportunities and the elimination of discrimination in the workplace.

THE SCOPE OF THE SEX DISCRIMINATION ACT 1975

The Sex Discrimination Act 1975 applies to all workers, and not just those engaged on a permanent employment contract. Thus protection is afforded to:

- job applicants;
- part-time staff;
- temporary staff;
- agency personnel;
- subcontractors;
- casual workers;
- homeworkers;
- freelance workers;
- apprentices.

The principles of the 1975 Act apply equally to men and women although, in practice, it is women who are most commonly the victims of discrimination.
Discrimination may occur:

(a) at any stage during the recruitment process;

(b) during employment, for example denial of a promotion or training opportunity;

(c) at termination of employment, including dismissal and arrangements for redundancy;

(d) in general treatment at work, for example sexual harassment.

Exemptions from Sex Discrimination Legislation

There are a small number of exclusions from the scope of the sex discrimination legislation. The following people are not protected.

1. Employees who are working wholly or mainly outside Great Britain. Great Britain means England, Scotland and Wales (not Northern Ireland, although similar provisions exist there). Personnel working on offshore oil and gas installations *are,* however, expressly covered.

2. Employees working on a ship which is registered outside Great Britain and operates wholly outside Great Britain.

3. Ministers of religion, where it is lawful to restrict employment to one sex in order to comply with the doctrines of the particular religion.

How Part-timers are Protected by Sex Discrimination Legislation

Part-time employees share all the same statutory employment rights as their full-time counterparts. Such statutory employment rights include, for example, the right to bring a claim for unfair dismissal, the right to a redundancy payment, maternity rights, etc.

At present, however, there is no law which compels employers to afford part-time staff the same *contractual* benefits as full-time employees (e.g. contractual terms relating to sick pay, bonuses, etc.) although the forthcoming Employment Relations Act, when implemented in the UK, create equal (pro rata) rights for part-timers.

In theory, therefore, employers could for the time being 'discriminate' against part-time workers by not offering them an annual bonus to which full-timers were entitled or not making available access to an occupational pension scheme. There is, however, a catch in adopting such a policy.

Less favourable treatment of part-timers can constitute indirect sex discrimination against female employees because the vast majority of part-timers are, in practice, women. Thus a rule or condition which placed part-timers at a disadvantage (when compared to full-time staff) would have a disproportionately adverse effect on female employees. Unless the employer could objectively justify the rule or condition, the result would be indirect discrimination entitling those affected to take a complaint to an employment tribunal.

Employers are therefore advised to ensure that all part-time staff receive the same level of pay and the same benefits (on a pro rata basis) as full-time workers.

Discrimination on the Grounds of Marital Status

The Sex Discrimination Act also outlaws discrimination on the grounds of marriage. Thus, if a married employee or job applicant is treated less favourably than a single person on the grounds of their marital status, this would be unlawful. Paradoxically, it does not give protection to single people who are treated less favourably than married persons!

EQUAL PAY

The Equal Pay Act 1970, contrary to what its title may imply, covers all contractual terms and not just pay. Thus, any unfavourable treatment in terms of the contractual benefits afforded to employees would be covered by this Act. Only employees are covered, however, and not contractors, agency temps, casual workers, etc.

The Equal Pay Act provides for equal pay and benefits between men and women in the same employment where the woman's work, as compared to the man's, is:

- like work; *or*

- work rated as equivalent; *or*

- work of equal value.

Where a woman succeeds in a claim for equal pay, she will be entitled to receive not only equal pay to her male comparator, but equality in all the other terms of her employment contract as well.

It should be noted that the Act only allows for a woman to claim equal pay with a man (and of course vice versa). It does not cover the situation where an employee (of either gender) believes that their rate of pay is unfair in a general sense, nor does it give employees the facility to take a complaint based on a comparison of terms and conditions with someone of the same sex. For a claim to be valid under the Equal Pay Act, there has to be some evidence that the disparity in pay (or other contractual benefit) is due, wholly or partly, to a difference in gender.

Like Work

'Like work' in equal pay terms means work which is either the same or of a broadly similar nature. It is the work which employees actually carry out which is the relevant issue and not the duties listed in the employees' job descriptions. Trivial differences between two jobs would not be relevant for the purposes of establishing that two jobs constituted 'like work'.

Work Rated as Equivalent

This applies whenever the company has conducted a job evaluation study and graded jobs according to their overall worth to the company, usually based on factors, such as effort, knowledge and skill, decision making and level of responsibility. Provided the job evaluation study itself has been conducted in an objective and analytical way, a woman cannot challenge her pay status on the grounds that someone in a higher grade is earning more than she is earning. However, if a woman's job is graded in the same band as a man's job, then she will be entitled to enforce equal pay (although there may still be differences in pay for legitimate reasons – see 'The Genuine Material Factor Defence' below).

Work of Equal Value

Under the 'equal value' canopy, a woman can claim equal pay with a man even if the job she is doing is completely different from the man's job, provided it can be shown that the two jobs are equal in terms of their overall worth to the employer. The criteria for establishing whether or not one job is of equal value to another are similar to those used in setting up analytical job evaluation studies, namely:

(a) the effort required to perform the job to a satisfactory standard, for example in terms of concentration, attention to detail, etc;

(b) the knowledge and skill required for the job;

(c) the level of responsibility inherent in the job;

(d) the level of decision making involved in the job.

The 'Genuine Material Factor' Defence

Clearly an employer may elect to pay different employees different levels of pay, and there is nothing inherently unlawful in doing so provided the differences are not due to differences in sex.

In the event of an equal pay challenge, an employer may put forward a defence that there is a 'genuine material factor' which justifies the difference between a woman's pay and the pay of the male employee to whom she is comparing herself. So long as this factor has nothing to do with the sex of the individuals, and so long as it is clearly this factor, and not some other motive, which is the root of the difference, the defence is likely to succeed. The sorts of factors commonly cited as genuine material factors justifying differences in pay include:

(a) differences in the employees' levels of qualifications or experience;

(b) the individuals' job performance and/or productivity in the job;

(c) a higher level of responsibility or supervisory duties;

(d) a regional weighting allowance paid to compensate employees for higher costs of living, usually in London. This allowance should always be specified as a separate amount rather than incorporated into basic pay;

(e) the time of work, for example it is legitimate to pay an employee an extra allowance for night-shift working, or irregular/unsocial hours working. Such a premium should, however, always be identified as a separate sum payable only to those who work the specified pattern of hours;

(f) market forces, for example difficulties in recruiting suitable people into the organisation;

(g) the practice of 'red circling' i.e. retaining an employee on their existing (higher) level of pay following a transfer to a less senior job. A red-circled salary would probably only act as a material factor if it was applied on a temporary, rather than permanent, basis.

Case Study

The company appointed 24 employees to a newly created job grade. However, one of the female employees was paid a lower rate of pay than her male colleagues because she did not have the direct production experience which they had.

A year later, the employee claimed equal pay based on the concept of 'like work'. The tribunal ruled that at the time of her appointment the employee's lack of experience would have been a genuine material factor justifying a lower rate of pay but that because she had gained experience during the interim year, lack of experience could no longer be a valid defence against an equal pay claim. The employee succeeded in her case.

Post Office v. Page E.A.T. 554/87.

The Equal Opportunities Commission have produced a very helpful *Code of Practice* on equal pay which contains useful advice and guidance for employers, as well as examples.

SEXUAL ORIENTATION

There is presently no specific law governing discrimination against homosexuals and lesbians on account of their sexual orientation. The European Court of Justice has ruled that discrimination on the grounds of sexual orientation does not fall within the scope of European anti-discrimination law, and the UK Sex Discrimination Act 1975, similarly, does not include it within its scope because it specifies that for discrimination to be unlawful, it must occur on grounds of gender (or marital status).

The only possible route an employee could take if they believe they have been treated unfavourably on the grounds of their sexual orientation would be to demonstrate that their treatment was on account of their *sex* rather *sexual orientation,* for example if a homosexual man could show that he had been treated less favourably than a lesbian woman would have been treated in similar circumstances.

It is likely that the legal position on this will change in the future, either as a result of a future European Directive or by dint of a change to UK law.

If discrimination based on sexual orientation does become unlawful in the future, employers would need to conduct a review of their policies governing company benefits. Many companies nowadays offer benefits such as pension benefits, insurance cover, private medical care, relocation expenses and discounts to unmarried (as well as married) opposite-sex partners of employees. If this is the company's policy, and if the law changes in the future, then such benefits would also have to be offered on the same terms to same-sex partners of homosexual or lesbian employees. Without this parity, employees of homosexual orientation who lived with same-sex partners would be able to claim unlawful discrimination on the grounds of less favourable treatment.

THE SCOPE OF THE RACE RELATIONS ACT 1976

The Race Relations Act 1976 was introduced to eliminate discrimination against people in employment, and those trying to get into employment, on the grounds of race. Racial grounds, for the purposes of the Act, includes:

- colour;
- race;
- nationality (including citizenship);
- ethnic origins;
- national origins.

In Northern Ireland, a similar legal provision applies but with one additional category, which is that indigenous Irish travelling people are regarded as a racial group.

To be regarded as a separate group under the category of ethnic origins, for the purposes of the Race Relations Act, a group must have a long shared history, distinct traditions and culture, a separate social identity and common geographical origin, plus possibly a common language, common religion and literature unique to the group. As a result of various tribunal decisions, it has been held that Sikhs, Jews, Serbs and the Irish are separate ethnic groups, whilst Muslims and Rastafarians are not (but see 'Discrimination on the Grounds of Religion' below).

The category of 'national origins' was held, in a 1997 tribunal decision, to include the distinction between the English and the Scots (and, by extension, the Welsh).

Essentially, everyone is protected against discrimination on account of 'race' under the Race Relations Act from the white Englishman from Newcastle through to the black African from Zimbabwe.

Race discrimination, like sex discrimination, can be direct or indirect, and all workers are protected, i.e. not only employees, but also contract staff, agency personnel, freelance workers, etc.

Exemptions from Race Discrimination Legislation

Those excluded from protection under the Race Relations Act 1976 are:

(a) employees who are working wholly or mainly outside Great Britain. Personnel working on offshore oil and gas installations *are,* however, expressly covered;

(b) employees working on a ship which is registered outside Great Britain and operates wholly outside Great Britain;

(c) people working within a private household;

(d) certain Crown servants.

Discrimination on the Grounds of Religion

Religion is not one of the categories listed in the Race Relations Act, and it follows that discrimination against someone (for example refusal to recruit) on the grounds that they are of a particular faith would not be unlawful as such (although such a criterion is clearly inappropriate). Despite this conspicuous absence of anti-discrimination law in Great Britain, members of certain religious groups may, in certain circumstances, be able to claim that unfavourable treatment meted out to them constitutes indirect race discrimination. Apart from the classification of Sikhs and Jews as separate ethnic groups for the purposes of the Race Relations Act (see above), other groups, such as Muslims, may be able to show that they have been indirectly discriminated against on the grounds of colour, race or nationality as a result of a rule or condition applied to everyone but impacting on them in an adverse way. An example appears below.

Case Study

A large number of Asian employees, most of whom were Muslims, were employed by a company. When the company imposed a rule that no employee would be allowed to take holidays during the months of May, June or July on account of the company's high workload during those months, they overlooked the fact that this period spanned the Muslim religious festival of Eid. Various Muslim employees asked to take time off during Eid and offered to make up their hours at another time, but their request was refused.

Despite the company's rule, a large number of their Asian employees remained absent from work during Eid and, as a result, were given final written warnings. They made a claim for indirect race discrimination based on the premise that the requirement for employees to work during Eid, and the subsequent disciplinary warnings for their refusal to comply, had an adverse impact on Asian workers as compared to non-Asian workers, because fewer Asian than non-Asian workers could comply with it. They succeeded in their claim.

J H Walker Ltd v. Hussain and Others E.A.T. 406/94.

Discrimination on the grounds of religion is unlawful in Northern Ireland under the Fair Employment (Northern Ireland) Act 1989. This Act was expressly set up to protect both Catholics and Protestants from discrimination on the grounds of religious beliefs and/or political opinions.

EMPLOYING FOREIGN NATIONALS: THE PROVISIONS OF THE ASYLUM AND IMMIGRATION ACT 1996

Although the provisions of the Race Relations Act 1976 make it unlawful to discriminate against a job applicant on the grounds of nationality, employers also have to contend with the Asylum and Immigration Act 1996 which makes it a criminal offence to recruit someone of foreign nationality, who is subject to immigration control and who does not have permission to work in the UK. The Act places the onus on employers to ensure they do not employ anyone who does not have the right to work in the UK. Breach of the Act's provisions is a criminal offence rendering the company liable to prosecution and fine.

Citizens of countries in the European Economic Area (EEA – comprising the EU plus Norway, Liechtenstein and Iceland) have the automatic right to take up employment in the UK. Additionally, certain Commonwealth citizens with a grandparent born in the UK are eligible for a work permit lasting four years. Employers should take care, however, over Commonwealth 'working holidaymakers' who are not allowed to take full-time work for longer than one year. This status will be noted in the person's passport.

In order to avoid falling foul of the Asylum and Immigration Act 1996, employers need to take appropriate steps at the time of recruitment to:

(a) ask job applicants to produce a document which confirms their right to work in the UK. There is an official list of documents (available from the Home Office) which are valid for this purpose. The most common ones are documents showing the person's national insurance number, passports, work permits and birth certificate;

(b) check that the document appears to relate to the person in question and that it appears to be legitimate (although there is no need to make detailed or specific enquiries);

(c) keep the document or a copy of it on file during employment and for six months after termination of employment;

(d) if the person is not of British or EU nationality, check whether they require a valid work permit for the type of work they are applying for;

(e) ensure these checks are carried out before a job offer is confirmed.

It is not incumbent on employers to check out the validity or authenticity of a prospective employee's documentary evidence, nor are employers expected to be experts on the subject of who is or is not entitled to work in the UK. The key requirements are to gain sight of what appears to be a valid document indicating that the person has the right to work in the UK and to retain a copy of it on file.

The best way for managers to meet their responsibilities in this area and at the same time avoid potential accusations of race discrimination against candidates who are not of British nationality, is to ensure that *every* job applicant is asked to produce documentary proof of their right to work in the UK. If the employer checks documentation for all job applicants as a normal course, then there can be no suggestion that someone of a minority racial group was singled out and afforded less favourable treatment. It is also advisable, for the same reason, to inform job applicants that it is the company's policy to request documentary evidence and that all job applicants are required to comply.

A request for documentary proof of the right to work in the UK can be made of job applicants either at interview or, better still, at the time letters are sent out inviting candidates to attend interview. The check can be conveniently combined with a request for documentary proof of qualifications, thus minimising the inconvenience caused to both parties. If a job applicant refuses or fails to produce documentary evidence of their right to work in the UK, this would justify a refusal to make or to confirm an offer of employment.

The Asylum and Immigration Act applies to employers only at the time of recruitment. There is no obligation on employers to monitor the ongoing status of workers after they have been employed, nor is there any responsibility on the employer to back-track and check employees who were employed before the date the Act was introduced (27 January 1997).

DISCRIMINATION IN RECRUITMENT

Good recruitment, the same as any other business activity, requires a professional, unbiased approach and sound planning. The objective should always be to employ the person who is best suited to the job in question in terms of their knowledge, skills and ability. The person's sex, sexual orientation, racial background, age, religion and political views are likely to be completely ineffectual and irrelevant as criteria for predicting job performance. Despite this maxim, however, there are still many examples of recruitment decisions being influenced by prejudice, stereotyping, ingrained attitudes, personal preferences and assumptions amongst those responsible for selection decisions.

Case Study

An employer instructed a careers officer that he did not want to recruit anyone who lived in a particular area of central Liverpool. The particular area was one in which 50 per cent of the population was black. Since the black population for the whole of Merseyside at the time was approximately 2 per cent, the application of the condition had a disproportionately adverse impact on black people.

When the case was determined, it was judged that the employer's condition that candidates for employment must not live in the particular part of Liverpool had the effect of excluding a larger proportion of black people than white people. This was held to be indirect race discrimination.

Hussein v. Saints Complete House Furnishers [1979] I.R.L.R. 337.

Sound steps which an employer can take to minimise the chances of discrimination occurring during the recruitment process include:

(a) providing training in recruitment and equal opportunities to all those involved in the recruitment process;

(b) developing a recruitment policy, procedure and guidelines, and ensuring they are communicated and implemented consistently;

(c) monitoring those recruited in terms of gender, marital status, race, age and disability;

(d) ensuring any criteria laid down as conditions for recruitment into a particular job are not potentially indirectly discriminatory against women (or men) or members of any minority racial group;

(e) revising application forms to remove questions which are potentially discriminatory, e.g. title, marital status, nationality, age, number and ages of children. This information can, if necessary, be collected after the person has been employed;

(f) ensuring interviews are conducted only by those trained in interviewing skills, and that all candidates are treated consistently and fairly at interview;

(g) developing an awareness of the inherent dangers of making assumptions about job candidates, stereotyping and allowing 'gut-feeling' to predominate as a factor influencing decisions;

(h) making short-listing decisions, and the final selection decision, based only on objective and relevant factors, e.g. concrete factual information obtained from the person's CV and at interview and not on personal attitudes or assumptions.

(i) keeping full records of interviews, short-listing methods and selection decisions on file for at least six months (in case a rejected job applicant takes a complaint of discrimination to an employment tribunal).

Genuine Occupational Qualifications: Sex and Race

When recruiting, there are certain exceptions to the requirements not to discriminate on the grounds of sex and race, known as 'genuine occupational qualifications' (GOQs). These GOQs mean that in certain circumstances an employer can justify employing a person of only one sex or race because of the specific nature of the job. The list of exceptions as regards employment of men/women are as follows.

1. Where the job holder must live at the place of work and there is accommodation for one sex only. An example could be employment on an oil-rig if the washroom facilities were communal.

2. For reasons of decency or privacy, where the job involves close physical contact with people, or working in the presence of people who are in a state of undress.

3. Where the job involves the provision of personal services linked to welfare or education.

4. Where the job involves working in a single-sex establishment for people requiring special care. This could include work in a single-sex, old people's home if the residents required special care.

5. Where, for reasons of authenticity, either a man or a woman is required. This covers acting and modelling jobs.

6. Where employment is in a private household, for example the recruitment of a private nurse to attend someone in their home.

7. Where the job involves working overseas in a country whose laws or customs prevent the employment of a woman. For example, in Saudia Arabia women are not permitted to drive.

8. Where the job is one of two to be held by a married couple.

The list of genuine occupational qualifications which can justify employing a person of a particular racial group are as follows.

1. Where the job involves the provision of personal services, which involve promoting the welfare of a particular racial group.

2. Where, for reasons of authenticity, either a man or a woman is required. This covers acting and modelling jobs.

3. Where, for reasons of authenticity, a person of a particular racial group must be employed in a particular setting, for example waiting staff in a Chinese restaurant.

This list, like the list of GOQs applying to sex discrimination, is exhaustive, and employers are not permitted to invent their own reasons for excluding people of a particular sex or race from a job, no matter how strong their views might be on the matter.

Interviewing without Discrimination

Much discrimination takes place at interviews and is often unconscious in so much as the interviewer may be unaware that their personal views and attitudes are influencing the interview or prejudicing the selection decision. In order to avoid discrimination, questions at interview should relate to the requirements of the job, and not to the personal lives of the applicants. The types of question which, when asked of a woman, would constitute sex discrimination include those about the candidate's:

• children – how many children or their ages;

• childminding arrangements;

• family commitments;

- husband's employment;
- plans to have children in the future;
- marriage plans or intentions.

Instead questions may be asked (for example) about the candidate's availability to work at weekends, how they would cope with being called out to work unexpectedly during the evening, whether they are willing to work away from home from time to time, what their goals and aspirations are for the next few years, etc.

The principle of asking male and female candidates the same questions at interview is a sound approach in an overall sense, but it may be unrealistic since the interviewer will want to follow up on each candidate's responses and not be restricted to a fixed list of questions. In any case, it is not just the questions which are asked which can be discriminatory, but also the *purpose* for which they are asked and the use to which the answers are put.

Ultimately, the decision as to whom to appoint should be taken based on factual evidence, following interviews. In the event that a manager decides to offer a job to a candidate whose qualifications and/or experience are not as suited to the job specification as another candidate, then they should be prepared to justify the selection decision based on other objective factors. If a candidate has been passed over for recruitment in favour of someone of the opposite sex or different racial group, and the person appointed appears to have lower qualifications or less experience, this could lead an employment tribunal into drawing an inference that the selection decision was discriminatory, unless the employer can produce strong evidence that there was some other objective, job-based reason for the selection.

DISCRIMINATION AT RETIREMENT

In general terms, employers are free to nominate any age as a retirement age for their employees, as there is no age prescribed in statute at which employees must cease working. If no retirement age is specified in employees' contracts of employment, then the age of 65 will apply. However, it is a requirement in law that the retirement age for a group of employees must be the same for men and women.

Pension Scheme Membership and Pension Benefits

Where a company operates an occupational pension scheme, access to the scheme and benefits received on account of scheme membership must be the same for men and women. The continuing distinction in UK state pension ages has nothing to do with employers' obligations not to discriminate against their employees on the grounds of sex. The Pensions Act 1995 made it compulsory for company pension schemes to contain an equal treatment rule to ensure that men and women are afforded the same rights to join a company scheme and to receive the same benefits from the scheme. This includes equality of treatment as regards the provision of survivors' benefits for employees' widows/widowers.

VICTIMISATION

Both the Sex Discrimination Act 1975 and the Race Relations Act 1976 give protection to employees against victimisation over and above the basic right not to be discriminated against. Victimisation can include a broad range of detrimental treatment, including refusal to employ or promote, removal of perks or denial of expected benefits (e.g. overtime), unfair discipline, dismissal, general hostility or harassment.

The aim of the victimisation provisions is to protect employees who have:

(a) raised a genuine complaint of discrimination with their management;

(b) taken a case of sex or race discrimination to an employment tribunal;

(c) given evidence of alleged discrimination on behalf of another employee either internally or at a tribunal hearing;

(d) done anything in relation to anti-discrimination legislation (this is a catch-all provision);

(e) indicated an intention to do any of the above.

Essentially, the inclusion of victimisation in the law affords substantial protection to any worker who is penalised for any type of involvement in a complaint of sex or race discrimination. So long as the employee's involvement in a complaint of discrimination can be shown to be the cause of their subsequent unfavourable treatment, they will have grounds to bring a complaint of sex or race discrimination to tribunal.

One limitation, however, on the victimisation provisions is that a claim will not succeed unless it can be shown that there was conscious motivation on the part of the person responsible for the victimisation, and that their conduct towards the employee resulted directly from the employee's behaviour.

POSITIVE ACTION

In certain, limited circumstances, an employer may take positive action to recruit or promote members of one sex or members of a particular racial group. However, positive action can only lawfully be taken where one of the sexes, or a particular racial group, is under-represented in a specific type of work to the extent that there have been few or no members of that sex or racial group in a particular type of work for the previous twelve months. Where this is the case, the employer may give (limited) preferential treatment to a member of the minority sex (either men or women) or to those from minority racial groups.

Positive action is only permissible in recruitment, promotion and training and is restricted to:

(a) encouragement for members of the minority sex or a minority racial group to take up opportunities for work. This includes recruitment campaigns and job advertisements which may specifically state that members of one or other sex or members of a particular racial group will be particularly welcome.

(b) access to training for members of one sex or racial group for particular work. This could include (for example) language training for employees of foreign nationality or special training aimed at women who have recently returned to work after a period away from full-time employment.

Although it is permissible for employers to place advertisements which openly encourage members of the minority sex or of a minority racial group to apply to them for work, it must also be made clear that selection will be carried out on merit without reference to sex or race. This is because the law does not permit reverse discrimination, i.e. it is unlawful to treat an employee more favourably on account of their sex or race. It is only in promoting employment opportunities (and in training) that positive action may lawfully be taken.

It is thus important to bear in mind that:

(a) at the point of selection for employment or promotion all applicants must be treated equally and judged on their merit without any reference to sex or race;

(b) giving automatic priority to women or people from a minority ethnic group with a view to achieving equal representation is unlawful;

(c) applying a quota system whereby a target is set to achieve a defined percentage of female employees or employees from minority racial groups is unlawful.

HOW EMPLOYMENT TRIBUNALS ADDRESS CLAIMS OF DISCRIMINATION

In addressing a case of alleged sex or race discrimination, the tribunal's job is to establish whether the employer would have treated a person of the opposite sex or a different racial group differently from the complainant. However, it is not necessary for there to be a *real* comparator and, instead, the individual who is taking the discrimination complaint, only has to show that a *hypotheti-*

cal person of the opposite sex or different racial group would have been treated more favourably than they were treated.

Technically, it is for the complainant to prove at tribunal that they were discriminated against, but the burden of proof is not a high one. Tribunals apply the 'balance of probabilities test' and in practice concrete proof is not required. Instead, if the person can show that they were the victim of unfavourable treatment, and if there is evidence that someone of a different sex or racial group was, or would have been, treated more favourably, then the case will have been made out. The onus will then be on the employer to demonstrate to the tribunal that there was a reason for the employee's less favourable treatment which had nothing to do with sex or race. If there is no such evidence, or if the tribunal finds the employer's explanations inadequate or unsatisfactory, they may legitimately draw an inference that the unfavourable treatment of the complainant was on the grounds of sex or race. Thus whilst evidence of unfair treatment on its own will not be enough for the employee to win their case, absolute proof is not required.

Employers are liable for the discriminatory acts against their employees which take place in the course of their employment. Individual employees may also be liable to pay compensation to the victim of discrimination. It is good policy, therefore, to make all employees aware that they may be held personally accountable for any discriminatory actions in an employment tribunal, and that they may have to pay compensation out of their own pockets if the tribunal finds that they were responsible for unlawful discrimination perpetrated against the employee.

Case Study

An employee, who was of Irish nationality, was a special needs lecturer. His problems began when one of his colleagues disparagingly called him an 'Irish prat'. The employee found the remark offensive and upsetting and regarded it as racial harassment. He raised a grievance under the college's grievance procedure on account of the incident, but this was not taken seriously or handled in an appropriate manner. The employee's line manager delayed and procrastinated in taking any action over the grievance. Furthermore, the colleague who made the remark persistently refused to offer an apology. Some time later, the employee was denied a place on a short-list for a promoted post on account of the fact that he was persisting in pursuing his grievance.

As a result of the original remark and the excessive length of time that it took the college to address the matter, the employee suffered a great deal of stress and was absent through illness arising from this.

When the employee took a case of race discrimination to an

employment tribunal, he succeeded in his case and was awarded a total sum of £29,900 compensation for racial discrimination. The case was particularly interesting because the tribunal allocated elements of the compensation to individuals, as well as to the employer. The college principal was ordered to pay £2,000; the line manager £6,500; the curriculum director £1,500; and the colleague who made the 'Irish prat' remark £5,000.

Bryans v. Northumberland College of Arts & Technology [1995] C.O.I.T. 36674/94.

Compensation for Sex/Race Discrimination at Employment Tribunal

The usual remedy for successful complaints of sex and race discrimination is compensation for the complainant. The main factor influencing the amount of compensation is the employee's (or job applicant's) actual financial losses flowing from the act of discrimination. This may include estimated future loss as well as losses to date.

Since 1993, there has been no ceiling on the amount of compensation which an employment tribunal may award in cases of sex or race (or disability) discrimination. Although some awards can be very high, the average for sex discrimination cases runs at about £4,500 whilst for race cases, the average compensation award tends to be approximately £8,000 (these figures are taken from statistics for 1997).

In addition to compensation for financial loss, there is usually an additional element of compensation for injury to feelings.

Reinstatement and re-engagement are not available under discrimination legislation, although where the complainant has brought a claim for unfair dismissal as well as sex or race discrimination, reinstatement or re-engagement may be ordered (see 'Remedies Available to an Unfairly Dismissed Employee at Employment Tribunal' in Chapter 17).

Case Study

One of the highest awards to date for a case of unlawful discrimination was made to an employee who suffered repeated
race discrimination and victimisation over a period of four years.
He had, over the years, succeeded in four complaints of unlawful race discrimination at an employment tribunal. Two of his
complaints were on account of victimisation following complaints
he had raised internally about racially discriminatory treatment.
On one occasion disciplinary action had been taken against him
for complaining, and on another he had been suspended following a complaint. Additionally, his race had influenced a decision
to deny him a place on a short-list for a promoted post. Finally,
he was dismissed.

The Employment Appeal Tribunal observed that this was the
'worst case of unlawful race discrimination' it had ever had to
deal with. They awarded him £358,229 in compensation. A considerable portion of this amount was on the basis of estimated
future losses, as the tribunal formed the view that it was unlikely
that the employee, who was in his fifties, would work again.

D'Souza v. London Borough of Lambeth [1997] I.R.L.R. 677.

CHAPTER EIGHT

MATERNITY RIGHTS

Female employees have a number of special statutory rights which protect them and afford them specific benefits when they are pregnant and/or on maternity leave. These are:

(a) the right to take (paid) time off work for ante-natal care;

(b) the right to be paid statutory maternity pay (SMP), subject to a minimum period of qualifying service of six months;

(c) the right to take maternity leave and return to work;

(d) the right not to be dismissed or discriminated against on account of pregnancy;

(e) the right to have all periods of maternity absence counted towards continuous service (once the woman has returned to work).

There is no limit to the number of times a woman may claim statutory maternity rights in employment.

TIME OFF WORK FOR ANTE-NATAL CARE

All pregnant women have the right to take time off work, with pay, to attend ante-natal appointments. This applies irrespective of the employee's length of service or the number of hours she works.

The employer is not permitted to compel an employee who takes time off for ante-natal care to make up for lost time by working extra hours nor is it permissible to expect an employee to arrange medical appointments outside working hours.

The employer may, however, insist on the employee producing an appointment card, except in the case of her first ante-natal appointment.

PREGNANCY AND MEDICAL SUSPENSION

If a pregnant woman's work could in any way place her at risk, the employer must take steps to remove her from that risk. The risk might arise from working conditions, work processes or specific job duties, including everyday tasks, such as heavy lifting.

Where a risk has been identified, the first option for the employer to consider is whether the woman's duties, or working conditions, can be altered to remove her from the risk. This might be achievable simply by rearranging her job duties. If she is a night-shift worker, the employer is obliged to move her to day work, if so recommended on health grounds by a medical practitioner. If it is not possible to adjust the job, so as to remove the employee from the risks to her health, the employer should review whether she can be moved to another job for the duration of her pregnancy (with her level of pay maintained). There is no obligation to create a job specially for her but if a job exists which is appropriate for her to do, she should be offered it.

If transfer to another job is not possible, or where the change of job would not remove the employee from the risks to her health, the woman has the right to be suspended from work on full pay until the commencement of her maternity leave.

Employers have no choice in this matter despite the obvious difficulties which these provisions could cause, especially to small employers. If an employee is dismissed on account of inability to continue in her job during pregnancy, this would constitute an automatically unfair dismissal and direct sex discrimination, leading potentially to a very high award of compensation.

These provisions are not applicable where the woman is signed off sick by her doctor, but rather where she is able to come to work but is unable to perform her particular job duties for health or safety reasons. An example of this could be where the job involves heavy lifting and the woman, whilst fit and healthy, is unable to lift heavy objects due to her pregnancy.

MATERNITY PAY

There is no obligation in law to continue normal salary or wages when a woman is on maternity leave. Some employers do elect to pay full salary or wages for a defined period of maternity absence and it may be that entitlement to pay exists as part of the employee's contractual rights. However, this is not mandatory.

Contractual Maternity Pay

Where an employee's contract of employment contains a clause entitling her to receive full (or part) salary during periods of maternity leave, this will mean that she will continue to be paid in the normal way whilst she is absent on maternity leave. The employer may offset statutory maternity pay against the woman's normal pay (see the next section).

In circumstances where the employee has contractual rights which are in excess of the statutory rights, she can combine her statutory maternity rights with elements of contractual maternity rights. This is commonly referred to as an employee's 'composite right'. The practical effect of this is that the employee's statutory rights are modified so as to give effect to any more favourable contractual terms.

Statutory Maternity Pay

Employees are eligible to receive statutory maternity pay (SMP) if they have had at least six months' continuous service, calculated as at fifteen weeks before the expected week of childbirth (known as the 'qualifying week') and provided they also meet the following conditions:

(a) the employee must still be employed during the qualifying week;

(b) her average weekly earnings must be over the 'lower earnings contribution' limit (£64 at the time of writing);

(c) she must provide notification of her intended maternity leave at least 21 days before her maternity leave is due to begin and in accordance with her employer's rules;

(d) she must provide medical evidence of the expected date of her confinement;

(e) she must have actually stopped work.

Eligibility to receive SMP is not in any way dependent on whether or not the woman returns to work following maternity leave.

SMP may be paid for up to eighteen weeks in total, unless the woman returns to work before the end of this period in which case it must be stopped. There are two levels of SMP – a higher rate and a standard rate. The higher rate, which is equivalent to 90 per cent of the woman's normal average earnings, is paid for the first six weeks and then the standard rate is paid for a further twelve weeks. The standard rate of SMP is a fixed amount, currently £57.70 per week.

SMP is treated as pay, therefore tax and national insurance contributions must be deducted from it. Amounts paid are in part recoverable by deduction from the employer's gross national insurance contributions.

MATERNITY LEAVE

The rights of employees to take maternity leave are somewhat complex because there is a two-tier system of statutory rights in operation in the UK, depending on whether a woman has two years' (or more) continuous service.

Firstly, all pregnant employees have the right to take fourteen weeks' maternity leave and resume work. This provision applies to all female employees irrespective of their length of service or whether they work full or part-time. The employee does not have to give any notice of her intention to resume work, unless she wishes to return before the expiry of the fourteen weeks, in which case she must give seven days' notice. The employer is not permitted to postpone a woman's return beyond the fourteen weeks.

The government is proposing, in the forthcoming Employment Relations Act, to increase this period of fourteen weeks' statutory maternity leave to eighteen weeks.

If an employee's baby arrives late, and she has exhausted her fourteen weeks' maternity leave, there are special provisions which means that she does not lose her right to resume work. This is because there is a compulsory period of maternity leave of two weeks after the date of birth (four weeks for a factory job) and the woman's maternity leave may be extended to allow for this compulsory period of leave.

The second tier of rights, which exist independently of the basic statutory entitlement to fourteen weeks' maternity leave, is available to women who have two or more years' continuous service, calculated as at eleven weeks before the expected week of childbirth. Eligible employees are entitled to a period of extended maternity absence consisting of up to eleven weeks before the baby is due and up to 29 weeks after the week their baby is born. This means that there is an overall maximum entitlement of up to 40 weeks' leave (which incorporates the 14-week period of leave described above). The 2-year period of qualifying service for eligibility for extended maternity absence, is to be reduced to one year once the Employment Relations Act is implemented.

Apart from the minimum service qualification, a woman must, in order to qualify for extended maternity absence:

(a) still be employed at the beginning of the 11th week before the expected week of childbirth. She does not have to be physically at work but her contract must still be in force;

(b) she must provide her employer with written notification of her intention to take maternity leave and return to work, together with a note of the date of her expected week of confinement. This information must be provided at least 21 days before she wants her absence to begin;

(c) she must provide a certificate of the expected week of confinement, if asked to do so by her employer;

(d) when she is ready to return to work, she must give 21 days' written notice of the date on which she intends to return.

Timing of Maternity Leave: An Employee's Right to Choose

A pregnant woman may commence her maternity leave at any time after the beginning of the 11th week before the expected week of childbirth. She may, if she wishes (and provided there is no health risk) continue in employment right up until the baby is born. The choice is the employee's, and managers do not have the right to delay or bring forward the commencement of the employee's maternity leave.

One exception to this is that, if the employee is absent from work due to a pregnancy-related condition at any time after the beginning of the 6th week before the date her baby is due, the employer may trigger the maternity leave period automatically. This triggering facility only comes into play, however, when the employee's absence is due to a pregnancy-related illness and not if she is off work for some other reason, for example if she has flu.

Following the woman's confinement, the employer may write to the woman and ask whether she still intends to return to work. This request cannot be made earlier than the 12th week of her maternity leave. If she receives such a request, the woman must reply to it in writing within fourteen days (or as soon as is reasonably practicable) confirming that she still intends to return to work. The employer cannot oblige the employee to decide her actual return date at this point and her only obligation is to confirm that she still intends to return. Failure to reply to this type of request, in theory, leads to the woman losing her right to return to work.

The woman has complete freedom to decide when to return to work following maternity leave, so long as her return date falls within the 14-week statutory period of leave or (if she has two or more years' service) within the 29-week period. This is subject to the law that a return within two weeks of childbirth (four weeks for factory jobs) is illegal.

Employees' Rights During Maternity Leave

During the 14-week period of statutory maternity leave to which all employees are entitled, the employee's contract continues in force, which means that she is entitled to the continuation of all benefits under her contract, apart from pay. This means that benefits, such as the provision of a company car, private medical insurance provided by the company, accrual of holiday entitlement and employer's pension contributions, must be continued. Although salary is not payable, most women will qualify for SMP for up to eighteen weeks (see above).

The status of an employment contract during extended maternity absence is not defined in statute, although a proposal has been put forward by the government, in the Employment Relations Bill, to clarify this matter by introducing a provision under which contracts of employment will be deemed to continue in force throughout all periods of maternity absence.

EMPLOYEES' RIGHT NOT TO BE DISMISSED ON ACCOUNT OF PREGNANCY OR MATERNITY LEAVE

It is automatically unfair in law to dismiss a woman for a reason which is in any way connected with her pregnancy or maternity leave. Where a woman is dismissed for pregnancy or maternity-related reasons, she may bring a case of unfair dismissal to an employment tribunal irrespective of her length of service. Dismissal on account of pregnancy or maternity leave is also highly likely to amount to sex discrimination in law.

Case Study

In one British case which reached the European Court of Justice (ECJ) in 1998, the employee had been dismissed following 26 weeks' continuous sickness absence during pregnancy. This was in accordance with a contractual policy operated by the employer whereby any employee who had 26 weeks' continuous sickness absence would be automatically dismissed.

The ECJ held that the employee's dismissal due to sickness absence during pregnancy amounted to discrimination on the grounds of sex. This was based on the premise that dismissal due to incapacity for work arising from pregnancy is "linked to the occurrence of risks inherent in pregnancy and must therefore be regarded as essentially based on the fact of pregnancy". The logic of this is that because only women, and not men, can be pregnant, dismissal on account of a pregnancy-related condition is directly discriminatory against women.

The ECJ took the view that the employer's policy of automatically dismissing employees after 26 weeks' sickness absence and the fact the policy was applied equally to men and women, was irrelevant.

Brown v. Rentokil E.C.J. C–394/96.

The Protected Period

Female employees are entitled to special protection from dismissal on account of illness throughout pregnancy and maternity leave. This period of time running from the start of pregnancy through to the end of the woman's maternity leave is known as the 'protected period'. Dismissal on account of illness during this protected period will be automatically unfair and will also be discriminatory on the grounds of sex.

Additionally, any sickness absence which occurred during the protected period must not be taken into account if, at a future date, dismissal for extensive sickness absence is being contemplated.

Redundancy during Maternity Leave

If a woman's job becomes redundant whilst she is on maternity leave, and if any suitable vacancy occurs at any time from the date the redundancy is notified right up to the latest date the woman can exercise her right to return to work, the employer is obliged to offer her this vacancy. This means that, in effect, if any suitable job becomes available at any time during maternity leave (following the decision that her own job is to be made redundant), a woman is entitled to be offered it in place of her old job.

Employers should also ensure that they do not overlook the obligation to consult an employee on maternity leave whose job is potentially affected by a redundancy programme. The fact that an employee is on maternity leave does not entitle the employer to exclude her from her rights relative to redundancy (see Chapter 18).

The Concept of a Deemed Dismissal

A woman may claim a 'deemed dismissal' where she is refused the right to return to work following extended maternity absence. She will have this right provided her proposed return is within the statutory period (29 weeks after the week her child was born) and provided she has given her employer the correct written statutory notice of her intention to return (21 days).

The concept of a 'deemed dismissal' was necessary because of the possibility that a woman's contract of employment was, in reality, suspended during extended maternity absence. Technically, if no contract is in existence then there is nothing from which an employee can be dismissed. The existence of the concept of deemed dismissal therefore allows a woman, whose contract of employment has not subsisted during extended maternity absence, to bring a claim for unfair dismissal if she is refused the right to return.

Sickness at the End of Maternity Leave

If a woman is unable to resume work at the end of her statutory 14-week maternity leave period, she is protected in law from dismissal for a period of four weeks provided she has produced a medical certificate stating that she is incapable of working.

The key point to bear in mind in these circumstances is that a woman who takes up to fourteen weeks' statutory maternity leave, continues to be employed for all purposes except pay and the performance of work. It follows from this that when maternity leave is at an end, her position is no different to any other employee, i.e. she has the right to receive full benefits under her contract of employment. This would include entitlement to statutory and contractual sick pay (see Chapter 10).

Where a woman has taken extended maternity absence and is unable to return to work at the end of her absence as a result of illness, she will not lose her right to return to work provided that:

(a) she has given the correct statutory notification of her intention to return on a specified date;

(b) she has produced a medical certificate stating she is incapacitated and signed and dated before the date she was due to return to work.

Thus, although in theory a woman who fails to exercise her right to return to work within the time allowed loses her right to return altogether, in the event that illness prevents return, the woman may preserve her position by giving notice of her intended date of return together with a medical certificate stating that she is unable to attend work. An actual physical return to work on the notified day is not, therefore, necessary because the revival of the contract of employment is activated by the giving of statutory notification of the intended return date. This means that the woman's employment continues whether or not she is physically at work.

If an employer refuses to allow a woman in these circumstances to take sick leave and resume working at a later date once she has recovered, this will constitute a dismissal which, in all probability, will be unfair. It is also likely that a woman in these circumstances would succeed in a claim for sex discrimination based on the argument that a man who, due to sickness, was unable to return to work afer a period of leave would not have been dismissed on account of his inability to resume work on the first day he was due back.

Additionally, there is a provision that a woman may postpone her date of return for up to four weeks beyond the maximum period of leave if she is ill (see 'Postponing the Return Date', below).

The correct approach for employers who are faced with the difficulties of an employee who is unable to return to work on account of sickness following maternity leave, is as follows.

1. If the employee is in receipt of SMP, continue to pay this for up to eighteen weeks.

2. If there is no entitlement to SMP, or if entitlement has been exhausted, institute statutory sick pay (SSP) according to the usual rules (see 'Statutory Sick Pay', Chapter 10).

3. If the employer operates a contractual sick pay scheme, this grants the woman her contractual rights under the scheme in the same way as any other employee. SMP for the first four weeks can be offset against any contractual sick pay paid. In effect, the day on which she would have returned to work (had she not been sick) is to be regarded as the first day of her sickness absence.

4. If payment of contractual sick pay is discretionary, exercise discretion in the woman's favour and grant her contractual sick pay under the scheme. Failure to do so could be held to be direct discrimination on maternity-related grounds.

THE RIGHT TO RETURN TO WORK

As explained earlier in this chapter, all employees, regardless of length of service, have the right to take up to fourteen weeks' statutory maternity leave (soon to be increased to eighteen weeks) and resume work. This right to resume work is automatic and is not dependent on the woman giving notice of her intended date of return. In effect the woman can simply turn up, sit down at her desk and resume working. Any attempt to postpone a woman's date of return, or a refusal to permit her to return, would be unlawful.

Following extended maternity absence to which women with two or more years' service are entitled, the woman's right is to return to a job under the same contract of employment. This means either the same job, or, if it is not reasonably practicable for the employer to allow her to return to the same job, a suitable alternative position. A suitable alternative position in this context is one in which "the work is suitable in relation to the employee and appropriate for her to do in the circumstances" and where "the provisions of the contract as to the capacity and place in which she is to be employed . . . are not substantially less favourable".

The only exception to the rule that employees have the right to return to work following extended maternity absence, is where the employee works for a 'small employer', defined as an employer who, at the time the woman wishes to return to work, employs five or fewer employees. In this case the woman does not have the automatic right to return after extended maternity leave. This exception, however, does not apply at the end of the 14-week period of maternity leave.

Postponing the Return Date

Following a woman's notification of her intention to return to work after extended maternity absence, the employer may postpone her return for up to four weeks, provided there are 'specified reasons' for doing so (usually business reasons). Such a postponement can only be implemented following extended maternity absence and not where the woman wishes to return to work at the end of the period of fourteen weeks' leave.

Similarly, following notification of the intended date of return after extended maternity absence, the employee may postpone the date of her return for up to four weeks in the event that the woman is sick, provided she gives the employer a doctor's certificate. There can be only one postponement, however, which means that if the woman has postponed her return by two weeks, she cannot subsequently add on a second postponement of one week even though the two periods combined would be less than the permitted four weeks.

The Effect of a Woman's Failure to Return to Work on the Notified Day

If an employee fails to return to work at the end of extended maternity absence (or after a postponement), she technically loses her right to return once and for all, with her contract of employment terminating automatically. In these circumstances the woman has not been dismissed, but instead it is as if the contract has evaporated and disappeared. The same principal would apply in the event that the woman failed to give the correct statutory notification of her intended date of return (21 days' written notice).

However, if a woman is sick, and provided she has given the employer the correct statutory notification of her return dates, and produced a medical certificate dated before the day on which she was due to return, she will not lose her right to resume work at a later date when she has recovered (see 'Sickness at the End of Maternity Leave', above).

Additionally, irrespective of whether the employee has correctly exercised her right to return to work, if there is evidence that her contract has subsisted throughout her extended maternity absence, refusal to allow her to return to work when she is ready to do so could constitute a dismissal and also sex discrimination. Evidence of the contract subsisting could arise if the company had continued to make some of the benefits under her contract available to her, for example use of a company car, cover under a company insurance scheme, etc.

Best practice in the event that a woman does not return to work within the statutory timescale is to:

(a) check whether the employee has provided the requisite notification of her intended date of return – if so, she has the right to continue in employment;

(b) review whether the employee has provided a medical certificate and if so whether it has been signed and dated by a medical practitioner before her notified date of return;

(c) refrain from assuming that the employee's contract has terminated automatically in the event of a failure to recommence work on the notified date of return or a failure to provide proper statutory notification of her return date.

(d) examine her contract of employment and maternity procedures to establish whether there might be an express or implied agreement that her contract of employment has subsisted throughout maternity leave – if so she has the right to continue in employment;

(e) if it is obvious that her employment has been reactivated by the giving of statutory notification, grant her statutory and (if the contract provides for it) contractual sick pay according to the same criteria as would be applied to any other employee who has not been on maternity leave.

DEALING WITH REQUESTS TO RETURN TO WORK PART-TIME

Today, many women are choosing to work part-time following the birth of a child. This may present a dilemma for an employer who may be faced with a request from an employee to switch from full-time to part-time work around the time they are due to return to work following maternity leave. Similarly, a woman may ask to be removed from shift-working or expect not to have to work extensive overtime once she has returned to work.

Contractually, no employee has the right to demand a change of hours. The terms of a contract of employment can be varied only with the agreement of both parties and the employer is not, on the face of it, obliged to agree to an alteration to an employee's hours of work just because it might suit the employee's personal purposes.

Despite the contractual position, however, it may be unlawful to refuse a woman's request to move to part-time working or to job-share on her return from maternity leave. This is because it has been held that such a refusal can constitute indirect sex discrimination which will be unlawful unless the employer can objectively justify the need for the woman's job to be performed on a full-time basis. The logic of this proposition is that a condition that a particular job must be performed on a full-time basis is one with which a considerably smaller proportion of women than men can comply, because more women than men need time away from work on account of childcare responsibilities. If a woman, who is entitled to return to work following maternity leave, cannot comply with the requirement to work full-time, and if she is forced to leave her job as a result of the employer's refusal to permit part-time working, she will have suffered a detriment on account of her sex. Unless the employer has an objective reason for refusing her the option of moving to part-time work, this will constitute unlawful sex discrimination.

This raises the obvious question of what sorts of reasons an employer may legitimately put forward to justify a refusal to permit a woman returning from maternity leave to move to part-time working. Relevant factors would include:

(a) the nature of the woman's job, including the extent to which her work is specialised;

(b) the need for continuity in the work and the potential effect of part-time working on that continuity;

(c) the number of other staff employed in similar work and the degree of cover available for the work;

(d) the employer's overall size and administrative resources;

(e) the level of genuine inconvenience to the business or to customers which would result from the woman's switch to part-time working;

(f)   the extent to which the employer has made a genuine effort to accommo-
      date the employee's request to work part-time (for example if no one
      suitable has replied to a job advertisement seeking a job-sharing partner,
      this would in all probability constitute justification for refusing to permit
      the woman to work part-time).

Case Studies

A clerical worker employed in the tax department of a local council
requested a job-share following her maternity leave but was refused. When the employee took a complaint of sex discrimination to a tribunal, the council maintained that job-sharing was
impracticable because it could lead to inefficiency, that members of the public would find it confusing to have to deal with
two people instead of one and that the council would incur increased training costs if two people were engaged to job-share
one position.

The employment tribunal which heard this case was not impressed by these arguments. They held that there was no real
reason why the council could not have introduced job-sharing
arrangements and that therefore the requirement for the employee
to work full-time was not objectively justifiable. The employee's
claim for indirect sex discrimination succeeded and, because she
had resigned on account of the council's failure to offer her a
job-share, she succeeded in a claim for constructive dismissal as
well.

Puttick v. Eastbourne Borough Council [1995] C.O.I.T. 3106/2.

An employee who had been employed as a full-time receptionist
by an ultrasound-instrument manufacturer put forward a request
to switch to part-time working on her return from maternity leave.
The company relied heavily on the telephone to conduct its business and therefore refused the employee's request on the grounds
that there was a need for a full-time receptionist to ensure continuity and familiarity with customers.

The employee complained of indirect sex discrimination and,
when the case went to appeal, the EAT accepted that in the
particular circumstances of the case, the company had an objective reason for refusing the employee's request to work part-
time. This was based on the company's contention that the job
of receptionist was a key role in promoting customer relations
and continuity. The employee's case, therefore, failed.

Eley v. Huntleigh Diagnostics Ltd [1997] E.A.T. 1441/96.

Administrative inconvenience, a manager's personal objection to part-time working or an argument that part-time working would run contrary to policy or traditional working practices, would be unlikely to convince an employment tribunal that it was impracticable for the employer to permit part-time working. If an employer refuses to comply with a woman's request to return to work on a part-time basis, the reason for the refusal must be objective and related to the needs of the business and not the preferences of management.

Where a request is received therefore, the employer should always:

(a) consider the request carefully;

(b) approach the issue with an open mind;

(c) take all reasonable steps to accommodate the woman's request;

(d) ensure that any refusal to grant an employee's request is based only on objective, job-based factors;

(e) recognise that refusing a request out of hand is likely to lead to a claim of sex discrimination against the company.

CHAPTER NINE

DISABILITY DISCRIMINATION

THE DISABILITY DISCRIMINATION ACT 1995

The Disability Discrimination Act 1995, which came into effect in December 1996, imposed new requirements on employers with regard to the recruitment and employment of disabled people and afforded protection to disabled people against discrimination in employment. The Act extends protection to employees and job applicants in the areas of:

- recruitment;
- terms and conditions of employment;
- training, transfer and promotion;
- dismissal;
- selection for redundancy;
- general treatment at work.

Further disability discrimination legislation is to come into effect in the future, which will affect the provision of services and will compel service providers to adjust their policies, practices, and premises to accommodate the needs of disabled people.

The employment provisions of the Disability Discrimination Act apply to all employers in Great Britain and Northern Ireland provided they employ fifteen employees or more. Small employers are thus exempted from the provisions of the Act (see below).

The Act makes it unlawful for an employer to treat an employee or job applicant who has a disability less favourably than they would treat someone who does not have a disability in similar circumstances. Such unfavourable treatment will amount to unlawful discrimination unless the employer can show that the particular treatment was objectively justified.

The Act also places an obligation on employers to make reasonable adjustments to working practices and premises to accommodate the needs and requirements of disabled employees (and job applicants).

Exemptions and Exclusions from Disability Discrimination Legislation

As stated above, employers are exempt from the Disability Discrimination Act if they have fewer than fifteen people working for them. However, in calculating the number of people employed, the employer must count everyone who works for the business, i.e. the total number of workers at all branches and locations. The only exception to this rule is for franchise holders who are exempt from the Act if they, as individuals, employ fewer than fifteen people.

The number fifteen must include:

- part-time staff;
- contract workers;
- casual workers;
- temporary staff;
- workers supplied by an employment agency;
- self-employed people who are performing work for the business;
- apprentices.

There are no other employers who are exempted from the provisions of the Disability Discrimination Act, but there are a number of conditions which are specifically excluded from the scope of the Act. They are as follows.

1. Addiction to alcohol, nicotine, drugs or any other substance, except where the addiction is to a drug which has been medically prescribed.
2. Mental conditions, including, a tendency to start fires, a tendency to steal, a tendency to physically or sexually abuse others, exhibitionism, and voyeurism.
3. Tattoos which have not been removed.
4. Body piercing.
5. Hay fever.

Establishing Whether an Employee is Disabled

The wording of the definition of 'disability' in the Act is such that a very wide range of conditions, both physical and mental, can come under its umbrella. The Act states that a disabled person is someone who "has a physical or mental impairment which has a substantial and long-term adverse effect on his ability to carry out normal day to day activities". There is no official list of impairments for the purposes of the Act; the key criteria for assessing whether an impairment is substantial enough to merit protection under the Act is its effect on the person in relation to normal activities. Further clarification follows.

Impairment

An impairment is regarded as affecting a person's ability to carry out normal day to day activities if it affects any of the following:

- mobility;
- manual dexterity;
- physical co-ordination;
- continence;
- ability to lift, carry or otherwise move everyday objects;
- speech, hearing or eyesight;
- memory or ability to concentrate, learn, or understand;
- the perception of the risk of physical danger.

In addition, severe disfigurement is regarded as a disability under the Act, whether or not this has an impact on the person's ability to carry out normal day to day activities.

Substantial

The term 'substantial' has been described as meaning "more than minor or trivial", which may not be altogether helpful! One point to note is that the cause of the person's impairment is not relevant to whether or not it will be regarded as substantial. Thus, if an individual becomes disabled as a result of kidney failure, and the kidney failure has been occasioned by persistent heavy drinking, the individual is still to be regarded as disabled under the Act irrespective of any argument that the disability might have been self-imposed or preventable.

Long-term Effect

'Long-term effect' means an effect which has lasted, or can reasonably be expected to last, twelve months or more. If it is uncertain whether a particular condition will last twelve months, the employer would be advised to play safe and regard the person as if they were protected under the Act.

If, as a result of an illness which amounts to a disability under the Act, an employee is diagnosed as having a life expectancy of less than twelve months, the person is automatically covered by the Act, assuming the effect of the illness is likely to last for the whole of the rest of their life.

Adverse

The presence of the word 'adverse' ensures that only detrimental or damaging effects can entitle the person to be classed as disabled under the Act.

Normal Day to day Activities

It is important to note the implications of the phrase 'normal day to day activities'. The 'activities' which are meant are those which are carried out by most ordinary people on a fairly regular and frequent basis, such as walking, climbing stairs, reaching, etc. The 'activities' in question do not have to form part of the employee's particular job.

This produces the effect that an employee could be unable, due to an impairment, to carry out the duties of their particular job, for example an employee with two amputated fingers could be incapable of performing a job which involved intricate manual dexterity, but not be incapable of carrying out 'normal day to day activities' in life generally. Such an employee might not be classed as disabled under the Disability Discrimination Act 1995. Conversely, another employee may be classed as disabled under the Act due to an impairment which affected day to day activities (for example severe arthritis in the hands), but be perfectly capable of performing their job (where the job did not require manual dexterity).

Case Study

An example which demonstrates this paradox, occurred in a case which concerned a general assistant at a garden centre who was dismissed shortly after beginning his job because he was unable to lift large, heavy bags, which formed part of the job. The employee had undergone open-heart surgery ten years earlier and was consequently unable to carry out heavy lifting without risk to his health.

When the individual claimed at employment tribunal that his dismissal amounted to disability discrimination, the tribunal found from the evidence that, even though his condition meant that he could not carry out his job, he was not disabled within the meaning of the Disability Discrimination Act because he was able to lift and carry everyday objects such as books, full kettles, shopping, briefcases and chairs. The outcome was, therefore, that the claim failed because the employee did not suffer from a disability within the meaning of the Act.

Quinlan v. B & Q plc [1998] E.A.T. 1386/97.

Examples of Impairments

A very wide range of conditions, injuries and illnesses can potentially fall under the definition of disability for the purposes of the Disability Discrimination Act. Both physical and mental impairments are covered.

Mental impairments include clinically well-recognised mental illnesses and learning disabilities. The definition of 'mental impairment' is, therefore, potentially very wide-ranging and would include, for example, clinical depression, schizophrenia, learning difficulties, severe dyslexia, anorexia, bulimia and (potentially) certain stress-related illnesses.

Some specific examples of the types of effect, which would be regarded as substantial adverse impairments, are provided below under the various headings used in the Act.

Mobility

Mobility covers a person's ability to walk, move about, change position, bend and reach. Clearly, a very wide-range of physical conditions could impact on mobility ranging from amputation to chronic back trouble. Disability may manifest itself in:

(a) limited ability to walk at a normal pace without getting short of breath;

(b) inability to walk upstairs or downstairs without support, due to an injury or a stroke;

(c) serious inability to bend or reach as a result of chronic back pain;

Manual Dexterity

This relates to an individual's ability to use their hands and fingers and to co-ordinate the two hands together. Clearly, reduced functioning in the dominant hand would be more likely to constitute a disability than loss of function in the non-dominant hand. The type of effects which could entitle the individual to protection under the Act include:

(a) inability to grasp or handle cups and saucers due to arthritis;

(b) lack of power in the hands to grip tools;

(c) severe difficulty in using a keyboard due to repetitive strain injury;

Physical Co-ordination

This category would cover activities requiring co-ordination and balance, for example the ability to co-ordinate the movements of different parts of the body. Examples of adverse effects could include:

(a) severe difficulty in pouring coffee from a jug into a cup without spilling due to cerebral palsy;

(b) inability to drive a car due to a lack of ability to co-ordinate the hands and feet;

(c) lack of ability to co-ordinate eye and hand movements, e.g. catching a ball, due to brain damage.

Continence

This covers a person's ability to exercise normal control over their bladder and/or bowels. If loss of control is reasonably regular or frequent, then the person would be regarded as disabled under the Act.

Ability to Lift, Carry or Otherwise Move Everyday Objects

This would include a person's ability to lift ordinary objects of a moderate weight, carry them steadily and securely, and move objects around safely. A common cause of this type of impairment is back trouble. Examples of the effects of this could include:

(a) inability to pick up a book with one hand, due to muscle weakness;

(b) inability to carry ordinary objects without risk of dropping them, as a result of arthritis in the hands or upper limb disorder;

(c) severe difficulty in holding a tray loaded with coffee cups steadily.

Speech, Hearing or Eyesight

Severe speech impairments are covered under the Disability Discrimination Act, as are conditions which affect the senses. With regard to visual impairments, however, the assessment of the person's eyesight is made taking into account any spectacles or contact lenses they wear to correct vision. This contrasts with hearing impairments in which the use of a hearing aid is to be disregarded when assessing whether the person's impairment is substantial. Examples include:

(a) significant difficulty in reading a typed report at a normal distance due to a visual impairment which cannot be corrected by spectacles or contact lenses;

(b) serious difficulty in hearing individual words when taking part in a group discussion in a moderately noisy environment (with or without a hearing aid);

(c) lack of ability to speak articulately, as a result of a stroke or speech impediment.

Memory or Ability to Concentrate, Learn or Understand

This category could cover a person's ability to remember ordinary things, to organise a simple work plan, concentrate for short periods and understand spoken or written instructions by reason of a variety of mental conditions. Effects could include:

(a) significant difficulty in understanding written text, other than very slowly;

(b) severe difficulty in concentrating over a short period of time;

(c) inability to adjust to new work routines, due to learning difficulties.

Perception of the Risk of Physical Danger

This category is most likely to be caused by mental illness or brain damage. The result may be that the person either underestimates or overestimates health and safety risks and could include:

(a) severe lack of understanding as to why machinery must be operated with safety guards in place;

(b) a tendency to exhibit reckless behaviour without any appreciation of the resultant risks to other people's safety;

(c) an irrational belief that working practices are inherently unsafe, due to manic depression.

Severe Disfigurement

The question of how 'severe' a disfigurement must be to constitute a disability is a relative one, depending primarily on the level of its effect on the individual. One exception is tattoos, the presence of which is not regarded as a disability under the Disability Discrimination Act.

Progressive Illnesses

Where an employee is diagnosed as having a progressive illness, such as multiple sclerosis, they will be protected by the Disability Discrimination Act immediately, even though the effects may not at that stage be substantial or continuous. So long as there are *some* symptoms and effects on day to day activities and, so long as the diagnosis has been confirmed, protection under the Act comes into play. The logic of this is the degree of certainty that the illness will, in time, produce a substantial disability.

The following progressive illnesses are expressly covered under the Disability Discrimination Act:

• cancer;

• multiple sclerosis;

• muscular dystrophy;

• AIDS.

Because the structure of the Disability Discrimination Act allows an employee to be classed as disabled only once symptoms of the progressive illness begin to be experienced, it would appear that a diagnosis of HIV would not entitle the person to protection under the Act. Once full AIDS has developed, however, the employee would be protected against disability discrimination. Managers should ensure, therefore, if it comes to light that a particular employee has AIDS, that the person is not treated in any way unfavourably on account of their condition.

Past Illnesses

Although the Disability Discrimination Act only came into effect in December 1996, it affords protection against discrimination to employees and job applicants who have suffered a disability (e.g. a long-term illness) in the past, from which they may have partially, or fully, recovered. This is the case irrespective of whether the illness occurred before or after the date the Act was implemented.

The effect of this provision is that a person is permanently protected against disability discrimination on the grounds of a past impairment. This part of the Disability Discrimination Act is most likely to affect employers when they are recruiting. If it comes to light during an interview, or as a result of a medical questionnaire or pre-employment medical examination, that a candidate has, for example, a history of cancer or heart disease, it will be unlawful for the employer to refuse employment to the person on these medical grounds unless such refusal can be objectively justified in relation to the needs of the job.

THE EMPLOYER'S DUTY TO MAKE REASONABLE ADJUSTMENTS

In addition to the duty not to discriminate directly on grounds related to a person's disability, the Disability Discrimination Act 1995 imposes a duty on employers to make reasonable adjustments to working practices and the working environment, in order to accommodate the needs and requirements of disabled employees (and job applicants). Essentially the requirement to make adjustments arises where any of the company's procedures, practices, working arrangements, or physical features of the premises cause a substantial disadvantage to an employee with a disability when compared to a non-disabled employee. In these circumstances the employer must take appropriate steps (within reason) to reduce the adverse effect of the working arrangements on the disabled employee. Examples of the sorts of adjustments, which employers could be obliged to make, are given in the following sections.

It is possible under the Act to justify not making a particular adjustment, provided the reasons for not doing so are objective, material and substantial (see 'Circumstances in which Disability Discrimination may be Justified by the Employer', below).

There is no overriding or global obligation on employers to make adjustments to facilitate the employment of disabled people. Instead the obligation to make adjustments arises only when a specific disabled employee is recruited or when an existing employee becomes disabled.

Adjustments to Premises

Under the Disability Discrimination Act, employers have a duty to make modifications to the physical features of their premises, including access to the premises and to fixtures, fittings and furnishings, in order to facilitate the employment or retention of disabled employees. Examples of adjustments could include the duty to:

(a) widen doorways to accommodate a wheelchair user;

(b) provide a ramp for wheelchair users to access the building or to move between different areas within the building;

(c) redesign a work station for a disabled employee, for example by modifying the desk height to accommodate someone in a wheelchair;

(d) provide a special chair for someone who is unable to stand for long periods, where the job would otherwise require the person to stand;

(e) lower shelves or counters for someone who has difficulty reaching;

(f) relocate door handles or light switches so that they can be reached by a person in a wheelchair;

(h) reduce the level of the lighting to accommodate the needs of someone with epilepsy;

(i) install signs in extra-large print to help a visually impaired person;

(j) rearrange furniture to make it easier for a wheelchair user to move about.

Some adjustments would involve minimum cost, but where the cost would be excessive in relation to the employer's available resources, the employer would in all likelihood be able to justify not carrying out the adjustment (see 'Justifying Not Making Adjustments', below).

Adjustments to Working Practices

There is potentially a very wide-range of possible adjustments which an employer may be expected to make in order to accommodate the needs of a disabled employee. Some examples of action an employer could take are as follows.

Adjusting the Job

1. Discuss the possibility of transferring a newly disabled employee to an alternative job.

2. Allocate any heavy duties to another employee, for example if an employee has developed a heart condition.

3. Transfer the driving duties of a particular job to another employee where, for example, the employee cannot drive on account of epilepsy.

Adjusting the Method of Doing the Job

1. Arrange for an employee with severe dyslexia to dictate letters and reports for someone else to write using an audio cassette, rather than writing them personally.

2. Organise for the colleague of an employee, with a mobility impairment, to deliver physically work to the work station at regular intervals.

3. Allow an employee with a mobility impairment to do part of the job by telephone rather than having to travel to meetings at distant locations.

Adjusting the Equipment Used in the Job

1. Provide a specially adapted keyboard for someone with arthritis in their hands.

2. Adapt telephone equipment for use by an employee with a hearing impairment.

3. Alter the height of a machine so that a wheelchair user can operate it from a seated position.

Adjusting Procedures

1. Tolerate a higher than normal level of sickness absence from an employee who has developed a serious illness.

2. Adjust working hours so that the person has additional flexibility to attend medical appointments.

3. Offer the option of part-time work where a disabled employee's energy levels are affected by their impairment.

Adjusting the Work Location

1. Allow a person with limited mobility to work at a work station on the ground floor.

2. Move an employee who uses a wheelchair to an area where access to and from the area is easier.

3. Allow an employee with a mobility impairment to do some of their work from home.

Adjusting Instructions and Reference Manuals

1. Produce instruction manuals in braille for a blind person.

2. Arrange for company procedures to be recorded on to audio cassette for an employee with a serious visual impairment.

3. Provide written material in a different form, e.g. using pictures for someone with learning difficulties.

Adjusting Training

1. Arrange for an employee with learning difficulties to be given more training than would normally be required.

2. Deliver training in a different form, for example for an employee who is blind.

3. Provide specialised coaching during training for a disabled employee.

Adjusting Recruitment Procedures

1. Arrange for a job applicant to take a test orally rather than in writing, where their disability affects their ability to write.

2. Relinquish the need for a disabled job candidate to take a particular selection test where it is likely that they would perform poorly in comparison to non-disabled candidates.

3. Reserve a parking space near the front door for a disabled applicant who can drive.

CIRCUMSTANCES IN WHICH DISABILITY DISCRIMINATION MAY BE JUSTIFIED BY THE EMPLOYER

Unlike the laws on sex and race discrimination, the Disability Discrimination Act contains a provision whereby an employer can justify discriminating against an employee or job applicant on grounds related to disability or justify not making an adjustment.

Justifying Discrimination

An employer will be able to justify treating a disabled employee unfavourably on grounds related to disability, if it is clear that the person's disability would either prevent them performing the job altogether (for example a blind person would be unable to work as a driver) or render it excessively difficult for them to do the job (for example an individual with a mobility impairment might find it extremely difficult to perform certain types of manual work). Such unfavourable treatment will, however, only be lawful if the employer can also show that there is no adjustment which can be made which would remove or substantially reduce the factors which are impeding the person from doing the job.

It is important to note that, in order to justify less favourable treatment, the employer must be able to demonstrate that the reasons for it are both *material* and *substantial*. This means that that the reasons for the discrimination must be relevant to the specific circumstances (rather than based on generalised assumptions) and must be significant (as opposed to minor).

Case Study

In one case an application for employment as a train guard was rejected on the grounds that the applicant suffered from depression and took the drug Prozac. The individual brought a claim of disability discrimination to a tribunal. It was held that, for the purposes of the Disability Discrimination Act, the applicant was disabled and the employer had discriminated against him in refusing to employ him by reason of his depression.

However, the tribunal also found that the refusal to engage the individual was justified on the basis that his disability was both material to the duties of the job of train guard and substantial. The view was that the possible side effects of Prozac could affect levels of concentration and judgement which in turn could prejudice the safety of passengers in the event of an emergency.

Toffel v. London Underground Ltd [1998] 220488/97.

To address the issue of making adjustments, where difficulties are being encountered as a result of an employee's disability, the manager should:

(a) discuss the effects of the disability directly and openly with the person in order to identify what adjustments might help (it is likely that the employee will understand what is required better than the manager);

(b) refrain from making assumptions about the employee's ability to transfer to different work or learn new skills;

(c) consider every option as to what measures could be taken to accommodate the needs of the disabled employee in order to remove the factors which prevent effective or satisfactory job performance;

(d) approach the issue with an open mind;

(e) where necessary, seek the co-operation of other employees.

Justifying Not Making an Adjustment

There are certain situations in which an employer would be able to justify not making an adjustment to working practices or premises. The most likely of these are as follows.

1. If the cost of making the adjustment would be very high in relation to the employer's available resources, taking into account the employer's overall size and number of staff.

2. If it can be shown that it would be impossible, extremely difficult or impracticable to make the adjustment.

3. Where making the adjustment would cause severe disruption to the business (for example a major adjustment to premises at a particularly busy time).

4. Where the adjustment would contravene health, safety or fire regulations.

5. Where the employer does not own the work premises and the owner refuses to consent to a structural alteration or where planning permission is refused.

6. Where the employer does not know, or could not reasonably be expected to have known, that an employee (or job applicant) is disabled.

7. Where the adjustment would make no tangible difference to the disabled employee's ability to carry out the job effectively.

8. Where the disabled employee is unwilling to co-operate with the employer's proposal to make a particular adjustment.

If an employer cannot justify a failure or refusal to make an adjustment which it would be reasonable and practicable to make and which would help to reduce or remove the disadvantage to the disabled employee, this will constitute unlawful discrimination.

RECRUITING DISABLED EMPLOYEES

The Disability Discrimination Act affords protection against disability discrimination to job applicants through all stages of the recruitment process.

This includes:

- job advertisements;
- application forms;
- job descriptions;
- employee specifications;
- short-listing procedures;
- arrangements for interview;
- the interview itself;
- selection testing;
- the criteria for selection and selection procedures.

Examples of discrimination in recruitment could include:

(a) a job advertisement which imposes the requirement that applicants should be 'energetic', where the job is an office-based job which does not require any special characteristics or degree of fitness. If a particular candidate is subsequently turned down for the job on account of this requirement because, for example, they have a condition which causes them to tire easily, this could constitute unlawful disability discrimination;

(b) a decision not to short-list an applicant with a disability based on the manager's assumption that the person would need excessive time off work – unless there was factual evidence that the person would be unsuitable for the job in question;

(c) inflexibility or rigid adherence to procedures in making arrangements for an interview, for example in terms of timing and location. All job applicants should be routinely asked whether they require any special arrangements to be made for them so that adequate preparations may be carried out;

(d) asking questions at interview about a person's disability where their condition is largely irrelevant to the job in question or where the answers are used to the disadvantage of the candidate (see 'Questions at Interview', below);

(e) refusal to employ an individual on account of a past serious illness which lasted for twelve months or more;

(f) insisting that a candidate with an impairment which affects manual dexterity should take a written selection test, where their impairment would cause them to be disadvantaged in terms of performance in the test;

(g) singling out a disabled candidate for a medical examination prior to confirmation of employment, where it is not the company's normal policy to require a pre-employment medical and where there are no special factors justifying such action.

It should be recognised that many disabled people are fit and healthy and capable of performing a wide range of tasks as competently as able-bodied employees. In fact, research has shown that disabled employees have the same productivity levels as able-bodied workers, a better than average safety record, and *lower* rates of absenteeism and sickness.

Questions at Interview

It is not unlawful under the Disability Discrimination Act to raise the issue of a job applicant's disability at interview, nor to ask direct questions about the person's impairment, illness or other condition and its effects. It may in any event be judicious to discuss the disability in order to assess the potential difficulties, which the person might encounter at work if recruited, and how these could be reduced or removed through particular adjustments. The issue should not be avoided, because if the interviewer does not ask the appropriate questions, it would be impossible for them, subsequently, to give full and fair consideration to the types of adjustments which could potentially be made to facilitate the employment of the candidate.

Questions should be phrased in a positive way and should of course not give the impression that the interviewer is looking for problems. A focus on the person's *ability* rather than on their *disability* is advisable. Only those questions which are clearly relevant to the person's capacity to perform the job in question should be asked.

Interviewers should also bear in mind that there is no obligation on job applicants to reveal that they have a disability. Unless they are asked a direct question about it, they are entitled to keep their condition confidential. Thus, the onus is firmly on the interviewer to ask suitable questions in order to obtain important information to facilitate as assessment of the candidate's suitability for the job, taking into account any adjustments to working arrangements or premises which could reasonably be made.

The types of questions which could reasonably be asked could include the following.

1. Do you suffer from any illness or other condition which could affect your ability to do this job?

2. To what extent have you recovered from the illness which you had five years ago? Are there any symptoms which persist and (if the job requires a high level of stamina), if so, how do these affect your stamina?

3. Where the job involves attending regular meetings: How does your hearing impairment affect your ability to understand what people are saying

in a noisy environment, e.g. a meeting? How do you overcome this problem?

4. I see you have difficulty in using your hands – to what extent would you say this could affect your ability to perform keyboard work? How did you overcome this difficulty in your last job?

5. How have you overcome the effects of the disability caused by your amputation?

6. (Where the job involves lifting.) How did you cope in your last job with the lifting duties, bearing in mind your recurring back problems?

7. If we offer you the job, what adjustments or arrangements would you suggest we could make in order to help you overcome any disadvantage which your disability might otherwise cause you?

Questions at interview should be asked only for the following purposes.

1. To gain information relevant to the employee's ability to perform the specific job for which they have applied.

2. To address the difficulties or disadvantages which the person may face in performing the job with a view to taking steps to overcome them.

3. To discuss and assess what specific adjustments to working practices or premises may be required to overcome any disadvantage which the person might otherwise experience in performing the job.

4. To examine whether there might be any health and safety implications which the employer would need to take into account if the person was recruited.

5. To give the job applicant a fair chance of competing with other applicants in terms of being offered the job.

DEALING WITH EXISTING EMPLOYEES WHO BECOME DISABLED

Where an existing employee becomes disabled, whether gradually or suddenly (for example as a result of an accident) the employer should make every possible effort to continue to employ the person. If the person is dismissed on account of their disability without first giving full consideration to adjustments which could reasonably be made to allow them to continue in employment, this would be discriminatory and unlawful.

The need to make adjustments could also by triggered where an employee's existing condition gets worse. In these circumstances, the employer must be prepared to support the employee and make reasonable adjustments to accommodate their changing needs, rather than penalise them on account of the fact their condition is deteriorating.

Managers should take care not to make negative or blanket assumptions about an employee's capacity to overcome a disability or to be flexible in terms of adapting to new duties or working methods, etc. The disabled employee should always be fully involved in discussions about the impact of their disability and steps which the company can take to help them to overcome any difficulties imposed on them by their impairment or illness.

Sickness Absence

There is evidence to show that the majority of disabled people are fit and healthy and do not require any more time off work than other employees. With the exception of illnesses which amount to a disability for the purposes of the Disability Discrimination Act, the majority of physical and mental impairments will have no impact on the disabled person's general health, even though they may affect day to day activities.

Nevertheless, certain illnesses may be severe enough to be classed as disabilities under the Act, and where an employee develops such an illness, clearly they will require time off work for medical treatment and recuperation. The employer should be prepared to adjust normal sickness absence or attendance procedures, so as not to place the disabled employee at a disadvantage as a consequence of their illness. This may involve allowing the disabled employee more time off work than would normally be considered acceptable or being flexible as regards working hours.

The Disability Discrimination Act does not prevent dismissal on account of extensive sickness absence. However, in order to justify such action, the employer would have to be able to demonstrate that there was a material and substantial reason for the dismissal and also that there was still a significant problem even after all reasonable adjustments had been considered and applied. Otherwise dismissal on account of sickness absence or poor attendance would in all probability constitute unlawful disability discrimination.

Medical Advice

Where an employee develops a disability, it would usually be appropriate for the employer to seek expert medical advice. This would enable the manager to establish:

(a) what adjustments might help the employee;

(b) whether, and to what extent, recovery is likely;

(c) within what timescale the employee might be able to resume normal working;

(d) whether the disability is likely to be temporary or permanent;

(e) whether the person's condition is likely to worsen in time.

Case Study

A case concerning the dismissal of a long-serving employee following his collapse at work produced an interesting outcome. Although the employee was an epileptic (which would be classed as a disability under the Disability Discrimination Act), he had not suffered previous problems in performing his job, which involved working with heavy machinery, hot metal and dyes.

The employer sought a medical report from the employee's general practitioner. The report stated that he should not be allowed to continue to work in his present job and, in particular, should not be permitted to operate machinery. Following the GP's report, the company dismissed the employee. He brought a claim to tribunal for disability discrimination (and unfair dismissal).

The tribunal, in assessing the evidence, found that the company had failed to give sufficient consideration as to whether any adjustments could be made either to working conditions or in terms of allowing the employee more time to bring the epilepsy under control. Furthermore, the tribunal judged that dismissal based on the GP's advice was not justified in this case because the employer had not questioned whether the advice was appropriate. The tribunal was of the opinion that the employer should have obtained further medical evidence from either a specialist in epilepsy or an occupational health practitioner in order to establish whether the GP's recommendations were appropriate.

The employee, therefore, succeeded in his claim for disability discrimination, and was awarded £6,322 compensation.

Holmes v. Whittingham & Porter [1997]1802799/97.

It follows, from the case above, that employers should not act too hastily in concluding that an employee's condition renders him unsuitable for continued employment. Medical advice should be sought from an expert in the employee's condition and from a company doctor (if there is one) who may be in a better position than a general practitioner to assess the employee's capabilities in relation to the job they are employed to do.

Redeployment of a Disabled Employee

One of the possible adjustments which an employer should consider, if an existing employee becomes incapacitated to the extent that they can no longer perform their job effectively, is a transfer to a different job.

It is important to bear in mind that an employer is not entitled to move an employee to a different job without the employee's consent, otherwise the transfer would constitute a breach of contract (see Chapter 3). Additionally, even in circumstances where the employee can no longer perform their job to a satisfactory standard as a result of a disability, an enforced transfer to a different job would constitute unlawful disability discrimination. The issue should be viewed in a positive light taking into account the employer's duty to make reasonable adjustments. The manager should, therefore, review what steps can be taken to facilitate the retention of the employee, and not attempt to force unwelcome changes upon him.

As an alternative to transfer, the employer may wish to consider altering the job duties of the disabled employee's current job, particularly those duties which are not central to the job function. Managers should:

(a) identify which of the employee's job duties are causing the disabled employee difficulty;

(b) review the person's job description and working practices to assess whether these duties are central to the performance of the job, or whether they are subsidiary or peripheral;

(c) where the duties which are causing difficulty are not central to the function of the job, examine whether these duties can be transferred to other employees;

(d) discuss these matters fully, firstly with the disabled employee and secondly with the employee(s) to whom the duties may be transferred;

(e) consider whether any training or coaching would be required if certain job duties were allocated to others;

(f) explain carefully the reasons behind the proposal for an adjustment and ensure employees understand the employer's duty under the Disability Discrimination Act to make such adjustments, the need to offer the disabled employee support and the benefits in allowing the person to remain in employment;

(g) make the decision about the adjustment, taking into account the views of the disabled employee and their colleagues as well as the company's business needs.

THE IMPLICATIONS OF DISMISSING A DISABLED EMPLOYEE

Where a disabled employee is dismissed for a reason which is related to a disability, this will constitute unlawful discrimination unless the employer has first taken appropriate steps to make whatever adjustments are reasonable and practicable to help the employee to come up to the standards of the job.

It can happen, however, that, even after making reasonable adjustments, the employer may find that the disabled employee has become incapable of performing the job to a standard which is acceptable, or that job performance has dropped to the extent that it has a material and substantial detrimental effect on other employees or on the business as a whole. The point may come where continued employment is no longer practicable and further adjustments unworkable. The reasonableness of a decision to dismiss will depend on the individual facts of the case, but would always have to be justified on objective grounds, if a claim for unlawful discrimination was to be successfully defended.

Dismissal will only be fair in circumstances where *all* the following criteria are met.

1. The employer can justify dismissing the employee for lack of capability.

2. The employer has made all possible adjustments to accommodate the needs of the disabled employee.

3. There is no alternative job within the company which the employee could reasonably do (to an acceptable standard).

4. The employer is certain that no further adjustments are possible or practicable, or that, even if further adjustments were made, they would not lead to a satisfactory improvement in performance.

5. Expert medical advice regarding the employee's condition and ability to perform the job has been obtained and considered.

6. Reasonable procedures have been followed prior to dismissal.

The same principles should be applied when considering disabled staff for redundancy. The following points are important.

1. There must be a genuine redundancy situation.

2. The methods of selecting staff for redundancy must not discriminate in any way against employees with disabilities, for example a strict adherence to using attendance as a criterion for selection could have a discriminatory impact on a disabled employee whose condition meant that they had a significant amount of sickness absence.

3. The employee must have been fully consulted as to the likelihood of their being selected for redundancy.

4. The employer must have made all possible adjustments to facilitate the continuing employment of the disabled employee prior to selection for redundancy.

5. Expert medical advice, regarding the employee's condition and ability to perform the job, should have been obtained and considered.

6. Full consideration must be given to whether suitable alternative

employment is available for the disabled employee and to the training which would be required as an adjustment to facilitate transfer into such a job.

Case Study

A chemist in a sugar factory was selected for redundancy following a procedure whereby employees were assessed on a points system based on several criteria. The employee concerned had very poor eyesight, even when wearing special glasses, to the extent that this condition amounted to a disability under the Disability Discrimination Act. Following his dismissal for redundancy, he brought claims to a tribunal for disability discrimination and unfair dismissal.

The tribunal found that the redundancy selection points scoring was prejudiced and that the attitudes of various managers towards the employee had been biased, resulting in a much lower score than he would have been given if he had not been disabled. Furthermore, there was evidence of marking down as a result of two ill-health absences which had occurred in the previous year, one of which was for treatment in connection with the employee's disability. The tribunal thus concluded that the employee had been the victim of less favourable treatment on disability-related grounds and that this treatment could not be justified under the circumstances. The decision was upheld on appeal.

Kirker v. British Sugar plc [1997] 2601249/97.

British Sugar plc v. Kirker [1998] EAT 170/98.

CHAPTER TEN

SICKNESS ABSENCE AND SICK PAY

SICK PAY

The effective management of sickness absence and sick pay is very important for employers, as a high level of absence amongst employees can cause the employer a great deal in terms of lost time and disruption to productivity. Ill-health and absence from work should, therefore, be managed in a positive, consistent and objective manner with a view to balancing the business needs of the organisation against the welfare needs of the employees.

Most employers operate a contractual sick pay scheme, i.e. a policy whereby employees continue to receive full or part salary for a defined period of time if they are off work due to sickness. Statutory sick pay (SSP) is an entirely separate concept. SSP is governed by statute, and imposes certain obligations on employers to pay a prescribed rate of sick pay to employees who are absent from work due to personal sickness, administered according to fixed and rather convoluted rules.

Contractual Sick Pay

There is no legal requirement to continue to pay a salary or wages to an employee who is unable to come to work due to sickness. Essentially, this is a matter for each employer to decide as part of company policy and to define and communicate as part of employees' contractual entitlement. There must, however, be a statement in writing (as part of the employee's written particulars of employment – see Chapter 1) explaining terms and conditions relating to sickness absence and any contractual entitlement to sick pay. If the company does not operate a contractual sick pay scheme, each employee's written statement must say so.

Many employers pay contractual sick pay according to a defined formula which provides for entitlements to sick pay, which augment with length of service. Some adopt the policy of paying full salary for a fixed period, followed by an equivalent period at half pay. Other employers operate a discretionary policy and, where this is the case, it is important that the company produces guidelines for managers and supervisors to maximise the chances of discretion being applied consistently and fairly across departments.

Statutory Sick Pay (SSP)

SSP is a fixed amount of money which employers are obliged to pay to employees who are absent from work due to personal sickness. Both full-time and part-time employees are eligible. Liability to pay SSP arises where an employee has been absent from work due to sickness for four days or more, and it is paid for a maximum period of 28 weeks at a time.

Eligibility for SSP

Eligibility for SSP depends on a number of factors.

Employee status. SSP is not payable to self-employed people or others not engaged on a contract of employment.

Age. Employees under age sixteen or over age 65 are not eligible.

Earnings. To qualify for SSP, an employee must have average weekly earnings at least equivalent to the lower national insurance earnings limit (at the time of writing this is £64.00 per week).

State benefits. Employees who have claimed incapacity benefit, maternity allowance or severe disablement allowance during the preceding eight weeks are ineligible for SSP.

Pregnancy. An employee cannot receive statutory maternity pay (SMP) and SSP at the same time.

Notification. The employee must have notified their employer that they are sick in accordance with the company's rules.

Medical evidence. Either a self-certificate (which is the normal requirement for absence of up to seven days) or a doctor's statement must be provided.

Employees who are on strike or in legal custody when an illness begins are excluded from SSP benefit.

There is no minimum length of service for eligibility for SSP. In theory a new employee could start work and qualify for SSP the next day, provided they met the above conditions. One exception, however, is that those engaged on a contract for three months or less do not qualify unless the contract is extended. In this eventuality, the employee becomes eligible for SSP immediately an extension has been confirmed provided the extension will take the total period of continuous employment beyond three months.

If an employee is not entitled to receive SSP, the employer must issue an exclusion form, so that the person is able to claim any state benefits to which they may be entitled.

Entitlement to SSP arises when:

(a) an employee is sick and incapable of work for four or more calendar days. This forms a 'period of incapacity for work' (PIW);

(b) three 'waiting days' have elapsed (during which no SSP is payable). Thus SSP becomes payable on the fourth day of sickness absence;

(c) the days on which the employee is sick are 'qualifying days'. Qualifying days are normally the employee's usual working days (although in the event of irregular working patterns the qualifying days may be agreed specifically between the employer and the workforce).

Payment of SSP ceases when the employee returns to work, or after 28 weeks have elapsed. However, where the employee falls sick again within eight weeks of the end of an earlier period of sickness absence, the two periods are linked and count as one period of incapacity for work. Two results of this are that:

(a) the employee does not have to serve three waiting days on the second occasion he falls sick; and

(b) the two periods are added together for the purposes of calculating when 28 weeks of SSP entitlement expires.

Where a new period of sickness absence occurs, more than eight weeks after an earlier period of absence, the employee will be eligible for SSP for up to a further 28 weeks.

Payment of SSP and Rates

The rate of SSP is a single standard weekly or daily rate which is reviewed by the government from time to time. At the time of writing the rate is £57.70 per week. This weekly rate may be divided up to calculate an employee's daily rate which will be the weekly rate divided by the individual employee's number of qualifying days in the week. SSP is treated as pay for tax purposes and therefore income tax and national insurance contributions must be deducted in the normal way.

It is not permissible to pay SSP on top of normal salary and so where the employer operates a contractual sick pay scheme, through which employees receive full pay whilst absent from work due to sickness, SSP must be offset against this salary. Where only part salary is paid during periods of sickness absence, SSP may either be paid on top or offset against salary (provided the amount paid to the employee does not fall short of the standard rate of SSP).

Administration and Recovery of SSP

The cost of SSP today is met largely by employers rather than by the government. However, where an employer's SSP bill has been particularly high in a given month, certain amounts can be reclaimed. This is done through what is known as the 'percentage threshold scheme'. Essentially employers can recover the amount by which their SSP payments, for a particular month, exceed 13 per cent of their total Class 1 national insurance contributions (employer's and employees' combined) for that month. There are no longer any special rules or exemptions for small employers.

Employers may, if they wish, opt out of the SSP scheme, provided they operate a contractual sick pay scheme which pays employees an equivalent or higher benefit. In the event of an opt out, the employers may still claim back amounts that would have been recoverable under the percentage threshold scheme, provided they keep the records necessary to calculate entitlements. This does not in any way undermine employees' rights, as their statutory entitlement to SSP remains and will kick in if they do not receive equivalent or better sick pay under their contract for any given day on which they are off sick.

Except where the employer pays contractual sick pay at a level equivalent to, or in excess of, SSP, it is a legal requirement to keep certain records of SSP payments. The records must be held for a minimum period of three years and, interestingly, a failure to comply with this requirement is a criminal offence!

EMPLOYEES' RIGHT NOT TO BE DENIED CONTRACTUAL LONG-TERM SICKNESS BENEFIT

Some employers operate a permanent health insurance scheme whereby employees are protected against loss of income in the event of long-term sickness absence. A permanent health insurance scheme, or long-term disability scheme, will thus guarantee a continuing income for an employee who is permanently injured or who suffers from an incapacity, which renders them unable to work for a long period of time. Most schemes operate on a percentage basis and are designed to start after a defined period of sickness absence has elapsed. For example, employees may be entitled to receive 50 per cent of their normal salary commencing six months after the beginning of incapacity and continuing until they are able to resume work or until retirement age (or death).

One of the difficulties, which employers have encountered with such a scheme, is the effect on the employee's entitlement to benefit under the scheme if they are dismissed. It is very important to be clear whether the terms of the scheme allow for the employee to continue to receive benefit if their employment is terminated and, if so, whether any special rules govern such entitlement. If the terms of the scheme are such that only employees (and not ex-employees) are eligible for benefit, the employer may find that dismissal of an employee, on the grounds of long-term ill health, would constitute a breach of contract, because such a dismissal would effectively deny the employee their contractual right to receive benefit under the scheme. It would be somewhat incongruous to give employees a contractual right to financial protection in the event of long-term sickness and then deny them the opportunity to benefit from such protection by dismissing them when they become ill and potentially qualify for the benefit.

Case Study

An employer operated a scheme whereby employees could receive both short and long-term disability protection under a scheme, which was designed to protect income in the event of an employee's incapacity for work due to illness. This was a contractual entitlement for employees. When the employee became ill, he received payment under the short-term scheme for three months but, following this period, was dismissed. Payments under the scheme ceased at that point.

The Court of Session, in determining the employee's claim for breach of contract, held that that the employer had denied the employee the protection, to which he was entitled under his contract of employment, by dismissing him. This was unlawful and the employee's claim for breach of contract was upheld.

Adin v. Sedco Forex International Resources Ltd [1997] I.R.L.R. 280 Court of Session.

Some employers adopt a practice of 'automatically dismissing' employees who have reached a specified number of days' sickness absence in a given period. Although a dismissal in these circumstances would be contractually correct, such an approach may lead to claims of unfair dismissal unless the employer can show that the decision to dismiss was reasonable in the circumstances of the individual case, and that a fair procedure was followed. There could also be claims of disability discrimination or (in the event that sickness absence is connected with pregnancy) sex discrimination.

In essence, a policy of automatic dismissal is not to be recommended because it may remove the element of good management and fair treatment of individuals by substituting an automated response without due regard being given to the person's individual circumstances. It could also have the effect of putting pressure on employees to return to work, before they were physically or mentally fit enough to do so, simply to avoid losing their job.

GAINING ACCESS TO EMPLOYEES' MEDICAL RECORDS

The Access to Medical Reports Act 1988, limits employers' rights as regards gaining access to medical reports prepared by the employee's own doctor. The Act also gives employees considerable rights as regards access to any medical report prepared by their GP for employment purposes.

However, because the Access to Medical Reports Act does not normally apply to medical reports prepared by independent company doctors, it follows that there is no need to seek an employee's express permission to gain access to a medical report which has been prepared by an occupational health specialist, unless the doctor in question happens also to be the employee's GP or regular specialist.

GP's Reports

Employees have a statutory right to refuse to allow their employer to apply to their GP for a medical report and an equivalent right to refuse to allow a particular report which has been prepared by their GP to be passed to their employer. They have further rights to gain access to any medical report prepared about them by their own doctor and to ask their doctor to amend the report, if it is inaccurate or misleading.

An employer who wishes to obtain a medical report from an employee's (or job applicant's) GP, must therefore seek the individual's written consent before making such an application. This request must be made to the employee in writing. When making the request, the employer is also obliged to inform the employee of their rights under the Access to Medical Reports Act.

It is important to note that any term written into a contract of employment which purports to create an obligation on the employee to consent to provide a GP's report to their employer will be void, because such a term would contradict the freedom given to individuals under statute.

Company Doctors' Reports

Because the Access to Medical Reports Act limits employers' ability to procure medical information from an employee's GP, using the services of a company doctor may be the only route an employer can take to obtain professional medical advice concerning a particular employee.

Although the Access to Medical Reports Act does not cover medical reports prepared by company doctors, the employer cannot just demand that employees must consent at random to medical examinations or medical reports. In order to have authority to obtain medical information about an employee, there must first be a clause in the particular employee's contract of employment stating that it is a condition of employment that they agree to consent to attend medical examinations by a company doctor or nominated specialist at the company's request. If no such written clause exists, employees cannot be lawfully obliged to agree to undergo a medical examination by a company doctor. Even where such a clause is written into the contract of employment, the employer cannot force an employee to undergo a medical examination, but a refusal in these circumstances could justify the employer in taking disciplinary action against the employee for breach of contract (provided disciplinary rules make this clear).

DEALING WITH FREQUENT, PERSISTENT, SHORT-TERM ABSENTEES

Where an employee's attendance record is poor as a result of frequent or persistent, short-term absences, the manager should consider whether these might be the consequence of genuine ill health or, alternatively, whether the employee is taking time off without real cause, which could be regarded as misconduct. It is important for the employer to try, through investigation and consultation with the employee, to establish into which category such absences fall. Depending on the outcome, the matter might be handled as one of incapability or of misconduct. Employers might benefit from the guidelines set out below.

Investigate and gather the facts. Establish the exact nature of the employee's absence record and examine whether it is tangibly worse than that of other employees, or worse than any standard laid down by the company.

Set up and operate a stringent return-to-work interview procedure. This can act as a deterrent to casual absence.

Speak to the employee about their frequent absences (in a non-blame way). Discuss the problems their absences are causing, ask for an explanation for each absence.

Be prepared to be open-minded and to consider any mitigating circumstances.

If the problem is thought to be health-related, seek medical advice. This can be done either by asking the employee's permission to obtain a medical report from their GP or, alternatively, by arranging for the employee to be interviewed and/or examined by a company doctor (if this is a term of the employment contract).

Consider the implications of the Disability Discrimination Act. See 'Sickness Absence and The Implications of Dismissing a Disabled Employee' in Chapter 9.

Review whether the cause of the employee's absences may be work-related. For example, work-related stress, bullying, boredom at work, etc.

Warn the employee of the likely consequences of continued poor attendance. That eventually they could be dismissed.

Set a time limit for appraising the situation and stick to it.

Keep full records of all absences.

If there is no improvement after the agreed time-frame for review, take all factors into account before taking a decision whether to dismiss the employee. Such factors would include the employee's age, length of service, general job performance, the explanations put forward by the employee, availability of suitable alternative work, and the effect the absences have on the business and on other employees.

It may be useful to remember that frequent absences from work are usually a symptom of some other problem. If the employee is in good health, then it is usually reasonable to assume that the problem may either lie with the company (management style, type or amount of work allocated to the employee, unrealistic deadlines, poor relationships with colleagues, etc.) or with the employee (personal or family problems, poor attitude, disinterest, etc.). It should not be automatically assumed that the employee is to blame for the problem but instead a fair and objective approach should be taken to resolving the issue.

Dismissal for long-term absence due to ill health is dealt with in 'Procedure when Dismissing for Ill Health', Chapter 17.

CHAPTER ELEVEN

SENSITIVE ISSUES IN EMPLOYMENT

Whenever people are employed, managers will inevitably encounter awkward and sensitive problems from time to time. A range of sensitive issues in employment are explored in this chapter.

SEXUAL, RACIAL AND DISABILITY HARASSMENT

There is no employment law in the UK which specifically outlaws harassment in the workplace. It has been established, however, that an individual who suffers sexual or racial harassment, or harassment on account of a disability, may take a complaint of unlawful discrimination to an employment tribunal under the relevant discrimination legislation, namely the Sex Discrimination Act 1975, the Race Relations Act 1976 or the Disability Discrimination Act 1995. No minimum period of qualifying service is required to bring such a complaint and compensation is unlimited (see 'Compensation for Sex/Race Discrimination at Employment Tribunal', Chapter 7). In order to succeed in a case at tribunal, the individual would only have to show that the treatment they suffered amounted to a detriment (i.e. a disadvantage) and that it was associated with their sex, race or disability.

Apart from taking a complaint of unlawful discrimination to tribunal, the individual may also succeed in a claim for constructive dismissal (subject to two years' service with the company). Such a case would be especially likely to succeed if the employee had complained internally about the harassment and the matter had not been dealt with adequately.

The term 'harassment' may cover a wide range of behaviour, the effect of which is to make the victim feel intimidated, embarrassed or distressed. Most harassment at work is perpetrated by the employee's immediate supervisor/ manager. Harassment may consist of a single serious incident or, alternatively, a series of minor incidents which, cumulatively, constitute a detriment to the individual.

Sexual harassment has been described in the EC Code of Practice (on measures to combat sexual harassment) as "unwanted conduct of a sexual nature or other conduct based on sex affecting the dignity of women and men at work". The code further states that such conduct may be physical, verbal or non-verbal and will constitute harassment where it is "unwanted, unreasonable and offensive to the recipient". A similar approach is taken to racial harassment (and by extension to disability harassment).

Effectively, therefore, the assessment of whether particular conduct constitutes harassment is a subjective one. For example, one employee may laugh off sexist or racist jokes, whilst another may find them offensive.

It is, therefore, particularly important, if a manager is approached by an employee alleging that they have been harassed by a colleague, that the manager takes the complaint seriously rather than concluding that it is trivial and telling the employee to just ignore it. Such an approach would give the employee strong ammunition to take a case to an employment tribunal. The important issue is whether *the employee* genuinely finds someone's behaviour towards them offensive, and not what *the manager* perceives.

Case Study

In one of the earliest cases of sexual harassment brought before a tribunal, an employee complained that she had been the victim of a campaign of 'vindictive unpleasantness' by colleagues who wanted to force her to transfer to another workplace. The harassment included suggestive remarks of a sexual nature and being forced to brush up against male employees in order to pass by.

The court upheld her complaint on the basis that the treatment she had suffered contained a significant sexual element and was, therefore, to be regarded as treatment on the grounds of her sex. The employer's argument that an equally disliked man would have been treated equally badly was held to be irrelevant. Equally irrelevant were the motives behind the harassment and the objectives of it; the relevant issues were the treatment the employee had received, whether it was detrimental towards her and whether it contained a sexual element.

Strathclyde Regional Council v. Porcelli [1986] I.R.L.R. 134.

Sexual harassment may affect men or women and would include conduct such as:

- unwanted touching;
- unwelcome sexual advances;
- sexist jokes or innuendoes;
- unwanted sexually implicit or explicit messages sent by e-mail or in a written note;
- leering or making offensive gestures, etc.

Racial harassment may include:

- racist jokes or banter;
- using racist terminology or offensive name-calling;
- the display of racist publications;
- written notes or e-mail messages containing racially offensive language, etc.

Disability harassment may include:

- patronising or offensive behaviour towards a disabled employee;
- calling the person an offensive name linked to their disability;
- insensitive jokes about people with disabilities;
- isolation or non-co-operation at work.

Clearly any behaviour of this (or similar) types is unacceptable in terms of morale, working relationships and productivity, quite apart from its unlawfulness. Managers should take the following action.

1. Devise a policy statement which stipulates that conduct at work which is in any way intimidating, humiliating or offensive to others will be regarded as gross misconduct rendering the perpetrator liable to disciplinary action up to, and including, summary dismissal (such a policy can incorporate bullying as well as harassment).

2. Appoint and train a member of staff to whom employees may turn if they feel they have been harassed.

3. Ensure all complaints are taken seriously, fully investigated and dealt with appropriately and fairly.

4. Ensure the alleged harasser's rights are respected, that they have the opportunity to put forward their side of events and that, where appropriate, they receive counselling or guidance from a suitable person.

5. Monitor and follow up complaints of harassment to ensure neither party is suffering victimisation as a result of the complaint being raised.

BULLYING

Bullying at work is clearly just as destructive and damaging to morale and productivity as harassment. A victim of bullying, however, will have no claim under discrimination legislation (unless the bullying contains a significant sexual or racial element or is linked to the person's disability). Bullying can take many forms, for example:

(a) ridiculing an employee in front of others;

(b) direct verbal aggression or threatening language;

(c) any type of physical assault;

(d) unrealistic targets or excessive workloads imposed deliberately;

(e) any form of intimidating behaviour, whether perpetrated in writing, electronically or verbally;

(f) victimising someone by giving them only unpleasant or exceedingly trivial tasks to do;

(g) unfair and excessive criticism, etc.

The key feature of bullying is its effect on the recipient who may feel upset, humiliated, intimidated or stressed.

Where an employee is suffering serious bullying at work, they may be able to succeed in a claim for constructive dismissal (see 'Claims for Constructive Dismissal', Chapter 4). The argument is that the employee's treatment amounts to a breach of the duty of trust and confidence reaching a situation where the employee finds it intolerable to the extent that they feel that they cannot continue in their job. Thus the bullying forces them to resign because they can no longer reasonably put up with it.

Bullying most often consists of a series of incidents, rather than a single incident, although where a single incident is serious enough, it may be sufficient to amount to a breach of contract.

Case Study

An employee who had been employed as a telephone supervisor in a hotel for thirteen years was severely reprimanded one day on account of the fact that she had taken time off work without permission to attend an emergency dental appointment. She had been suffering from severe toothache and overlooked the employer's requirement to obtain permission from her manager before taking time off work for such appointments.

The employee was extremely upset because of the reprimand and resigned forthwith. She subsequently brought a complaint of constructive dismissal to tribunal.

The tribunal, in assessing the evidence, formed the view that the reprimand had been "officious and insensitive", that the employee had not merited that sort of treatment and that she had, as a result, been "humiliated, intimidated and degraded to such an extent that there was a breach of trust going to the root of the contract of employment". The case succeeded based on this single incident.

Hilton International Hotels (UK) Ltd v. Protopapa [1990] I.R.L.R. 316.

More usually, bullying consists of a series of incidents which have the effect of wearing the employee down. It may be that there is a 'last straw' incident which, although not sufficiently serious on its own to justify a claim of constructive dismissal, may combine with earlier behaviour to form a breach of trust and confidence going to the heart of the working relationship. Alternatively, if the employee has raised an internal grievance on account of bullying behaviour, and if this complaint has been ignored or inadequately addressed, this denial of support could of itself give rise to a breach of trust and confidence. In either case, the employee may be able to win a case of constructive dismissal against the company.

To prevent, and/or tackle bullying at work, managers should:

(a) take immediate action as soon as it is known (or suspected) that a problem exists;

(b) take complaints of bullying seriously and ensure they are tackled promptly;

(c) investigate any incidents of bullying thoroughly;

(d) adopt a supportive attitude to the employee who is alleging bullying;

(e) ensure the alleged perpetrator of the bullying is treated fairly and given a full opportunity to state their case in confidence;

(f) handle the matter in a sensitive but objective way.

STRESS AT WORK

Stress and stress-related conditions constitute the biggest single cause of employee illness and absence from work. Much of the source of employees' stress may lie in factors in the workplace such as:

• workplace change, especially cutbacks;

• fear of redundancy;

• high workloads, long hours and tight deadlines;

• lack of control over work and/or work methods;

• lack of purpose and/or conflicting goals;

• lack of support or training;

• difficult working relationships, etc.

Most people at work are reluctant to admit that they are suffering from stress for fear that they may be seen as inadequate or weak, or that such a disclosure would result in disapproval or insinuation of failure. Nevertheless, stress at work, which is neglected, may lead to legal claims against the company.

The most likely claim against an employer would be a claim for constructive dismissal, based on an alleged breach of the implied duty to take care or of the implied duty of trust and confidence. This type of claim would require the employee to have a minimum of (presently) two years' continuous service. To succeed, the employee would have to show that the employer was sufficiently negligent in taking care of their health, welfare or safety to justify their resignation or that the pressures on them at work were intolerable to the extent that they had no choice but to resign.

Alternatively, if workplace stress has caused the employee to become ill, and if they can prove that this damage to their health was foreseeable, they might be able to succeed in a claim for personal injury and damages in a civil court. To succeed the employee would have to show that:

(a) the employer had breached their duty of care by being negligent;

(b) the employee had suffered an injury to health. Stress in itself does not amount to an illness, but a condition arising from stress, for example a nervous breakdown or severe depression, would constitute damage for the purposes of this type of claim;

(c) the injury to health was caused largely by work and not by factors in the employee's personal life;

(d) the injury to health was reasonably foreseeable.

From the last point above, it can be seen that, where an employee has approached their manager and complained that they are not coping with their workload, that their health is suffering or that they are feeling 'stressed out', the complaint should be taken seriously and positive action taken to alleviate the employee's stress. It would be difficult to argue that injury to health was not foreseeable, if the employee had plainly made their manager aware that a problem existed.

There is also the possibility that a stress-related illness, such as depression, could lead to the individual being able to claim that they were disabled under the provisions of the Disability Discrimination Act 1995. If the illness lasted twelve months or more, or was expected to last twelve months, and if it had a substantial adverse effect on the person's ability to carry out normal day to day activities, then the individual would be protected against discrimination (see Chapter 9 for details of the provisions of the Act).

Under health and safety legislation, employers are under a duty to provide and maintain systems of work and a working environment which are, as far as is reasonably practicable, free from risks to health. This includes risks to employees' mental health. It follows that managers should pay as much attention to employees' mental well-being as they do to their physical safety at work, and treat both as equivalent health issues. Managers are responsible for ensuring that employees are not put at risk as a consequence of excessive work pressures or other workplace factors, which could put their mental health at risk.

Stress at work is, therefore, a significant and relevant management issue which needs to be addressed positively, rather than ignored. The consequences of stress can be severe – apart from potential legal claims, there are the unseen costs such as high absenteeism, resentment and demotivation amongst employees, and impaired job performance and productivity. Prevention is always better than cure and a proactive approach towards employees' health (including mental health) together with a caring management attitude, flexibility and open communication systems, will go a long way towards stopping stress from becoming a major problem in the organisation.

AGE DISCRIMINATION

Currently there is no age discrimination legislation in the UK, although a code of practice exists which aims to provide advice on best practice in avoiding unfair age discrimination in recruitment and employment. The government has not ruled out legislation on age for the future, but has preferred the option of providing a voluntary code of practice as an alternative in the meantime.

Although it is not unlawful, managers may wish to review the rationale behind excluding vast numbers of highly experienced people from the pool for selection on account of their age. Upper age limits are usually arbitrary, or the result of someone's personal whim, and they rarely form an objective or auspicious method of selection. By applying age limits, the employer is in effect failing to take full advantage of experience and ability and ignoring a rich source of talent and skill. There is evidence that people in their forties and fifties stay in their jobs five times longer than employees in their early twenties and that they have *lower* rates of absenteeism.

Placing an upper age limit on a job as a condition for recruitment can, in some instances, constitute indirect sex discrimination against women. The logic of this can be gleaned from the following case study.

Case Study

A 35-year old woman applied to the civil service for a job as executive officer but on receiving the information pack describing the job and terms of service, she noticed that there was an upper age limit of 28. She was thus barred from eligibility for the job on account of the age limit.

She brought a complaint to an employment tribunal claiming that the upper age limit of 28 was indirectly discriminatory against women because it had a disproportionately adverse impact on them. The contention was that a considerably smaller proportion of women than men could have achieved the necessary experience to qualify for the job by age 28 due to the fact that more women than men take time out from work to raise children.

The case went to appeal and the EAT upheld it, finding that the age requirement could not be justified by the civil service. They had put forward the contention that employees needed sufficient time ahead of them to acquire the skills and experience necessary to progress to more senior positions, but the EAT rejected this argument. Thus they ruled that the age limit was discriminatory. The civil service subsequently amended their policy on age limits.

Price v. Civil Service Commission [1977] I.R.L.R. 291.

Full information on the implications and rationale behind indirect sex discrimination appears in 'The Concepts of Direct and Indirect Discrimination', Chapter 7.

Information about retirement ages is to be found in 'Retirement' in Chapter 15.

DRESS AND APPEARANCE

Employers are entitled to devise rules regarding the standards of dress and appearance, to which they wish their employees to conform, in the same way as they are entitled to formulate rules on conduct at work. Difficulties may arise, however, if some employees resent being restricted in their mode of dress or fail to conform to the standards laid or where the standards are perceived as over-rigid, unfair or discriminatory.

Where there is a problem with an employee failing to conform with the rules of dress and/or appearance without good reason, the appropriate course of action for the manager would be to deal with the matter under the company's disciplinary procedure (see 'Disciplinary Procedures and Handling Disciplinary Issues Correctly', Chapter 17).

Care should be taken, however, to ensure that any rules imposed are based on objective factors (for example a rule that employees handling food must tie their hair back is justifiable on the grounds of hygiene). Rules on dress should never be introduced arbitrarily or as a result of an individual manager's personal opinions. There is also the risk that rules on dress or appearance may indirectly discriminate against men or women or against persons from a particular racial group. This could occur in any of the following situations.

1.   Where the standards of dress are on the whole more restrictive for women than men (or vice versa).

2. Where a rule is applied only to women, or only to men, without good reason (for example a ban on men wearing earrings).

3. Where the rules are enforced more strictly on women than on men (or vice versa).

4. Where a rule is such that members of a particular racial group cannot comply with it, for example a ban on beards would discriminate indirectly against Sikhs, whose culture requires that they do not shave (although the rule could be justified if it was introduced for reasons of hygiene).

There is no need for rules on dress and appearance to be *the same* for men and women (in any event this would be silly!), but rules should be designed so that they apply an equivalent standard of smartness and/or conventionality to both sexes.

A ban on women wearing trousers to work would, in all likelihood, constitute indirect sex discrimination against women, unless the employer could justify the rule on objective, job-based reasons (which would be hard to envisage). Conversely, a ban on men and women wearing jeans to work introduced for reasons of smartness would not be discriminatory.

To avoid discrimination and promote good practice, managers should:

(a) examine rules and standards of dress and appearance and check that they are genuinely based on the requirements of the job (for example safety, hygiene or company image) rather than on personal opinions, stereotyped assumptions or arbitrary decisions;

(b) ensure that any rules on dress and appearance are not more restrictive for one sex, or racial group, than another;

(c) when introducing rules on dress and appearance for the first time, consult employees to seek their views before proceeding, and avoid imposing new rules without regard for individuals' concerns or objections;

(d) apply flexibility where an employee's racial origins mean that they cannot comply with the rules;

(e) ensure any rules are clearly communicated and that the penalties for failure to comply are clearly stated;

(f) investigate any breach of the rules thoroughly in case the individual has a valid reason for refusing to conform.

SMOKING AT WORK

In recent years, it has become commonplace for companies to ban smoking in the workplace altogether. Some firms take a softer stance and provide a 'smoking room' or set aside an area of a staff canteen for smokers. In the light of available evidence of the damaging effects of passive smoking, it is sensible for employers to apply rules on smoking at work so that employees are free from the potentially harmful, and undoubtedly unpleasant, effects of breathing in other people's cigarette smoke.

The Workplace (Health, Safety and Welfare) Regulations 1992 compel employers to provide rest areas where non-smokers can eat without suffering discomfort from tobacco smoke. The Regulations also stipulate that employers must make "effective and suitable provision to ensure that every enclosed workplace is ventilated by a sufficient quantity of fresh or purified air". Doing nothing to control employees' smoking could, arguably, be in breach of these provisions.

One possible remedy for an employee who is subjected to the effects of cigarette smoke at work is to resign and claim constructive dismissal.

Case Study

An employee who was a non-smoker had been employed as a secretary in a firm of solicitors for eight years. Following a move to an open-plan area, she suffered discomfort as a result of cigarette smoke, and so complained about it to management. A policy was introduced banning smoking in the open-plan area but this did not solve the employee's problem because smoke from nearby offices and an adjacent smoking room still wafted through to where she worked. Ultimately, her manager told her she would just have to put up with it, following which she resigned and brought a claim of constructive dismissal to an employment tribunal.

The case went to appeal and the decision was that the employer, in failing to take proper action to reduce the effects of tobacco smoke to an acceptable level, had breached an implied term in the employee's contract that she was entitled to work in an environment which was reasonably tolerable and suitable for her to perform her duties. Thus the employee succeeded in her case.

Waltons & Morse v. Dorrington [1997] I.R.L.R. 488.

The principle from the *Dorrington* case (above) is that, if employers fail to take appropriate steps to render the working environment reasonably free from tobacco smoke, this could amount to a breach of contract entitling employees who find the atmosphere intolerable, to resign and claim constructive dismissal.

Managers should handle any breaches of smoking rules in the same way as any other type of misconduct and in accordance with the company's specific rules, procedures and circumstances. The manager responsible should treat the matter as one of discipline and ensure that the employee is treated fairly and reasonably (see 'Disciplinary Procedures' and 'Handling Disciplinary Issues Correctly', Chapter 17). The severity of the penalty imposed on the employee will obviously depend on the seriousness of the offence, e.g. a verbal warning might be the appropriate penalty for a first offence where the employee had been caught absentmindedly lighting up a cigarette in their office, whilst summary dismissal may be the appropriate outcome following an instance of smoking near flammable materials.

DRINK AND DRUGS

An employee whose conduct, job performance or attendance at work is impaired by the abuse of alcohol or drugs can present their manager with a serious problem. The problem should never be ignored and instead should be tackled in a positive and supportive manner.

If the employee has been caught drinking or using illegal drugs in the workplace, this should be regarded as gross misconduct leading to disciplinary action up to and including dismissal. The employer may elect to apply the same principle to drunkenness or drug-taking at works functions, provided the company's disciplinary rules make this clear.

Where impaired performance or frequent absence from work occurs as a result of out-of-work drinking or drug-taking, however, the matter is more difficult. The first course of action for the manager should be to endeavour to establish whether the employee's problem relates to an illness (i.e. an addiction) or to casual use of alcohol or drugs. This can only be done by talking directly to the employee and adopting a sympathetic and understanding approach.

In employment law, an employee who is an alcoholic, or who is addicted to a particular drug, should be treated in the same way as an employee suffering from any other illness which affects their work (see 'Procedure for Dismissing for Ill Health', Chapter 17). Dismissal would be likely to be unfair unless the employer had first explored other possibilities, for example time off to rehabilitate or for counselling.

If there is any doubt as to the employee's overall state of health, the employer should initially give the employee the benefit of the doubt and regard the matter as one of genuine illness. A useful course of action would be to obtain a medical report on the employee (see 'Gaining Access to Employees' Medical Records', Chapter 10).

If the problem is one of occasional bouts of heavy drinking affecting attendance at work or job performance (and provided the employee is not an alcoholic), the manager may treat the matter as one of misconduct and deal with it under the company's disciplinary procedure. All the circumstances of an individual incident should be taken into account before any decision is made as to whether to discipline or dismiss the employee and the employee should, of course, be afforded the opportunity to explain their actions. If a single very serious incident occurred, for example if an employee, came to work drunk and began a fight with another employee, then this would normally be gross misconduct justifying summary dismissal, unless there were mitigating circumstances.

Recreational use of drugs outside of work may or may not constitute grounds for disciplinary action depending entirely on the employer's rules and on the impact the drug-taking has or might have on the employee's performance at work. It is legitimate for the employer to apply a rule which states that an employee, who is found to have been using illegal drugs outside of work, will be dismissed. This would be particularly relevant where the nature of the work was such that:

(a) impaired performance could lead to a safety risk; or

(b) the job involved working with machinery; or

(c) the job involved intense concentration; or

(d) the employee had responsibility for the care of others (for example a driver).

In general, if an employee is found to have been using an addictive drug, such as heroin, this should be regarded as a 'capability' issue (i.e. treated as an illness), whilst use of cannabis, which is not generally regarded as being addictive, may be viewed as misconduct.

If no rule on drug-taking outside of work is in place, and if the employer decides to dismiss an employee on account of such behaviour, it would have to be shown that the employee's out-of-work drug-taking had some tangible impact on the performance of their job, otherwise a dismissal would probably be ruled unfair (see also 'Dismissing an Employee for Behaviour Outside of Work', Chapter 17).

Case Study

The employee, who was a manager, had smoked cannabis at a party which had been held for staff and their guests at a local hotel. Following a complaint, the employer interviewed the employee in connection with the incident and she admitted openly that she had indeed smoked cannabis at the party. She was subsequently dismissed on account of the incident despite the fact that it had taken place away from the workplace and in her own time. The employee consequently took a complaint of unfair dismissal to an employment tribunal.

> The tribunal held that the dismissal was fair on account of the fact that the employee was in a managerial position and had smoked an illegal substance in front of junior staff for whom she was responsible. The company's contention that it had genuinely lost trust and confidence in the employee's ability to manage staff as a result of the incident was accepted.
>
> *Focus DIY Ltd v. Nicholson* [1994] E.A.T. 225/94.

The dismissal of an employee for drug-taking outside of work is more likely to be fair in law than a dismissal for drunkenness outside of work simply because the use of drugs is illegal.

Even if an employee is charged by the police with a drink or drugs offence outside of work, a dismissal would only be fair (in the absence of a company rule on the matter) if the employer could show that there was a direct link between the employee's off-duty conduct and the drink or drugs offence. The fairness of a dismissal would depend on all the circumstances of the individual case, in particular whether the employer could justify the employee's out-of-work conduct as sufficient reason to dismiss and on whether they treated the employee in a reasonable manner.

It is plainly in the interests of employers and employees alike to have clear policies and rules in place covering the subjects of drink and drugs. This will clarify for employees exactly what the rules are and what the penalties will be following drinking at work, drunkenness and drug-taking, and will make matters more straightforward for the employer.

GRIEVANCE PROCEDURES

Employers have a legal responsibility towards employees to:

(a) specify in writing the name or designation of the person to whom they should apply if they have a work-related grievance; and

(b) afford them a reasonable opportunity to obtain redress for any work-related grievance they may have.

There should be a formal written grievance procedure in place (except in very small companies) which specifies how employees should raise work-related complaints, the stages of the procedure and the time scales within which grievances will be dealt.

The objective of a grievance procedure should be to settle any dispute fairly and as near as possible to the point of origin. The relevant code of practice recommends that:

(a) the grievance procedure should be simple and rapid in operation;

(b) grievances should normally be discussed first between the employee and their immediate superior;

(c) the employee should be offered the opportunity to be accompanied by an employee representative during formal discussions with management about a grievance;

(d) there should be a right of appeal;

(e) the employer should keep written records of grievances raised, the various stages and the outcome.

A procedure for grievances to be dealt with promptly and fairly can be significant in affecting employee morale and motivation. Apart from the implications under employment law, there is the wider area of good employment practice.

The starting point from a good employment practice perspective is that, if an employee feels aggrieved or upset about something, it is best for this to be known, discussed and resolved – and for this process to be completed quickly. This requires managers and supervisors to adopt a positive, rather than defensive, attitude towards employees who raise grievances and to see grievance handling as a positive way of identifying and eliminating causes of employee discontent.

Without a constructive managerial attitude, employees may well be reluctant to voice grievances for fear of rejection or because of cynicism about the extent to which complaints will be taken seriously.

It is, of course, not possible for every grievance to be resolved in the way the employee concerned would wish. Part of a manager's skill in handling a grievance effectively is the ability to say 'no' where it is clearly inappropriate for the employee to be granted the outcome they want – and to do so firmly, without any hint of rancour and with a clear explanation of the reasons why.

One of the worst, and unfortunately most common, failings, is where a manager listens to a complaint, considers it unfounded, but instead of saying so, speaks vaguely about 'seeing if anything can be done' and then does nothing. The resulting lack of feedback to the employee is likely to cause resentment, apathy and, at worst, resignation followed by a complaint to a tribunal for constructive dismissal. This is because employees have an implied right in law to an opportunity to obtain redress for any grievance they may have. This does not mean that every grievance must be resolved in the employee's favour, but rather that employees must be afforded the opportunity to have their grievance heard, taken seriously and given full and fair consideration. It follows that employers should never dismiss employees' complaints out of hand and should instead ensure they are dealt with in a professional, prompt and positive manner.

CHAPTER TWELVE

TRANSFER OF UNDERTAKINGS LEGISLATION

The provisions contained in the Transfer of Undertakings (Protection of Employment) Regulations 1981 (TUPE) form a very detailed and complex sector of employment law. This chapter aims to explore the key issues surrounding this domain. The law in this area is likely to change in the future as the government is currently reviewing TUPE with a view to amending it.

The key purpose of TUPE is to protect people who are employed in a business which changes hands. Only employees are protected by TUPE, and not agency staff or workers engaged on a contract for service. Where there is a relevant transfer of a business under TUPE, employees have the right to the continuation of their employment contracts with the new employer. Thus employees' continuity of service, contractual entitlements and terms and conditions automatically become the responsibility of the new employer (the transferee) at the time the transfer takes place.

WHAT CONSTITUTES A TRANSFER UNDER THE TRANSFER OF UNDERTAKINGS REGULATIONS?

A transfer of an undertaking may occur when a business, or part of a business, changes hands. This may come about as a result of the sale of a business, a merger, the subcontracting of a discrete business activity, outsourcing or the re-letting of a contract or franchise. The effect is that employees, who were employed in the business (or part of the business) prior to the transfer, automatically have their contracts taken over by the new employer.

Determining whether or not the TUPE Regulations apply to a particular situation can be fraught with difficulties. The following are the key criteria.

1. The business must be a stable economic entity.

2. The business must retain its identity after the transfer, in other words the same or similar activities must be continued or resumed after the transfer (it is irrelevant whether or not this is done under a different name).

3. The new employer must either take over significant tangible or intangible assets, such as buildings and equipment, or take on a substantial number of the relevant workforce in terms of their numbers and skills.

No single element will be the determining factor as to whether there has been a transfer under TUPE but instead all the circumstances of the particular case will be considered together. If, for example, an employer tries to avoid TUPE by declining to take on any of the previous employer's staff, this is unlikely to succeed if other factors point towards a TUPE transfer having taken place. Equally, it is not necessary for the ownership of anything to be transferred because TUPE can apply where the transfer involves the responsibility for managing an activity or operation moving across from one company to another.

The transfer of a business may fall within TUPE even if the only tangible asset transferred is people. This can happen where a contract is sublet or where an existing contract changes hands without the transfer of any physical assets, for example in the catering industry. One catering company may lose a contract to another as a result of the contract being re-tendered and the incoming caterer may consequently take on a substantial number of the outgoing caterer's staff but not any buildings or equipment. TUPE will apply in this situation.

If in doubt, the determination of whether TUPE does in fact apply in a given situation is best left to qualified lawyers to assess.

EMPLOYER'S OBLIGATION TO CONSULT WORKERS' REPRESENTATIVES

Where the transfer of a business is proposed, both employers are obliged to consult workers' representatives in relation to the proposed changes. Workers' representatives may be either trade union representatives (where the employer recognises a trade union) or representatives elected by the employees. The representatives must represent *all* the employees who *may be affected* by the proposed transfer, including employees of the transferee (i.e. the company which is taking over the transferor's business).

If there is no trade union and it is necessary to elect workers' representatives for the purposes of TUPE consultation, there is currently no statutory method for electing them except for the criterion that representatives must be elected by the workforce, and not by the employer.

In order that consultation may take place, the employer is obliged to provide information in writing to the representatives as follows.

1. The fact that the transfer is to take place.

2. The approximate date of the transfer.

3. The reasons for the proposed transfer.

4. The legal, economic and social implications of the proposed transfer for the affected employees.

5. The measures the employer envisages taking in relation to the employees in connection with the transfer.

The necessary information must be made available to workers' representatives "in good time", which means long enough before the date of the transfer so that full and fair consultation may take place.

The law states that the *consultation* with workers' representatives in the event of a forthcoming transfer must cover the measures envisaged by the employer in relation to the employees, whilst the other points listed above need only be provided as *information* to the representatives. Consultation must consist of discussions between the employer and the representatives and must be conducted with a view to achieving agreement about the measures to be taken.

The transferee company is also under an obligation to provide information to the company being taken over about any measures they envisage taking in relation to the employees who are to transfer and these proposed measures should also form part of the consultation process.

If an employer fails to consult workers' representatives in connection with a forthcoming transfer, the representatives may bring a complaint to an employment tribunal against whichever employer failed to carry out proper consultation. If the complaint is upheld, the tribunal will make a declaration to that effect and may (on a discretionary basis) award compensation of up to four weeks' pay to all the employees who were adversely affected by the lack of consultation.

LIABILITIES OF THE NEW EMPLOYER

Where there has been a transfer of an undertaking under TUPE, all the old employer's rights, powers, duties and liabilities connected with the employees' contracts of employment are transferred automatically to the new employer. This can be a very onerous burden on the new employer because *all* liabilities connected with the contracts of employment of the employees who are transferred will be taken on. This could include, for example, liability for a claim for damages resulting from an injury at work or a claim for sex discrimination which has not yet been settled. It is therefore in the interests of an employer, who is contemplating taking over another business, to take the following steps.

1. Carry out a thorough review of employees' terms and conditions of employment, including any terms incorporated into contracts from a collective agreement.

2. Seek appropriate warranties and indemnities from the company which is being taken over as part of the agreed legal arrangements for the transfer.

3. Seek detailed legal advice from an appropriate source.

EMPLOYEES' RIGHTS WHEN THEIR EMPLOYER'S BUSINESS IS TRANSFERRED

When a business is transferred, the contracts of employment of the employees in the business shift across to the new employer with all existing terms, conditions, benefits and entitlements intact. The new employer has no choice in the matter, as the provisions of TUPE apply automatically. Employees have the following rights.

1. The right to continuity of employment.

2. The right to retain the same terms and conditions.

3. The right not to be dismissed on account of the transfer.

The Right to Continuity of Employment

Following a TUPE transfer, the employees, whose contracts have been taken over by a new employer, have the automatic right to continuity of service. This means that their length of service and accrued rights will be unaffected by the transfer.

Case Study

An employer who planned to close his plant and contract out the work to another company offered his employees a choice of three options, which were:
(a) to remain with the company and move to a different position; *or*
(b) to transfer to the new employer under TUPE – i.e. with continuity of employment and existing conditions preserved; *or*
(c) to opt out of the transfer and receive a redundancy payment.

The majority of the employees opted to take the redundancy payment and signed agreements to that effect following which they applied and were accepted, for employment with the new employer. Their contracts of employment with the new employer took immediate effect.

Just under a year later, there were redundancies in the company which had taken on the employees in question. Some of them claimed unfair dismissal and redundancy pay at an employment tribunal and as a preliminary issue the tribunal had to ad-

---

dress whether the employees had the requisite length of service to bring these claims. This, in turn, depended on whether their contracts of employment had transferred across from their original employer under TUPE or whether their continuity of service had been broken due to the fact that they had specifically opted out of the transfer and accepted redundancy payments from the old employer.

Two interesting conclusions emerged from this case. The first was the tribunal's finding that, because a TUPE transfer had occurred in law, the employees' contracts had transferred over to the new employer. The agreement the employees had signed opting out of their rights under TUPE was void because the operation of TUPE cannot be superseded by any private agreement. Thus the employees had sufficient continuity of service to entitle them to have their complaints heard by a tribunal.

Secondly, the tribunal addressed whether the redundancy package paid to the employees had any effect on their claim for redundancy pay against the second employer. Employees are barred from receiving a statutory redundancy payment twice for the same period of service and entitlement to future redundancy pay must begin afresh following receipt of a statutory redundancy payment for a past period of service. In this case, however, it was held that the payments which the employees had been given when they left their original employer could not in fact have been statutory redundancy payments, because the employees were not redundant (because when TUPE applies, employees have automatic continuity of service).

It followed from this that the money the employees had received from the original employer was to be regarded as an ex gratia payment and was irrelevant to the calculation of any future redundancy entitlement. The new employer was, therefore, liable to pay them each a statutory redundancy payment based on their total length of service incorporating the period of time they had worked for the original employer.

Senior Heat Treatment Ltd v. Bell and Others [1997] I.R.L.R. 614.

It can be seen from the *Bell* case above that, if a TUPE transfer applies, employees' continuity of service will be preserved when they are taken on by the new employer even if they have been paid a redundancy payment from the original employer. It is not the case that the granting of a redundancy payment absolves the new employer from liabilities arising from employees' periods of service before the transfer because, in law, TUPE has the effect of transferring the employees' contracts across to the new employer automatically. Thus, in the event that the previous employer has made staff redundant before the transfer and where the new employer decides to re-employ those staff, it will be a wise precaution to negotiate a full indemnity from the transferor company to cover any potential claims for redundancy pay against the new employer.

The Right to Retain the Same Terms and Conditions

Following a TUPE transfer, employees whose contracts of employment are transferred to the new employer have the right to continued employment on *the same terms and conditions.*

The only exception to this, which in any event is due to be removed in the near future, is the right for employees to receive equivalent occupational pension benefits from the new employer.

Employers who take over another business are, therefore, severely restricted in that they must honour the existing terms and conditions of the incoming employees indefinitely and cannot, at any time, alter those terms for a reason connected with the transfer. Furthermore, there is no time limit after which it becomes lawful to alter employees' terms on account of the transfer. Terms and conditions may be altered, with agreement, for reasons which are not related to the transfer but not otherwise. Even if an employee 'agrees' to a change, it will be ineffective if the transfer is the reason for it, quite simply because employers do not have the option to contract out of their obligations under TUPE.

This can impact severely on an employer who has taken over a business in which employees are earning higher rates of pay or enjoying more favourable contractual benefits than the company's existing employees. Current law does not allow for a rationalisation of terms and conditions on account of a transfer. If the incoming employees have their pay or benefits reduced as a result of a transfer, they would be able to take a complaint to an employment tribunal and through this route enforce their right to the terms and conditions of their original contracts which had transferred under TUPE. This would apply whether or not the employees had signed agreement to any changes.

The Right not to be Dismissed on Account of a Transfer

If an employee is dismissed for a reason which is connected with the transfer of a business, the dismissal will be automatically unfair unless it falls within an exception known as an 'ETO' reason (see the next section). This principle applies to dismissals of employees of both companies (i.e. the company taken over and the one doing the taking over) provided the dismissal is for a reason connected with the transfer and not some other reason.

The timing of the dismissal will not affect this principle. The issue is whether the reason for the dismissal is a transfer-related reason and not whether it takes place some time before or some time after the transfer. Thus, an employee who is dismissed before the transfer, at the time of the transfer or after the completion of the transfer will be, automatically, unfairly dismissed if the reason for their dismissal is connected with the transfer. There is no time limit after which it becomes potentially fair to dismiss employees for a transfer-related reason.

Employers cannot get round this provision by colluding to dismiss employees in advance of the transfer. Although the TUPE Regulations provide that employees must be employed by the transferor immediately before the transfer for their contracts to be transferred, a dismissal in advance of the transfer, which is implemented for reasons connected with the transfer, will not have the effect of dislodging the new employer's liability. Thus employees who are dismissed in advance of a transfer, and for a reason connected with the transfer, will retain their rights to protection under TUPE (unless the reason for their dismissal was an ETO reason – see the next section).

Any claim for unfair dismissal on account of a transfer will be against the new employer. One restriction, however, is that the employee requires to have a minimum of two years' service in order to bring such a complaint to an employment tribunal (this is to be reduced to one year upon implementation of the Employment Relations Act).

ETO Reasons for Dismissal Following a Transfer

There is one exception to the law which makes transfer-related dismissals automatically unfair. This is where there is an economic, technical or organisational reason for the dismissal entailing changes in the workforce. This is known as an ETO reason.

The most common ETO reasons are where, as a result of a transfer, the new employer has a surplus of employees, finds that work functions are duplicated or assesses that there is a legitimate need to restructure the workforce. In any of these circumstances, redundancies may legitimately be carried out under the ETO facility. It is important to note, however, that for such redundancies to be fair, selection must be made from amongst the *whole* workforce and not only from amongst those who joined the company as a result of the transfer.

Certain considerations which would *not* give rise to an ETO reason for dismissal include the argument that the employer had to dismiss staff in order to make the business more attractive to a purchaser or in order to obtain an enhanced sale price for the business.

As well as having an economic, technical or organisational reason to dismiss, the employer must also meet the second criteria, namely that any dismissals carried out because of the transfer must "entail changes in the workforce". This means that reductions in the workforce, which are for an economic, technical or organisational reason, must be part of the employer's overall plan and not just a possible or coincidental consequence of it. The courts have also held that changes to the identity of the people who make up the workforce cannot be regarded as a change in the workforce (for the purposes of establishing an ETO reason for dismissal) where the overall numbers and functions of the employees remain unchanged as a whole.

Where an employee is dismissed for a genuine ETO reason, they can still take a claim for unfair dismissal to an employment tribunal (subject to two years' continuous service) and the complaint will be dealt with in the normal way (see 'The Importance of Following a Fair Procedure', Chapter 17). To succeed in defending such a case, the employer would have to satisfy the tribunal not only that they had a genuine ETO reason for dismissing the employee, but also that they had acted reasonably towards the employee in carrying out the dismissal.

CHAPTER THIRTEEN

TRADE UNIONS

All employees have the right to choose whether or not they wish to belong to a trade union, and whether or note to take part in the activities of the union in their own time or at times permitted by the employer. Employers must grant employees the freedom of choice in this matter, and any unfavourable treatment meted out to an employee on account of their being a union member or taking part in union activities is unlawful.

Individuals' rights fall into three categories.

1. The right of a job applicant not to be refused employment on account of union membership or non-membership.

2. The right of an employee not to suffer any type of victimisation on union grounds.

3. The right of an employee not to be dismissed on the grounds of trade union membership or activities.

TRADE UNION RECOGNITION

At the time of writing, the government has put forward certain proposed reforms of trade union law in the Employment Relations Bill.

The position following implementation of the Bill is that employers will be compelled to recognise a trade union if the majority of the workforce wishes it. This will be the first time since 1979 that there will be provisions for statutory recognition of trade unions.

There are two ways in which a trade union can claim statutory recognition.

1. Where 40 per cent of the total workforce *eligible to vote* (rather than a percentage of the workforce who *actually vote*) vote in favour of union recognition at a ballot and this number also represents a majority of those actually voting.

2. Where the union can show that they have more than 50 per cent of the workforce actually in membership, in which case they can apply for automatic recognition.

Thus, employers will have no option but to concede to the wishes of the majority of their employees and clearly it is in the interests of everyone for employers to collaborate with unions with a view to promoting the best interests of both the company and the employees.

REFUSAL OF EMPLOYMENT ON TRADE UNION GROUNDS

It is unlawful to exclude a job applicant from employment on account of their membership of a trade union or on account of non-union membership.

Discrimination on trade union grounds can occur at any time during the recruitment process and may, for example, take the form of:

(a) refusal to deal with a job enquiry or process a job application;

(b) suspension of the job application;

(c) refusal or deliberate failure to offer employment;

(d) making an unreasonable offer of employment so that the offer is bound to be rejected;

(e) withdrawal of an offer of employment.

If an offer of employment is made conditional upon the person being (or not being) a trade union member, and if the candidate rejects the offer on these grounds, then they are deemed to have been refused employment on trade union grounds.

Technically it is only refusal to employ on the grounds of trade union *membership* which is unlawful and not rejection on account of *trade union activities*. In practice, however, the distinction between the two may be academic as the two are often inseparable.

Case Study

A social worker who had resigned from his job for family reasons later sought re-employment with a council. The employee had a reputation for being a strong and forthright union negotiator and the council took the view that during his earlier period of employment he had displayed a "confrontational and anti-management approach". On the grounds of these perceived attitudes, they declined to re-employ him. He subsequently claimed he had been refused employment on trade union grounds.

One of the issues dealt with in this case was the distinction between trade union activities and trade union membership. The employee would only succeed in his case if he could show that the refusal to re-employ him was on the grounds of his trade union membership. Thus the tribunal had to address whether the individual's past trade union activities were in fact part of the issue of trade union membership.

When the case went to appeal, an employment appeal tribunal held that it was not possible to separate the fact of trade union membership from the consequences of membership, such as union activities. They concluded, therefore, that because the council had refused employment for a reason related to the individual's trade union activities, it followed that he had been unlawfully refused employment on trade union grounds.

Harrison v. Kent County Council [1995] I.C.R. 434.

Because refusal to employ on the grounds of an individual's trade union membership is unlawful, managers should refrain from asking questions at interview about the job applicant's past or present trade union affiliations. Such questions would in all likelihood lead the applicant to form the view that the questions were being asked in order to screen out candidates who were union members or who had in the past taken an active role in union matters. Managers should therefore avoid asking questions about:

(a) whether the individual is or has been a trade union member;

(b) to what extend the person has taken part in trade union activities, such as attending meetings, campaigning, etc.

(c) whether the person has ever been a shop steward;

(d) whether the person would propose to join a trade union or to take part in union activities, if they were employed;

(e) what the person's general views are regarding trade unions and trade union membership.

EMPLOYEES' RIGHTS TO TRADE UNION MEMBERSHIP AND ACTIVITIES

All employees, regardless of their length of service or the number of hours they work, have the right to:

(a) elect to belong to a trade union of their choice;

(b) choose not to belong to a particular trade union;

(c) decline from being a member of any trade union;

(d) take part in trade union activities at an appropriate time.

The key point is that union membership is the employee's choice, and it is unlawful for the employer to attempt to exert influence on employees to belong, or not to belong, to a union or to penalise them in any way on account of their choice in the matter.

Similarly, the terms of employees' contracts of employment may not impose conditions relating to union membership. Any contractual clause which purported to compel an employee to be, or not to be, a member of a particular trade union, would be unenforceable and, if the employer attempted to enforce it, the employee would have the right to complain to an employment tribunal.

Trade unions may, of course, impose their own rules as to entitlement to membership. Most unions operate in specific industries, professions or trades, with membership being open only to individuals who are employed in a specific type of work. Similarly, membership may be open only to employees who work for a specific employer, or to those working in a specific workplace.

Trade unions are also entitled to set and maintain appropriate rules and standards of conduct for their members. It follows that a member who breaches the rules may be expelled from the union although this will not in any way affect the person's employment contract with their employer. It is, however, not open to a trade union to exclude or expel an individual from membership on account of their refusal to take part in a strike or other industrial action.

What Constitutes 'Union Activities'?

There is no definition of 'trade union activities' in law. A wide variety of actions may be classed as union activities, such as:

(a) attending union meetings;

(b) attending a union training course;

(c) seeking advice from, or raising a complaint with, a trade union official;

(d) canvassing on behalf of the union to encourage other employees to become members of the union;

(e) participating in an election campaign;

(f) voting in a ballot.

Employees have the right to take part in any of these activities at an 'appropriate time' and must not be penalised for doing so. An 'appropriate time' for trade union activities can mean:

(a) a time outside the employee's working hours, for example lunch or tea breaks; or

(b) a time within working hours which the employer has agreed as a time when employees may take part in union activities.

Employees' Rights to Time Off for Trade Union Activities

The law compels employers to grant employees who are members of a trade union, which is recognised by the employer, reasonable time off work to allow them to take part in the activities of the union. The time off granted must be time out of working hours and employees cannot be required to make up for the time taken by working additional hours at another time. There is no obligation on the employer to pay employees for time off taken for this purpose, although they may, of course, choose to do so if they wish.

The type of trade union activity which the time off provision would normally extend to cover would include time off to attend union meetings (including those called for the purpose of considering industrial action), time off to seek advice from a union official, time off for representation and time off to vote in ballots.

There is no minimum or maximum amount of time off for union activities prescribed by law, only the stipulation that the amount of time off granted must be 'reasonable'. Guidance on how much time an employer should permit is available in ACAS' Code of Practice on 'Time Off for Trade Union Duties and Activities'. The Code emphasises the need for co-operation and agreement between employers and unions in relation to determining how much time off should be granted.

Trade Union Officials' Rights to Time Off for Trade Union Duties

Employees, who fulfil the role of trade union official, have additional rights to time off work in order that they may carry out the duties of their position. This right to time off applies where the trade union is recognised by the employer and provided the union duty is a matter covered within the union recognition agreement.

Trade union officials have the following rights in relation to time off:

(a) to be granted reasonable time off during working hours to carry out the duties associated with the position;

(b) to be allowed time off to attend relevant training;

(c) not to be unreasonably refused time off for these purposes;

(d) to be paid for such time off.

The right for trade union officials to be paid for time spent conducting trade union duties does not apply if the time spent on union duties is part of the person's own time. Thus, if a trade union official elects to carry out some of their trade union duties at a time which falls outside their normal working hours, there will be no entitlement to extra pay. Equally, there is no right for the trade union official to be granted time off in lieu in these circumstances.

CHECK-OFF ARRANGEMENTS

Most union members elect to pay their union subscriptions by means of de-ductions from their pay, with the money deducted being paid over directly to the union. This arrangement is known as 'check-off'.

Each employee must give their written consent to check-off and no de-duction from an employee's pay on account of union membership can be made unless written authorisation has first been obtained. A deduction from pay, which is made without the employee's express written consent, would consti-tute an unlawful deduction from wages (see 'Deductions from Pay – When they are Lawful and when they are Unlawful' in Chapter 6).

Employees, who have agreed to check-off, have the right to end the ar-rangement at any time by informing their employer in writing that they have terminated, or intend to terminate, their trade union membership. In these circumstances, the employer must stop making deductions from the employ-ee's pay as soon as is reasonably practicable.

DISMISSAL FOR TRADE UNION MEMBERSHIP OR ACTIVITIES

It is unlawful for an employer to dismiss an employee, or select an employee for redundancy, on any of the following grounds.

1. Trade union membership, whether past, present or proposed.

2. Participation in the activities of an independent trade union at an appro-priate time, whether past or present.

3. Non-membership or refusal to join a trade union.

If an employee believes that their dismissal or selection for redundancy is linked with their trade union membership or activities, they may bring a claim to an employment tribunal irrespective of their length of service. Employees of any age (even those over retirement age) may bring this type of claim. Such dismissals are automatically unfair (see 'Automatically Unfair Dismissals', Chapter 17) and compensation levels can be very high.

In addition to the right to take a claim of unfair dismissal to tribunal, there is a course of action termed 'interim relief' which is open to employees who have been dismissed for reasons of trade union membership or activities. In-terim relief allows the employee to ask the tribunal to order the employer to re-engage them until the tribunal hearing. To be valid, a request for interim relief must be presented within seven days of the date of the employee's dis-missal and must be supported by a certificate signed by an authorised union official stating that there is evidence to show that the principal reason for the employee's dismissal was a trade union related reason.

If the request for interim relief is upheld, the employer will be ordered either to re-employ the person or to suspend them on full pay until the date of the tribunal hearing.

Employees who are dismissed for taking part in strike action are not regarded as having been dismissed on account of union membership or activities (see below under 'Dismissing Employees on Account of Strike Action').

ACTION SHORT OF DISMISSAL

In addition to the right not to be dismissed for trade union related reasons, employees have the right not to have action short of dismissal taken against them on the grounds that they:

(a) are, or propose to become, a member of an independent trade union;

(b) refuse to join or to belong to a trade union;

(c) have taken part in the activities of an independent trade union at an appropriate time.

All employees, regardless of age, length of service or hours of work enjoy this protection.

There is no statutory definition of action, short of dismissal, but in practice the type of victimisation covered could incorporate a wide range of management actions taken against the employee and designed to place them at a disadvantage, for example:

(a) a deduction from pay;

(b) the removal of a company benefit;

(c) discrimination in promotion;

(d) refusal to offer training opportunities;

(e) a disciplinary warning;

(f) the threat of dismissal.

EMPLOYEES' 'RIGHT TO STRIKE'

If employees take part in a strike, this in effect constitutes a fundamental breach of contract because a withdrawal of labour breaches one of the key terms of the working relationship, namely the provision of work by the employee. Thus, the employer may elect to dismiss employees who are on strike and such dismissals may be fair provided the employer fulfils certain criteria (see below) and acts reasonably in an overall sense.

Hence, although employees are free to take part in strike action if they wish, this so-called 'right to strike' places them in a vulnerable position in so much as they could lose their jobs.

Employees who are taking part in a strike (whether official or unofficial) are not entitled to be paid their wages for the time spent on strike. Equally, the period of time spent on strike will not, once the employee is back at work, count towards their continuous service with the company, although the gap does not act to break continuity. This means that, if at a future time an employee's total length of continuous service is being calculated (for example for the purposes of working out how much redundancy pay they are entitled to), the employer must count in all continuous service prior to the strike together with service after the strike but must subtract the number of days of the strike itself from the calculation.

DISMISSING EMPLOYEES ON ACCOUNT OF STRIKE ACTION

If a strike is unofficial, i.e. it has not been endorsed by the relevant trade union, employees who are dismissed whilst taking part in it are, at present, barred from bringing a complaint of unfair dismissal to an employment tribunal. Thus they have no statutory rights at all to protect them regardless of how the employer has handled the dismissals. Dismissal in these circumstances is, in a sense, automatically fair.

The position with regard to employees who are taking part in an official strike is set to change following proposals by the government (in the Employment Relations Bill). Previously employees dismissed whilst taking part in an official strike were barred from bringing claims to tribunal for unfair dismissal provided that:

(a) the employer acted consistently and dismissed *all* of the strikers rather than singling out certain individuals for dismissal;

(b) only those taking part in the strike or those clearly associated with it were dismissed and not those working normally;

(c) the dismissals were actioned whilst employees were taking part in the strike, and not before the strike began or after the strikers had resumed working;

(d) the employer did not selectively re-engage some (but not all) of those dismissed within three months of the date of their dismissals.

The new law will change the position for employees dismissed for taking part in official strike action. For the first eight weeks of strike action, dismissal will be automatically unfair. After this eight week period, the employer will be able to dismiss strikers, but those dismissed will have the right to bring a complaint of unfair dismissal to an employment tribunal, subject to a minimum period of qualifying service of one year. The fairness of such dismissals will be assessed according to the same criteria as are used for other types of dismissal (see 'How Employment Tribunals view Unfair Dismissal Claims', Chapter 17). It is likely that the question of whether the employer has acted consistently in dismissing strikers will be a key factor affecting the fairness or otherwise of such dismissals.

Other Industrial Action

Where employees take industrial action, which falls short of an outright strike, the employer may similarly elect to dismiss those taking part where their action constitutes a breach of one of the express or implied terms of the contract of employment. There is no definition in law of 'other industrial action' but it may include conduct such as:

- a 'go-slow';
- a work-to-rule;
- an overtime ban;
- refusal to carry out certain duties;
- picketing.

The key factor which distinguishes industrial action from other types of conduct is the motive behind it. If the action taken is done for the purpose of putting concerted pressure on the employer to negotiate or agree to certain employee demands, then it can be classed as industrial action.

If the industrial action is unofficial, those dismissed for taking part in it will be unable to bring a claim for unfair dismissal to an employment tribunal.

Lockouts

A lockout occurs where the employer either closes the workplace, suspends work or refuses to allow employees to come to work as a direct result of a dispute. Such action, on the part of the employer, will constitute a lockout provided the purpose behind the action is to put pressure on employees to accept certain terms and conditions affecting their employment. A lockout most usually takes place following industrial action.

If the industrial action which gave rise to the lockout was unofficial, those locked out as a result will be ineligible to bring a claim for unfair dismissal to an employment tribunal.

CHAPTER FOURTEEN

DATA PROTECTION LEGISLATION

THE DATA PROTECTION ACT 1998

A new Data Protection Act is to be implemented in the UK in early 1999 which will put into effect the provisions of the EU Data Protection Directive. The Data Protection Act 1998 includes a range of provisions regarding the collection, organisation, storage, retrieval, alteration, disclosure and destruction of information held about individuals in both manual and computer filing systems. The key difference between the new Act and previous UK legislation on data protection is that the new provisions apply to information held about employees in manual filing systems as well as information in computer systems, whilst the previous Data Protection Act 1984 only covered data held on computer. The new Act repeals the Data Protection Act 1984 as it incorporates most of its provisions.

The Data Protection Act 1998 defines computerised data as information which "is being processed by means of equipment operating automatically in response to instructions given for that purpose". A 'relevant filing system', for the purposes of manual files, is defined as a set of non-automated information relating to individuals which is "structured, either by reference to individuals or by reference to criteria relating to individuals, in such a way that specific information relating to a particular individual is readily accessible". This suggests that a manual file which contains a muddle of papers in no set order and with no structure is not covered by the Act. Structured filing systems held 'unofficially' by managers are, however, covered, although ad hoc notes made by a manager which do not form part of a structured filing system would not appear to come within the definition of 'relevant filing system'.

Under this Act employees have the right to request sight of documents, such as appraisals, warnings held on file, statements about pay and expressions of opinion or intention about (for example) promotion prospects. Confidential references, however, are exempted from the law.

Individuals also have the right to have inaccurate information corrected or erased from filing systems, although in relation to manual filing systems which existed prior to 23 October 1998, this provision will not come into force until October 2007. Individuals, however, do currently have the right to have inaccurate data about them corrected or erased from all computer systems and from manual files which were created after 23 October 1998 (e.g. those applicable to employees hired after 23 October 1998).

Another important feature of the Act is that it compels employers to inform employees when information has been collected about them, why it has been collected, to whom it may be provided and of their right of access to it.

Employers should, if they have not already done so, take the following actions.

1. Carry out a thorough audit of existing manual filing systems in order to identify what paper information is held and the purposes for which the files are held.

2. At the same time conduct a review of personal information held on computer.

3. Write to all employees informing them what information is held about them on both manual and computer files, the purposes for which the information may be used and to whom it may be provided.

4. Draft a letter informing employees of their rights of access to information under the Data Protection Act 1998.

5. Review what type of information they require employees and job applicants to provide and the purposes for which the information is used.

6. Draft a form to be used for obtaining employees' and job applicants' consent for the collection and use of sensitive data (see below).

7. Amend application forms to incorporate a statement informing job applicants about the information which is being collected about them, why it is being collected, to whom it may be provided, and of their right of access to it.

8. Review other existing documentation with a view to making similar amendments.

9. Formulate a clearly worded policy on this matter to ensure compliance with the part of the Act which deals with the collection of sensitive personal data.

THE DATA PROTECTION PRINCIPLES

The Data Protection Act 1998, like its predecessor, contains eight data protection principles governing the processing of personal data. These are broadly similar to the principles contained in the original Act of 1984, and read as follows.

1. **Personal data shall be processed fairly and lawfully.** To fulfil this principle, the employer must either obtain the employee's express consent for the information to be processed or else be able to show that processing is

necessary for the performance of the contract or in order to meet legal obligations.

2. **Personal data shall be obtained only for specified and lawful purposes, and shall not be processed in any manner incompatible with those purposes.** Clearly, compliance with this principle requires the employer to exercise control over why and how personal information about employees is used.

3. **Personal data shall be adequate, relevant and not excessive in relation to the purposes for which it is processed.** Under this principle, employers should not retain information about employees which is out of date or irrelevant. There must be a sound business reason for holding the information.

4. **Personal data shall be accurate and, where necessary, kept up to date.** The best method of ensuring that information is kept up to date is to periodically provide employees with a copy of their personnel file for them to check.

5. **Personal data shall be kept for no longer than is necessary for the purposes for which it is processed.** It follows from this principle that employers should not hold on to information about employees who have left indefinitely.

6. **Personal data shall be processed in accordance with the rights of data subjects under the Act.** It is the responsibility of the employer to ensure that employees are afforded their rights under the Act.

7. **Personal data shall be subject to appropriate technical and organisational measures to protect against unauthorised or unlawful processing and accidental loss, destruction or damage.** The employer needs to take measures to ensure that information is kept confidential and not made available to unauthorised parties. Additionally, a back-up system should be in place lest computerised files are accidentally lost.

8. **Personal data shall not be transferred to a country or territory outside the European Economic Area unless that country or territory ensures an adequate level of data protection.** This principle was not part of the Data Protection Act 1984. The "adequate level of data protection", however, is not required where the individual consents to the transfer of information held about them.

Employers are obliged to comply with both the spirit and the letter of all these principles.

EMPLOYEES' RIGHT OF ACCESS TO DATA HELD BY THE EMPLOYER MANUALLY AND ON COMPUTER

Employees' and job applicants' rights of access and rights concerning the correction and erasure of inaccurate personal data are contained in Part II of the Act.

Under the Act, all employees have the right of access to relevant manual files, as well as computer files. They also have the right:

(a) to be informed by their employer whether personal data about them is held or is being processed (whether manually or on computer);

(b) to be given a description of the data;

(c) to be informed of the purposes for which the data is being processed;

(d) to be given details of the persons to whom the data may be disclosed;

(e) to receive the relevant personal data in an intelligible form;

(f) to have any inaccuracies on the file corrected or removed.

To gain access to information held about them, the employee must make a written request to the employer and the employer may, if they wish, charge a fee for processing the enquiry (the current maximum level of such a fee is £10). The employer must comply with any request for access within 40 days. Access may be obtained "at reasonable intervals".

LIMITATIONS ON THE KIND OF INFORMATION WHICH MAY BE PROCESSED

The Data Protection Act limits the kind of information that can be collected and processed about individuals. In particular, there is a provision which will prevent the processing of certain sensitive information, i.e. data relating to any of the following aspects of an individual, except in the limited circumstances given below.

- Ethnic or racial origins.
- Political opinions.
- Religious or philosophical beliefs.
- Trade union membership.
- Physical or mental health.
- Sexuality.
- The commission of any criminal offence.

The processing of such sensitive data is also subject to the eight data protection principles (see above).

The Act prohibits the collection of sensitive data unless one of the following conditions is fulfilled.

1. The employee expressly consents to the information being collected.

2. It is necessary to collect the information in order to comply with employment law, for example the processing of data on sickness absence in order to comply with SSP requirements.

3. The processing of the information is necessary on account of legal proceedings, for example defending a tribunal claim.

4. Processing is necessary for the administration of justice or to comply with statute, for example the processing of information relating to an employee's criminal convictions for the purpose of compliance with an attachment of earnings order.

5. Processing is carried out for the purposes of monitoring to ensure equality of opportunity as between individuals of different races or ethnic origins.

In most instances, therefore, employers have to ensure that employees' (and job applicants') express consent is obtained prior to gathering information for processing or monitoring purposes, if the information includes any of the types of sensitive information restricted by the Data Protection Act.

TRANSITION PERIODS

Certain requirements under the Data Protection Act are subject to a transitional period. In particular, manual records, which were in existence on or before 23 October 1998 (the date on which the provisions of the Data Protection Directive should have been implemented), will be exempt until 23 October 2001 from the data protection principles, the access provisions and the rights of individuals concerning correction/erasure of inaccurate personal data. However, immediate compliance is required for all manual records created after that date.

A longer transitional period (up to 23 October 2007) is in place in respect of some of the data protection principles (part of number 1 and numbers 2, 3, 4 and 5) and the rights of individuals concerning correction/erasure of inaccurate data.

CHAPTER FIFTEEN

THE WAYS IN WHICH AN EMPLOYMENT CONTRACT CAN TERMINATE

There are many different ways in which a contract of employment can terminate. The two most common means of termination are, of course, resignation and dismissal. These, together with other ways in which an employment contract can come to an end, are explored below.

RESIGNATION

It is inherent in every employment contract that the employee may choose to terminate the contract if and when they wish to do so, provided they give the employer proper notice under the contract (see 'Employees' Notice Obligations', Chapter 16). If the contract contains no notice clauses, and no verbal agreement has been reached on the matter, then the employee need give only one week's statutory notice to terminate the contract, regardless of length of service.

Whilst an employer may wish in some instances to try to persuade an employee who has given notice to change their mind, refusing to accept an employee's resignation is not an option. This is because the provision of notice does not require the other party's acceptance in order for it to be effective.

The employee may give notice either verbally or in writing, although it is clearly preferable from the employer's point of view to obtain notice in writing. This avoids a situation arising where an employee may be thought, based on the words uttered, to have resigned, whereas in fact the manager may have misinterpreted what was said or the employee may have acted in the heat of the moment. In order to avoid confusion or misunderstanding, therefore, it is advisable for employers to include a clause in all employees' contracts of employment stating that notice to terminate the contract must be provided in writing. Managers should, of course, then ensure that this is put into practice on every occasion.

Confusion over whether Termination is Due to Resignation or Dismissal

In certain circumstances, there could be uncertainty over whether or not an employee has resigned. For example, if an employee makes a statement about leaving in the heat of the moment, the unwary employer may fall into the trap of assuming that the employee has resigned, make arrangements for the employment to be terminated and subsequently find themselves having to defend an unfair dismissal claim.

Case Studies

An employee had a dispute with his employer over pay. During discussions, the employee said "this money is no use to me" upon which the employer took this statement as a resignation.

The tribunal found that the statement had been ambiguous and made in the heat of the moment and the employer should not have interpreted it as a resignation.

Langlands & McAinsh Ltd v. Shearer [1988] I.R.L.R. 353.

An employee who discovered that some of her work had been allocated to a more junior person without her knowledge said to her manager "if that is how things are, I might as well leave".

The tribunal found that this was not a resignation and the employer's actions in terminating the contract constituted dismissal.

D A MacRae Ltd v. Bruce [1988] I.R.L.R. 352.

The moral of the story is to insert clauses into employees' contracts requiring them to provide notice in writing, and to avoid interpreting a verbal statement made in the heat of the moment as a resignation. Instead, if the employee does not return to work the next day, the employer should take steps to contact them to ascertain whether or not they have resigned, and, if they cannot be contacted, allow a reasonable period of time to pass before instituting termination procedures.

DISMISSAL

There may be many reasons why an employer may wish to terminate the contracts of one or more employees.

Express Dismissal

The employer may bring an employee's contract to an end at any time by giving the employee notice according to the provisions contained in the contract of employment. This will constitute an express dismissal. If the contract does not contain any notice clauses, the employee will be entitled to a minimum period of statutory notice according to a formula laid down in law (see 'Notice Periods on Dismissal', Chapter 16).

If the employee is dismissed without proper notice, this would constitute breach of contract on the part of the employer, giving the employee the right to take a claim for wrongful dismissal to an employment tribunal. If the claim was upheld the tribunal would award damages equivalent to net earnings for the outstanding portion of the notice period. It should be noted that 'wrongful dismissal' is a separate concept from unfair dismissal. Wrongful dismissal is explained in 'The Concept of Wrongful Dismissal', Chapter 3.

Provided proper notice is given, the contract will have been terminated lawfully, but this does not prevent the employee from bringing a claim for unfair dismissal to an employment tribunal if they have at least two years' continuous service (see 'Eligibility to Claim Unfair Dismissal at Employment Tribunal', Chapter 17).

Constructive Dismissal

A constructive dismissal occurs where an employee has resigned as a direct result of a fundamental breach of contract on the part of the employer. The breach of contract may be an express breach such as a pay cut, insistence on radically altering the employee's hours of work or removal or reduction in one or more contractual benefits without the employee's consent. There may also be a fundamental breach of contract where the manager treats the employee in a manner likely to destroy the relationship of trust and confidence between the parties. These issues are fully explored in 'Breach of Contract' in Chapter 3 and 'Constructive Dismissal' in Chapter 4.

To succeed in a claim for constructive dismissal, the employee would have to prove that:

(a) the employer's actions fundamentally breached one of the express or implied terms of the employee's contract; and

(b) the employee resigned as a direct result of that breach; and

(c) the employee did not wait too long before resigning in response to the employer's breach.

Pressure to Resign

If a manager puts pressure on an employee to resign, and the person succumbs to the pressure and does resign as a result of that pressure, then in law a dismissal has occurred. This 'resign or be fired' approach effectively leaves an employee without any choice as to whether or not they remain in employment – the only choice they have relates to the manner in which the contract will terminate. Thus, it is clear, on close examination, that this situation involves the employer, and not the employee, instigating termination of the employee's contract. This, of course, equates to dismissal.

To avoid this situation, the manager may seek to reach a mutual agreement with the employee to terminate the contract, which, if a suitable monetary incentive is offered, may lead to an acceptable solution for both parties. This subject is expanded in 'Termination by Mutual Agreement', below.

REDUNDANCY

Redundancy is a dismissal in law because it is the employer who gives notice to terminate the contract. This means that employees who have a minimum of two years' continuous service will have the right, if they wish, to take a claim of unfair dismissal to an employment tribunal.

The need for redundancies may arise as result of differing circumstances. The common factor is that, for redundancies to be genuine, there must be a genuine business need for the employer to reduce their workforce.

Circumstances in which redundancy may occur include:

(a) where the employer has ceased trading or intends to cease trading;

(b) where the employer has closed down, or intends to close down, a particular business premises, because either that part of the business has ceased trading or because it has moved to other premises;

(c) where the employer's requirements for employees to carry out work of a particular kind have ceased or diminished (or are expected to cease or diminish). This may be either generally or at one particular place of work.

In order for an employer to establish redundancy as a reason for dismissal, there must be an overall reduction in the amount of work to be done leading to the potential loss of one or more jobs. It is the disappearance of the job(s) which is the issue and not the performance or conduct of the individual doing the job. Thus, where the employer decides to reallocate the same amount of work amongst the same number of employees, reorganise those employees and possibly even give them new job titles, this will not constitute grounds for redundancy dismissals. Equally, an employee who is not coping with the responsibilities and duties of their job cannot be 'made redundant' on this basis, if the need for the work to be done is continuing. Such an attempt to disguise a dismissal as redundancy will provide the employee with solid ammunition to win a claim for unfair dismissal at tribunal.

Full information about redundancy is provided in Chapter 18.

Voluntary Redundancy

Volunteers for redundancy have the same rights in law as those who are selected for redundancy by the employer, provided there is a genuine redundancy situation to begin with. Individuals who volunteer for redundancy, and who the employer accepts, are regarded in law as having been dismissed. Volunteers consequently have the same statutory rights, including the right to redundancy pay, as those who are selected for redundancy by the employer.

It is important to bear in mind that the above principle applies only where there is a genuine redundancy situation in the first place. An employee who volunteers to leave the company in other circumstances will be deemed to have resigned.

RETIREMENT

When the employer terminates the contract of an employee on account of the employee having reached retirement age, this constitutes a dismissal in law. There is, of course, no reason why this would not be a fair dismissal unless the employer acts unreasonably towards the particular employee in the manner in which the contract is terminated.

The employer may, technically, specify any age for retirement in employees' contracts, provided it is the same for both men and women. If no contractual retirement age has been specified, and if there is no accepted practice within the company for employees to retire at a defined age, then the default retirement age of 65 will apply.

Employers who operate a clear and consistent contractual policy of retiring employees at a specified age should not encounter any difficulties. There will be no breach of contract, in addition to which the law (Employment Rights Act 1996) states that people over the age of 65 do not have the right to bring a claim for unfair dismissal to employment tribunal, except in certain specialised circumstances.

Early Retirement

In contrast with normal retirement, where an employee retires early (i.e. before the company's normal retirement age), this, in law, constitutes termination by mutual agreement rather than dismissal. This is important from the point of view of employees who may wish for, or be cajoled into taking, early retirement with false expectations of a redundancy payment. Because there is no dismissal, there cannot be an entitlement to statutory redundancy pay (although there is nothing to stop the employer from awarding the person an ex gratia payment). Early retirement cannot constitute redundancy even when circumstances exist where the employer would otherwise have to make redundancies, for example to cut costs. This contrasts with the situation of voluntary redundancy which is regarded in law as dismissal, provided it occurs in response to a genuine redundancy situation.

Essentially, an early retirement occurs when the natural end of the contract is brought forward by agreement. It is only in circumstances where such agreement is clearly absent, i.e. when early retirement has been forced upon the employee, that the employee could claim that they had been dismissed.

EXPIRY OF A FIXED-TERM CONTRACT

A fixed-term contract is one in which the date of termination is specifically stated in the contract at the outset. It is the existence of a defined termination date that makes the contract fixed-term. A fixed-term contract will come to an end automatically on the nominated termination date, however, it is important to note that, despite agreement between the parties that the contract will terminate on the due date, its expiry is regarded in law as a dismissal. Such dismissal will normally be fair, unless there are specific circumstances which render it otherwise.

Further information about fixed-term contracts is provided in 'Forms of Contract', Chapter 1).

Expiry of a 'Contract for Performance'

The key feature of a 'contract for performance' is its planned expiry on the completion of a specific task or occurrence of a specified event. An example of the former could be the contracts of workers engaged to work on a specific building project by a construction company. When the project is complete, the contract is said to be 'discharged by performance'. An example of the latter situation could be the contract of someone employed to cover the absence from work of another employee on account of sickness or maternity leave. In this case, the contract would be discharged on the date the absent employee returned to work. Thus, in the first case it is the completion of the task which effectively terminates the contract, while in the second case it is the return to work of the absent employee which triggers the termination.

In both cases, the contract terminates without the need for either a dismissal or a resignation. This is in contrast to the expiry of a fixed-term contract which constitutes a dismissal in law. The termination of a contract 'by performance' does not constitute a dismissal, therefore employees would be unable to claim unfair dismissal or redundancy pay.

Employers should take care, however, when setting up contracts for performance. The wording would have to make it quite clear that the employee is to be engaged for a specific task or until the occurrence of a specified event. In either case, the task or event should be clearly defined. Unless the contract is clear on this point, its termination may amount to a dismissal in law.

TERMINATION BY MUTUAL AGREEMENT

A contract of employment may be brought to an end by mutual agreement between employer and employee, in which case there is no dismissal. Termination by this method, therefore, means that the employee has no statutory right to claim unfair dismissal or redundancy pay. It is because of this that courts and tribunals are generally reluctant, in the event of a dispute, to make a finding that a contract has been terminated by mutual agreement, unless there is clear documentary evidence of such agreement between the parties. If there is any suggestion that the 'agreement' to terminate the contract was anything but a voluntary one on the employee's part, a court or tribunal is likely to rule that what took place was in fact a dismissal.

Termination by mutual agreement may occur with or without a period of notice and with or without any money changing hands. In other words, the terms of the agreement may be negotiated freely and agreed between the parties.

Where an employer wishes to enter into an agreement with an employee to terminate the contract on this basis, such agreement should be carefully drawn up in writing and should state unequivocally that termination is as a result of a mutual agreement. Obviously the agreement should be signed and dated by both parties.

It should be noted, however, that this type of agreement does not legally bar the employee from taking a claim for unfair dismissal to an employment tribunal, provided they have had a minimum of two years' continuous service. This is the case even where the agreement is signed by both parties and even where a sum of money has been paid to the employee. The only practical effect of such an agreement would be that, if the employee should subsequently succeed in a claim that the termination in fact amounted to a dismissal, any compensation awarded for unfair dismissal would be offset against the amount already paid.

To prevent an employee from pursuing a claim for unfair dismissal through a tribunal, the employer would need to engage an independent advisor for the employee and have a document known as a 'compromise agreement' drawn up. A compromise agreement, which is properly drawn up, will have the effect of procuring the employee's binding agreement not to pursue a claim of unfair dismissal at tribunal. Such agreement is normally obtained by offering the employee an appropriate sum of money.

For a compromise agreement to be legally binding to prevent the employee from taking a complaint to tribunal, the advisor engaged to draw up the agreement must be a qualified lawyer or other approved advisor and this person must explain the terms of the proposed agreement fully to the employee before it is finalised.

FRUSTRATION OF CONTRACT

A contract may be said to be 'frustrated' when an event occurs which was not reasonably foreseeable and which makes it impossible for the contract to continue to be performed. The frustrating event must be genuinely unforeseen and must be one which has not been instigated by either party. Furthermore, to constitute frustration of contract, the event giving rise to it must have effectively destroyed the whole essence of the contractual relationship.

Circumstances in which frustration of a contract may occur include:

(a) sudden unexpected serious illness or disability of the employee, especially if it occurs close to retirement age. However, because most employers have contractual sick pay schemes in place, it is difficult to argue successfully that sickness absence frustrates the contract (because putting a sick pay scheme in place is inconsistent with the assertion that sickness absence is unforeseen);

(b) imprisonment of the employee – in which case the contract is frustrated as a result of the prison sentence passed by the judge;

(c) a change in the law which makes continued performance impossible or unlawful;

(d) conscription of the employee into the armed forces;

(e) total destruction of the workplace rendering any further performance of the contract impossible, or radically different from that envisaged when the contract was set up.

The key point about frustration of a contract is that, when it occurs, there is no dismissal in law and, therefore, the employee has no unfair dismissal or redundancy pay rights. It is for this reason that courts and tribunals only rarely make findings of frustration of contract, because to do so effectively denies the employee any remedy in law for the fact that their employment has come to an end.

INSOLVENCY

When a business becomes insolvent, this does not of itself terminate employees' contracts of employment. If, however, a liquidator is appointed by the court, this will have the effect of automatically terminating all contracts because the company will be wound up. Termination of employment in these circumstances will constitute dismissal on the grounds of redundancy.

If a company goes into administrative receivership, or if an administrator is appointed, the receiver or administrator will be held to be the company's agent unless the company goes into liquidation. Usually the aim is to allow the business to continue to trade with a view to bringing it back into profit or else to allow time to find a buyer for the business. The appointment of an administrator or an administrative receiver will have no effect on employees' contracts of employment unless the business subsequently ceases to trade. During this period, if an employee leaves voluntarily, this will be regarded as a normal resignation, as a result of which the employee will lose any right to claim a redundancy payment.

In the event of termination as a consequence of insolvency, and where the company is unable to pay the employee all outstanding monies due, the employee can claim certain payments from the State, including arrears of pay, holiday pay, pay in lieu of statutory notice and certain other payments subject to defined limits.

If an insolvent business is sold to a purchaser as a going concern, this will normally constitute a transfer of an undertaking under the Transfer of Undertakings (Protection of Employment) (TUPE) Regulations 1981. This means that employees will have certain rights, including the right not to be dismissed on account of the transfer and the right to continuity of employment on the same terms and conditions. Chapter 12 provides full details of the TUPE Regulations.

CHAPTER SIXTEEN

NOTICE PERIODS

The law prescribes minimum periods of notice for both employees and employers. It is open to employers, however, to specify longer periods of notice in employees' contracts of employment. If an employment contract defines periods of notice which are longer than those laid down in statute, the contractual notice periods will apply. Employers, however, cannot impose notice periods which are shorter than those laid down in law, simply because statutory terms always take priority over contractual terms.

If no notice clauses are contained within the contract, then the period of notice required to terminate the contract will revert back to the minimum notice period defined in statute. Details are provided in the following sections.

EMPLOYEES' NOTICE OBLIGATIONS

An employee, who wishes to resign, must give notice according to the terms of their contract of employment, but if there is no contractual clause governing notice, the period of notice required under statute is only one week. This 1-week statutory notice period applies to both full-time and part-time employees after they have been employed for one month and does not augment with length of service.

Clearly, therefore, it is in the employer's interests to specify a contractual notice period which is longer than one week, especially for employees holding key positions within the company. In theory, this would prevent employees in senior or specialist positions from leaving the company at short notice, thus causing potential difficulties for the employer.

It is important to note that, where an employee indicates that they intend to resign at some future date, this does not constitute an actual resignation. Such a statement of future intent becomes a resignation only at the point when the employee clearly specifies either a date on which they intend to leave or a defined period of notice. It follows that, where an employee has merely spoken about the possibility of resigning in the future, the employee's manager should not put arrangements in place to bring the contract to an end nor make firm plans to replace the employee, as this could have the effect of converting a potential resignation into a dismissal.

Resignation Without Notice

If an employee resigns without giving proper notice under the contract, they are technically in breach of contract. The only occasion where an employee is entitled to resign without notice is in the event of a fundamental breach of contract by the employer.

Irrespective of this, there is not much an employer can realistically do to prevent an employee from leaving without working their full notice. This is because neither courts nor employment tribunals have the authority to compel an employee to work for an employer, either by injunction or by an order for specific performance. Furthermore, suing an employee for damages for breach of contract, although technically feasible, is not usually worthwhile from a financial standpoint, as the likelihood of success in recovering damages is very limited.

The only possible course of action which an employer might follow would be to apply to a court for an injunction to stop the employee from going to work for a competitor during the outstanding portion of the notice period. This would be based on the premise that the person was still employed until the expiry of the contractual notice period.

NOTICE PERIODS ON DISMISSAL

Where the contract of employment is brought to an end by the employer, the employer, like the employee, is contractually obliged to adhere to the notice provisions contained in the contract of employment. In the absence of contractual notice provisions, the statutory minimum notice periods will apply. Statutory notice on dismissal is based essentially on one week's notice for each completed year of service up to a maximum of twelve weeks. Thus, for example, an employee with eight and a half years' service would be entitled to a minimum of eight weeks' notice. Part years do not count. Both full and part-time employees are entitled to such minimum notice periods in law.

If an employer dismisses an employee without giving the proper period of statutory notice, the employee is entitled to 'add back' the notice period for the purposes of calculating continuous length of service. This could be important if the employee's length of service is on the borderline of two years (the minimum period of service required to take a claim for unfair dismissal and redundancy pay to tribunal). This provision has the effect of blocking any unprincipled attempt on the part of the employer to evade the unfair dismissal provisions by dismissing an employee without notice one week before they would otherwise have attained two years' service. However, this provision to 'add back' the period of notice to which an employee is entitled applies only to statutory periods of notice and not to any contractual notice (which might be longer than the statutory notice period).

Dismissal without proper contractual notice will be a straightforward breach of contract entitling the employee, whatever their length of service, to take a claim for damages equivalent to the outstanding portion of the notice period to either an ordinary civil court or an employment tribunal. This type of claim is known as a 'wrongful dismissal'.

Dismissal Without Notice

The only occasion where it is legitimate for an employer to dismiss an employee without any notice at all is where the employee has committed an act of very serious misconduct, known as gross misconduct. Dismissal without notice in these circumstances is known as 'summary dismissal'. Summary dismissal is thus dismissal for a single, very serious act of gross misconduct on the part of the employee and may be instituted without notice or pay in lieu of notice. The existence or otherwise of previous warnings for misconduct is irrelevant. The employer, however, must still take care to follow fair procedures prior to dismissing the employee if the dismissal is to be fair. Further information is available in 'Gross Misconduct and Summary Dismissal', Chapter 17.

WITHDRAWING NOTICE

Once notice has been given, it cannot unilaterally be withdrawn by the party who gave it. Withdrawal of notice may of course be agreed between the parties but neither employer nor employee has the right to automatically withdraw notice if they change their mind. Thus if an employee who has resigned makes a request to rescind their notice, the employer may choose whether or not to acquiesce.

Similarly, if an employee has been dismissed with notice and the employer offers during the notice period to retract the notice, the employee is not obliged to agree to stay on. The employee may, if they wish, elect to treat the original notice of dismissal as binding, in which case the original termination date specified by the notice, and the original reason for the dismissal, will prevail.

LENGTHENING OR SHORTENING THE NOTICE PERIOD

Similar principles apply if either the employer or the employee wishes to alter the length of the notice period. Notice, once given, is binding and can be extended or shortened only by mutual consent.

An attempt on an employer's part to shorten the employee's notice period against the employee's will, would constitute a breach of contract and would very likely have the effect of converting the person's resignation into an unfair dismissal. The situation would, of course, be different where the employee was fully compensated for the outstanding portion of the notice period (see the next section). Even if an employee gives longer notice than that required under the contract, the employer cannot lawfully oblige them to leave early. Effectively, therefore, both in the case of a resignation, and in the event of dismissal with notice, the employer cannot lawfully compel the employee to agree to a termination date which falls earlier than the date of expiry of the notice period.

NOTICE OF DISMISSAL TO AN EMPLOYEE WHO IS OFF SICK

Since sickness absence is not a form of misconduct, an employee who is dismissed on account of sickness absence is entitled to receive the appropriate statutory or contractual notice, whichever is the longer. One point to note is that, if an employee's entitlement to sick pay has been exhausted when the dismissal takes place, normal salary would have to be reinstated for the duration of the notice period, unless the contract of employment provided for a different arrangement upon termination under these circumstances.

PAY IN LIEU OF NOTICE

Many employers prefer employees not to attend work during the notice period, especially where the employee has been dismissed. There may be many reasons for this, for example the employer may be concerned about the employee's level of motivation, their loyalty or may even fear that the employee may take deliberate steps to cause the employer damage or disruption, perhaps through tampering with computer systems or taking copies of confidential documents. Thus, it is common practice to give pay in lieu of notice to departing employees.

Provided the employee is fully compensated at a level equivalent to the pay and benefits they would have received had they worked throughout the notice period, there is usually no problem. Technically, however, to be able to lawfully implement a 'pay in lieu of notice' policy, the employer should ensure that all employees' contracts contain a clause authorising them to elect to give the employee pay in lieu of notice (as opposed to allowing the employee to work out their notice). Although it can be difficult to calculate an amount which is representative of the value of all contractual benefits, failure to pay sufficient to cover perks as well as pay could lead to a breach of contract claim from the employee. A contractual right to pay in lieu should therefore be carefully thought out and should provide for payment of a sum which can be calculated precisely.

Particular difficulties may be encountered when considering how to deal with the notice pay of an employee who, as part of their contractual entitlement, has had a company car for personal (as well as business) use. The options open to the employer basically include:

(a) paying the employee an additional sum of money to compensate them for loss of the use of the car during the notice period; or

(b) providing a hired car of a similar type to the company car for a period of time equivalent to the notice period; or

(c) permitting the employee to continue to use the car throughout the notice period after employment has technically ended.

If there is a clause in the contract of employment authorising the employer to make payment in lieu of notice to employees who are leaving, then such pay in lieu equates to remuneration under the contract, which in turn means that it is taxable. In contrast, if the contract of employment does not expressly allow pay in lieu of notice instead of notice itself, then if payment in lieu is made the employer is technically in breach of contract and the amount paid equates to damages for breach of contract. In this latter situation, the amount paid out to the employee would not be taxable.

However, before employers assume that this second route is the preferable course of action (obviously the employee would benefit from receiving a tax-free sum of money), it would be advisable to consider the implications of a termination which is in breach of contract (known as wrongful dismissal), which is dealt with in Chapter 3.

Clearly it is in the employer's best interests to avoid a breach of contract when terminating employees' contracts and it is, therefore, advisable to have a clear statement in employment contracts to the effect that the company may elect to make payment in lieu of notice at its discretion both in the event of the employee resigning and when the employer dismisses the employee. So long as a sufficient sum of money is paid, there would then be no opportunity for the employee to make a successful claim for breach of contract.

THE DATE OF TERMINATION OF EMPLOYMENT

It is important for both the employer and the employee to be clear on the date on which employment ends. The reasons for this are that:

(a) if the employee wishes to claim unemployment benefit, they will be required to produce clear evidence of the date employment ended;

(b) in the event that the employee on the borderline of two years' service takes a claim for unfair dismissal or redundancy pay to an employment tribunal, it could be critical to establish the precise date of termination of employment so as to work out whether the person has sufficient service and also whether they have lodged their claim within the 3-month time limit allowed;

(c) if the employee had cover through their employment for life insurance, medical insurance and/or pension benefits, it would be important to ensure the employee was fully aware of when the cover is to run out.

The date of termination of a contract of employment is, in most cases, the day the employee stops work. This is not always the case, however, and the potential grey areas are listed below.

1. If an employee is summarily dismissed (i.e. without notice) following gross misconduct, termination takes effect at midnight on the day on which the employee is dismissed.

2. If the employee is given pay in lieu of notice following either resignation or dismissal, then the employment contract would normally terminate immediately, i.e. from the last day on which the employee worked. This situation is open to challenge, however, unless the employer makes it quite clear to the employee (in writing) that the contract is to terminate with immediate effect.

3. If a dismissed employee appeals internally against the dismissal decision, and where the appeal is unsuccessful, the termination date is normally the original date of dismissal and not the date on which the appeal is determined. Exceptionally, if the employer had continued to pay wages during the period between the dismissal and the appeal hearing, then the date of dismissal would be the date on which the outcome of the appeal was communicated to the employee.

4. If the employer and the employee expressly agree a specific date of termination, then that date will apply.

5. If the employee is placed on 'garden leave' (i.e. paid leave of absence) during the notice period (see the next section), the date of termination is the date on which the notice expires at the end of the notice period.

The Concept of 'Garden Leave'

'Garden leave' is paid leave of absence during the notice period. Although the employee is not required to work, the contract of employment continues in force, normal salary continues to be paid and all other contractual benefits, e.g. accrual of holiday entitlement, insurance cover, etc., continue. This has the advantage for the employer that the employee cannot lawfully take up alternative employment until the period of notice has expired. If the employee does so, they would be in clear breach of contract and the employer could take steps to stop them by seeking an injunction (although there is no guarantee that this will be granted). Employers often impose garden leave on employees who resign in order to prevent them from taking their skills and expertise (together with, possibly, important information about the market, customer preferences, etc.) directly to a competitor company.

The only difference between garden leave and ordinary notice is that the employee is not actually working. Presumably they are at home either digging the garden or (for the less energetic) sunning themselves in the garden!

Garden leave is lawful because employees have no automatic right in law to be provided with work (so long as they are in receipt of full pay). The exceptions to this rule are employments in which workers are paid according to the amount of work they produce (piece-work) or where it could be shown that the employee's skills would deteriorate if they were not used over a period of time.

In order to ensure that there can be no suggestion that garden leave is in breach of an employee's contract, the employer should include a clause in contracts of employment which provides authority to place employees on garden leave during periods of notice, whether this follows resignation or dismissal. This may be especially useful in the case of senior or specialist employees or those who have access to confidential or sensitive information.

CHAPTER SEVENTEEN

DISMISSING EMPLOYEES FAIRLY: FOLLOWING CORRECT PROCEDURES

ELIGIBILITY TO CLAIM UNFAIR DISMISSAL AT AN EMPLOYMENT TRIBUNAL

Any dismissed employee who has two or more years' continuous service may take a complaint of unfair dismissal to an employment tribunal, if they believe the dismissal is unfair. All employees have this right regardless of the number of hours they work per week. This means that part-time employees have the same protection in law as full-timers, provided their service is continuous. Thus an employee who works (for example) only two or three hours per week, has the same statutory right to claim unfair dismissal as an employee whose contract requires 40 hours per week.

Exclusions from Unfair Dismissal Rights

Certain people are excluded from the right to claim unfair dismissal, namely:

(a) workers who are engaged on a contract other than a contract of employment (see Chapter 1);

(b) people who normally work outside Great Britain;

(c) employees over the company's normal retirement age or, if no normal retirement age exists, then over age 65;

(d) members of the armed forces;

(e) police officers;

(f) some crown servants;

(g) share fishermen/women;

(h) those employed on a fixed-term contract for more than a year, where the contract expires without renewal on the planned date and where it contains a valid waiver clause in respect of unfair dismissal (see 'Fixed-term Contracts', Chapter 1).

Qualifying Service for Unfair Dismissal

The normal minimum qualifying period of service for a claim of unfair dismissal is two years (with the same employer or associated employers). The service must be continuous. The government has proposed, however, to reduce the qualifying period from two years to one year as part of its Employment Relations Bill. At the time of writing, it is not known when this change will come into effect.

Time Periods for Applying to an Employment Tribunal

The time limit for a complaint of unfair dismissal to be lodged with the tribunal office is three calendar months, starting on the date of termination of the person's contract of employment. Hence if the employee's date of termination was, for example, 4 April, then their application for unfair dismissal must be received by the tribunal office no later than 3 July if it is to be on time. A tribunal may, if asked, agree to allow a late claim to proceed if the employee can show grounds that it was not practicable for them to have presented the claim in time.

POTENTIALLY FAIR REASONS FOR DISMISSAL

When a case of unfair dismissal comes before an employment tribunal, the onus is on the employer to demonstrate the reason for the dismissal. Consequently, the employer normally gives evidence first at a tribunal hearing. Essentially, the tribunal will consider whether the employer acted reasonably in dismissing the person for the reason stated and whether the reason was sufficient to justify dismissal under all the circumstances of the particular case.

Potentially fair reasons for dismissal fall under five categories:

- capability;
- conduct;
- redundancy;
- legal restriction;
- some other substantial reason (SOSR).

The issues of *legal restriction* and *some other substantial reason* are described below, whilst capability and conduct are covered in later sections of this chapter. Redundancy is the subject of Chapter 18.

Legal Restriction

'Legal restriction', as a reason for dismissal, means that circumstances have arisen as a result of which it has become illegal for an employer to continue to employ a particular individual. Legal restriction is sometimes known as 'statutory ban'. Examples include:

(a) a driver who loses their driving licence;

(b) a foreign employee whose work permit runs out;

(c) an employee whose continued employment would contravene health regulations;

(d) a young person whose employment contravenes statutory provisions for young persons (for example a 17 year old employed in a licensed bar);

(e) an employee who fails to gain a qualification which is a legal requirement for the performance of their particular job.

As in all types of dismissal, the fairness or otherwise of a dismissal for legal restriction will depend on whether:

(a) the reason for the dismissal is genuine; and

(b) the employer has acted reasonably in dismissing the employee for the reason given; and

(c) the employer has followed proper procedures prior to dismissal.

It is also advisable for an employer, prior to contemplating dismissal on the grounds of legal restriction, to review whether or not it is possible to transfer the employee into another job within the organisation. Failure to investigate this may render the dismissal unfair, especially in the case of a driving ban which is quite short.

Some Other Substantial Reason (SOSR)

'Some other substantial reason' is effectively a 'catch-all' category allowing employers to (potentially) justify a dismissal which does not fall within one of the four other potentially fair reasons for dismissal. There is no prescribed list of reasons which fall under SOSR, as it would be impossible to list all the circumstances in which an employer could be justified in dismissing an employee. Technically, any reason may be put forward, the only criteria being that the reason must be substantial rather than trivial and that it must be capable of amounting to a reason which could justify dismissal.

Some reasons for dismissal, which tribunals have dealt with under the heading of SOSR, include:

(a) failure to disclose relevant information in a job application;

(b) an employee's refusal to agree to new terms and conditions of employment following a reorganisation of the business;

(c) pressure from a third party, for example a customer;

(d) a personality clash which cannot be resolved in any other way;

(e) a close personal relationship between an employee and someone employed by a competitor company which creates a potential breach of trust (for example where the employee concerned has access to confidential or sensitive information);

(f) an employee's unreasonable refusal to sign a restrictive covenant;

(g) dismissal of a replacement for an employee who has been absent on maternity leave or on medical suspension.

If dismissing an employee on the grounds of SOSR, the employer should bear in mind the requirement to ensure the reason is one which is valid and capable of objective justification and, of course, the requirement to act reasonably (see below).

THE IMPORTANCE OF FOLLOWING A FAIR PROCEDURE

In order for an employer to convince a tribunal that a dismissal is fair, they must show not only that there was a fair *reason* for dismissing the employee, but also that they *acted reasonably* in the manner in which they carried out the dismissal. The tribunal will assess in particular whether or not the employer followed a fair procedure prior to dismissal.

It follows that it is not enough for an employer to have a sound reason to dismiss an employee. To succeed in defending a claim for unfair dismissal, the employer must also be able to demonstrate that they acted reasonably in all respects when dealing with the matter which led to the employee's dismissal. Thus the test at tribunal is two-part: firstly the need to show that there was a potentially fair (and justifiable) reason for the dismissal and secondly to show that the dismissal was handled in a reasonable manner.

Case Study

In a case which aptly demonstrates the importance of following procedures, an employee had been arrested for burgling his own workplace and charged with that and a number of other offences. On being informed by the police that they believed the employee had committed the raid on the workplace, the employer dismissed him.

Despite the police evidence, when a case of unfair dismissal was brought to tribunal, it was held that the dismissal was unfair. This was because the employer had failed to carry out a reasonable investigation or give the employee a hearing.

Gael Force Marine Equipment Ltd v. Mitchell E.A.T. 761/92.

How Employment Tribunals View Unfair Dismissal Claims

The outcome of many unfair dismissal claims is easier to comprehend if the principles by which tribunals operate, and their overall approach, is understood. The tribunal's function is to assess the conduct of the employer, in order to establish whether the basis for the dismissal and the dismissal procedures, were reasonable. It is not the employee who is on trial. The tribunal must act objectively in assessing the employer's conduct and consider all the relevant circumstances of the case before reaching a decision.

This means that, even if an employee has committed an act of serious misconduct, the dismissal could still be unfair if procedures were not properly followed. This may seem strange to those unfamiliar with the doctrine of unfair dismissal, but the principle is firmly entrenched in employment law. The employee's conduct is not the matter 'under trial', and the consideration of whether or not the employee is 'guilty', is relevant only to the extent that it may affect the level of any compensation awarded to them.

CAPABILITY

'Capability' as a reason for dismissal is defined as "capability assessed by reference to skill, aptitude, health or any other physical or mental quality". The most commonly encountered examples of capability are problems with poor job performance and ill health. Procedures for handling these are discussed in the following sections.

Some examples of grounds for dismissal for capability include:

(a) a worker whose pace of work is unacceptably slow;

(b) an employee who consistently fails to reach the standards of work set by the employer;

(c) a worker who consistently makes unacceptable mistakes, despite having been given full training;

(d) a supervisor who fails to establish good working relationships with subordinates and/or other supervisors;

(e) an employee who is inflexible to the extent that work output is adversely affected;

(f) An employee who is incapable of performing their job because of ill health.

In one case which dealt with the issue of incapability (*Sutton & Gates (Luton) Ltd v. Boxall* [1979] I.C.R. 67), the Employment Appeal Tribunal stated that capability should be treated as applying to cases in which the incapability is due to inherent incapacity. If, however, an employee failed to come up to standard through their own carelessness, negligence or idleness, this would not be incapability but rather misconduct.

PROCEDURE WHEN DISMISSING FOR POOR JOB PERFORMANCE

There may be many reasons for an employee's poor job performance (apart from the employee's inherent lack of capability) for example:

(a) poor management or supervision;

(b) inadequate internal procedures or systems;

(c) lack of tools or equipment to do the job;

(d) the fact that the job has changed and involves new skills or methods;

(e) lack of training;

(f) lack of co-operation from colleagues or supervisors;

(g) bullying or victimisation caused by colleagues or supervisors;

(h) impossibly high workloads or over-tight deadlines;

(i) ill health;

(j) personal problems.

It is, therefore, very important for a manager to investigate the root cause of an employee's poor job performance before drawing any conclusions about its causes or taking any action. During such investigations, the above issues should be fully considered. If it is clear that none of these issues has had a significant impact on the employee's performance, then lack of capability may be the cause of the problem.

In some instances it may not be clear whether a person's apparent lack of competence is due to capability or conduct. Whilst an individual's conduct is within their control, capability, arguably, is not. This distinction is important when considering disciplinary action, or dismissal, because obviously it could be perceived as unfair to discipline an employee for something over which they had no control.

If in doubt as to whether an employee's poor job performance is due to incapability or misconduct, the safest approach is to address the issue as one of capability initially. If, following investigations, it is shown that the problem was caused by the employee's conduct, disciplinary procedures can be invoked at that stage.

In addressing an employee's poor job performance, the employer should, in the first instance, look for ways to give support to the employee to help them to improve to the required standard of competence. This may be done through the provision of training, coaching or informal supervisory guidance. If the employee is dismissed without such training or support having first been provided, then it is likely that an employment tribunal would find the dismissal unfair.

Notwithstanding this, dismissal could still be the eventual conclusion if, after being given support and any necessary training, the employee is still incapable of performing to the required standard. Provided the employer can justify the poor job performance as a sufficient reason for dismissal, the dismissal would be potentially fair.

The following are detailed guidelines for managers dealing with cases of poor job performance caused by lack of capability.

1. Ensure that the job duties and standards of work required have been fully and clearly explained to the employee. Managers often assume that employees know what is expected of them, whilst in reality, this is frequently not the case.

2. Investigate fully the reason(s) for the employee's inadequate job performance.

3. Listen to what the employee has to say in case there are any external factors which are adversely affecting job performance.

4. Tell the employee precisely, and in a non-blaming fashion, in what way they are failing to meet the required standards. Unless the employee is made fully aware of the nature of the manager's dissatisfaction, it is unrealistic to expect improvement.

5. Seek expert medical advice where the problem is thought to be health-related (see below).

6. Explain clearly (where there are no mitigating circumstances) the consequences for the employee of continued unsatisfactory job performance, i.e. eventual dismissal.

7. Arrange (where the reason for poor performance is lack of knowledge or skill) for the employee to receive further training or coaching.

8. Set reasonable time limits for the employee to come up to the required standards. This should be done in consultation with the employee to ensure that they feel that the training plan is realistic and reasonable.

9. Ensure the review date is adhered to. Dismissing an employee after allowing the review period to overrun without any further review is unlikely to be considered fair. Similarly, a dismissal before the completion of the review period would in all probability be unfair, unless the employee committed some act of serious misconduct or gross negligence in the interim period.

10. Consider the possibility of offering the employee a transfer to alternative work, if this is appropriate (bearing in mind that this can only be done lawfully with the employee's agreement).

11. Act consistently. For example, if a recent staff appraisal has recorded the employee's work as being satisfactory, or if the employee has recently received a merit pay increase, any resulting dismissal for poor job performance is likely to be found unfair.

12. Ensure at all times that the employee understands that the manager is on their side and that the desired outcome is improvement in job performance.

13. If, after the above procedures have been followed, the employee is dismissed, give them the opportunity to appeal internally against the decision.

PROCEDURE WHEN DISMISSING FOR ILL HEALTH

It is potentially fair to dismiss an employee on account of genuine ill health. This may arise on account of long-term absence due to a serious illness or injury, because of frequent short-term absences due either to a recurring illness or to a series of unrelated illnesses. Such a dismissal will only be fair, however, if the employer can justify dismissing the employee for absence from work and has followed reasonable procedures prior to the dismissal.

Unfortunately, there is no guidance in statute as to the time period after which it may be fair to dismiss an employee who is absent from work due to ill health. The key question which determines fairness (or unfairness) in a dismissal for ill health, is whether in all the circumstances the employer can reasonably be expected, in light of business requirements, to wait any longer for the employee to recover and attend work on a regular and reliable basis.

Thus, in the case of a small firm experiencing severe difficulties as a result of the absence of a key employee, dismissal may be contemplated after a relatively short period, particularly if it is clear that the employee is unlikely to recover and resume work in the near future. In contrast, a large employer would have difficulty justifying an over-hasty dismissal of, for example, a clerical worker if the person's workload could easily be covered by other employees or a temporary worker hired from an employment agency.

The factors which will be taken into account by an employment tribunal when determining a claim for unfair dismissal for ill health absence include:

(a) the size and resources of the employer;

(b) the degree of disruption the employee's absence is causing the organisation;

(c) the level of seniority or degree of specialism of the employee's job;

(d) the length of the employee's absence;

(e) the likelihood (based on medical evidence) of the employee being capable of returning to work in the near future;

(f) the nature and pattern of any previous absences;

(g) the feasibility of employing a temporary replacement;

(h) the urgency of having the employee's work done;

(i) the level of support afforded to the employee.

Where an employee is genuinely ill, disciplinary warnings are clearly inappropriate. Instead the employer should use a 'capability procedure' which may ultimately result in the employee's dismissal, but will have been achieved without the stigma of a disciplinary approach. Even where an employee's illness is genuine, it is ultimately possible for the employer to dismiss fairly, provided proper procedures are followed prior to the dismissal. It is, therefore, recommended that managers should adopt the following approach.

1. Review the employee's sickness absence record to ensure an accurate picture is obtained.

2. Consult the employee to discuss their absence. The purpose of this is to try (without putting pressure on the individual) to establish the likely duration of the employee's absence and whether on return they will be capable of full, or only partial, job performance.

3. Adopt a supportive stance and take full account of the employee's opinions and feelings regarding their condition.

4. Consider whether the employee's illness might be work-related. Explore possibilities such as pressure of work, stress, harassment, poor working relationships, cultural differences, etc.

5. Seek expert medical advice – either by asking the employee for permission to apply for a medical report from their own doctor or, alternatively, by arranging for an examination by a company doctor. (The law on gaining access to employees' medical records is explained fully in Chapter 10).

6. Consider whether the employee might be disabled under the terms of the Disability Discrimination Act 1995 (see the next section).

7. Set time limits for appraising the situation in order to make a decision and advise the employee of these.

8. Consider (where appropriate) the possibility of offering the employee alternative, lighter work or part-time work. If this is an option, ensure it is discussed directly with the employee at the earliest opportunity.

9. Tell the employee clearly and specifically if employment is at risk. It is particularly important to do this at the point at which termination of employment is being considered.

10. Follow up on any review period set and make the decision whether or not to dismiss.

The Implications of Dismissing a Disabled Employee

Before considering dismissing an employee on the grounds of ill health, it is advisable to take into account the provisions of the Disability Discrimination Act 1995. The provisions of the Act are explained fully in Chapter 9 but the pertinent points for ill health dismissals are stated here.

An employee is protected under the Disability Discrimination Act if they have an impairment which has lasted, or is expected to last, twelve months or more and which has a substantial adverse effect on their ability to carry out day to day activities.

Persons classed as disabled under the Act have the right not to be dismissed on grounds related to their disability unless the dismissal can be justified for reasons which are substantial and material. For example, dismissal could be justified where:

(a) an employee with a disability becomes totally incapable of performing the job for which they were employed; or

(b) the person's job performance drops to the extent that it has a substantial and material detrimental effect on the company; or

(c) a situation arises in which it would be unsafe to continue to allow the employee to do their job.

Thus, the point may come where continued employment is no longer feasible, at which time the employer may consider dismissal. However, it must be stressed that the employer must be able to justify objectively the dismissal of a disabled employee, if a claim for unlawful disability discrimination is to be avoided.

Additionally, under the Disability Discrimination Act, employers are obliged to make reasonable adjustments to premises and working practices to accommodate the needs of disabled employees. Thus, in the event of an existing employee suffering from a long-term condition, which is classed as a disability under the Act, the employer would be obliged to make adjustments in order to minimise the factors which were preventing the person from performing effectively. Such adjustments could include (for example):

(a) reallocation of the employee's heaviest duties to another employee;

(b) temporary transfer to another job;

(c) adjustment to working hours;

(d) provision of special tools or equipment, etc.

If a disabled employee is dismissed without such adjustments having first been made (where possible), then the employer would, in all likelihood, lose a case of disability discrimination taken against them and possibly lose a claim for unfair dismissal as well.

Chapter 9 gives full details of disability discrimination in employment.

MISCONDUCT

Misconduct is a potentially fair reason for dismissal, provided the employer genuinely believes that the employee's conduct justifies dismissal and this belief is based on reasonable grounds following reasonable investigation.

Misconduct at work may occur in many forms. There is no definition in law as to what constitutes misconduct and it is, therefore, up to each employer to:

(a) establish disciplinary rules and procedures, which should be in writing;

(b) specify the penalties applicable for breach of the rules;

(c) clarify the type of conduct which may warrant summary dismissal;

(d) ensure that the rules and related penalties are properly communicated to all employees;

(e) ensure rules and procedures are applied fairly and consistently.

Managers should refer to the ACAS Code of Practice on 'Disciplinary Procedures and Practice' which is a sound basis on which to decide how to proceed in cases of employee misconduct.

Some examples of misconduct are (please note the list is not intended to be exhaustive):

(a) poor time keeping;

(b) unauthorised absence from work;

(c) misuse of company resources, for example excessive use of company telephones for private calls, unauthorised access to the internet through a company computer, etc.;

(d) using abusive language (depending on the circumstances);

(e) disloyalty, for example where an employee works for another employer in their spare time and this employment has a detrimental impact on the employer's business interests or is in breach of company rules;

(f) breach of confidentiality, for example where an employee discloses or misuses confidential information;

(g) minor breaches of safety regulations;

(h) being under the influence of drink at work;

(i) smoking in non-smoking areas;

(j) refusal to carry out lawful and reasonable instructions from a supervisor/manager.

Disciplinary Procedures

The purpose of disciplinary procedures is 2-fold:

(a) to help the employer to ensure that rules and standards are adhered to;

(b) to provide a fair and consistent system for dealing with breaches of discipline or unsatisfactory job performance caused by lack of effort, negligence, carelessness or idleness.

The key purpose of an employer's disciplinary procedure should be to promote improvement in conduct and performance. The procedure should be regarded as a means of supporting an employee, rather than a means of punishment.

In most cases of misconduct the disciplinary procedure would be followed through from beginning to end, with appropriate warnings being given. This could lead eventually to dismissal if the misconduct persisted following warnings, or if the employee failed to improve within a reasonable time. Dismissal for a first offence is usually inappropriate unless the misconduct is of a very serious nature (see below).

It is interesting to note, however, that there is no requirement in law to give an employee three (or any other number) of warnings prior to dismissal. The key factor is not the number of warnings but rather that the severity of the penalty (i.e. the type of warning) should be appropriate in relation to the seriousness of the employee's misconduct.

Disciplinary procedures are generally structured in stages along the following lines.

Stage 1: Informal oral warning. An oral warning is the normal course of action for a minor first breach of the company's rules. Even though the warning is given verbally, managers are strongly advised to keep a record of what was said.

Stage 2: Formal oral warning. A formal verbal warning might follow an informal warning if the misconduct is repeated or it could be the first action taken following a relatively minor breach of discipline or unsatisfactory job performance (which is not due to lack of capability). Although the warning is given orally, a record of the fact the warning was given, the reasons for it and the surrounding circumstances, should be placed on file.

Stage 3: First written warning. A first written warning is appropriate where there has been no improvement following a verbal warning or possibly where there has been an accumulation of minor offences. A written warning may also be given as a first warning if the offence is fairly serious. A copy of the written warning should be given to the employee and a copy kept on file.

Stage 4: Final written warning. A final written warning is given where the employee has received previous warning(s) or where a first offence is serious enough to warrant only one written warning. It is important that a final written warning contains a clear statement that any further misconduct will lead to dismissal.

Handling Disciplinary Issues Correctly

At all stages of the disciplinary procedure, it is important for the manager dealing with the employee's conduct to follow certain guidelines. It is particularly important to follow the guidelines below before dismissing an employee. This is because if reasonable procedures are not followed prior to dismissal, then the dismissal will be unfair in law. It is also important, arguably, from the perspective of fair and consistent management. The following, therefore, represents guidelines for best practice.

1. **Tackle any apparent misconduct promptly.** If nothing is done, the chances are the problem will get worse.

2. **Investigate the problem thoroughly.** This may include checking the employee's personnel records, taking statements from witnesses or talking to other managers for whom the employee has worked.

3. **Avoid drawing premature conclusions about an individual's conduct which may be distorted by personal views or opinions.**

4. **Arrange an interview with the employee, informing them in advance that it is to be a disciplinary interview and giving reasonable notice.**

5. **Advise the employee in advance of the interview precisely what issue is to be discussed.** If the matter is complex, it is better to provide the person with a written summary of (for example) times/dates of absenteeism, etc.

6. **Advise the employee that they have the right (if they wish) to be accompanied at the interview by a colleague or trade union representative of their choice.** However, employees have no right (unless their contract of employment specifies otherwise) to bring an outsider to the interview, for example a solicitor, and it follows that the manager is justified in refusing any such request.

7. **Arrange for another member of management to be present (this person can act as note-taker).** Although this is not a statutory requirement, it is a safeguard in case an employee becomes aggressive or makes false or malicious allegations later about the manager or how the interview was conducted.

8. **Ensure discussions are held in private and kept confidential.** Employees should never be disciplined in front of others because this could be perceived as victimisation or bullying. It is also extremely bad for staff morale.

9. **Explain that the purpose of the interview is to establish the facts and to consider whether or not there are grounds for disciplinary action under the company's disciplinary procedure.**

10. **Give the employee a full and fair hearing at the interview (whatever the circumstances) and ensure they are encouraged to state their side of events fully.**

11. **Be prepared to take into account any factors raised by the employee of which management were previously unaware and which may have contributed towards the problem.** It may be necessary to conduct further investigation into these issues after the interview is over.

12. **State precisely what the problem is from management's point of view and why it is a problem.** Go through the background and evidence, focussing on facts, not opinions.

13. **Inform the employee of the content of any witnesses' statements and give them the chance to respond to the statements.**

14. **Specify precisely what improvements are required and discuss how the employee might achieve these.**

15. **Agree a (reasonable) time-scale for improvement.**

16. **Adopt a supportive attitude by encouraging the employee to work positively towards improving conduct/performance or to ensure mistakes are not repeated.**

17. **Offer training, coaching or guidance, where appropriate.**

18. **Tell the employee clearly that if conduct/performance does not improve to the standard required then (further) formal disciplinary action will be taken.**

19. **Be prepared to terminate the proceedings if it becomes clear that the employee has provided an adequate explanation of events, such that it is clear no misconduct has occurred.**

20. **Adjourn the interview once everything has been covered, in order for management to have time to make a reasoned decision about what, if any, penalty to impose.**

21. **Follow up by informing the employee of the outcome of the disciplinary interview.**

22. **Inform the employee of their right to appeal against any disciplinary action (this includes the right to appeal against dismissal).** The appeal should normally be to a higher level of management and, in any event, to a manager who was not in any way involved in the original disciplinary decision.

23. **Maintain a full record of the disciplinary interview.** This is important for various reasons, not least of which is to enable the employer to defend a claim for unfair dismissal at a later date.

24. **Follow up by monitoring the individual's conduct or performance within the time-frame agreed.**

25. **Follow the company's disciplinary procedure exactly at all times.**

Case Study

It is generally the case that an employment tribunal will find a dismissal unfair whenever there has been any breach of procedure. In one case, which aptly demonstrates this, an employer had discovered that one of their sales representatives had failed to make scheduled visits to various customers but had produced reports which stated that the visits had been made. The manager had investigated and put together details of the various calls which ought to have been made but had not taken place.

Following the manager's investigation, the employee was invited to attend a disciplinary meeting and was told that management had complaints about the way in which he was carrying out his job. At the meeting, the manager went through all the calls which had been reported but had not taken place and asked for his comments. The employee could not remember details and became confused. Later in the interview he fell silent. Eventually, after a further disciplinary interview, the employee was dismissed for gross misconduct.

When a claim for unfair dismissal was heard, the employment tribunal found that there was a potentially fair reason for dismissing the employee and that a thorough investigation had taken place. However, there was a key procedural flaw in the way in which the company had handled the matter. The manager had failed to inform the employee of the nature and seriousness of the allegations against him in advance of the interview. The employee should, at the very least, have been told in advance of the disciplinary meeting, that he was believed to have falsified his reports and failed to make scheduled visits to clients. Because he was not given this vital information, he was unable to prepare himself for the meeting (for example by checking his own records). Consequently the disciplinary meeting did not constitute a fair hearing because the employee was not afforded the opportunity to defend himself. The dismissal was unfair.

Spink v. Express Foods Group Ltd [1990] I.R.L.R. 320.

The above case demonstrates the fundamental principle behind effective and fair disciplinary procedures, which is that the employee must be allowed a full opportunity to put their case to the employer before any decision is taken about the type of penalty to impose.

Warnings

Where a written warning for misconduct is given, the warning should state the following:

(a) the nature of the employee's misconduct;

(b) the improvement required and the agreed time frame for improvement;

(c) the period for which the warning will remain 'live' on the employee's file;

(d) the disciplinary action which will be implemented if improvement is not forthcoming (i.e. the next stage in the disciplinary procedure);

(e) the means by which the employee may lodge an appeal against the warning and the time-scale for doing so.

Employers are entitled to decide, as part of their disciplinary procedures, how long a disciplinary warning should remain on an employee's file. There is no time period in law dictating how long warnings must remain on file, although normal practice is for warnings to be held for a period of between six and 24 months.

It is important to note, where an employee is told that a disciplinary warning will remain on file for a defined period of time, that the warning should be disregarded after this period has elapsed. To found a decision to dismiss on a previous warning which has expired could lead an employer into trouble, as the following case demonstrates.

Case Study

An employee had received a final written warning on 29 January 1992. This stated that the warning would remain on his personnel file 'for a period of twelve months from the date of this letter'. On 29 January 1993 a complaint was made against the same employee as a result of which he was dismissed following investigation and a disciplinary hearing. The dismissal was based on the employer's contention that the employee had committed an act of misconduct whilst subject to a final warning.

On considering the employee's complaint of unfair dismissal, the employment tribunal held that, based on the wording of the warning letter, the warning had expired at midnight on 28 January 1993. Thus, because the warning had lapsed, the employer had acted unreasonably in relying on it to dismiss the employee for misconduct. Since the second incident was not sufficiently serious on its own to justify dismissal, the dismissal was unfair.

Bevan Ashford v. Malin [1994] E.A.T. 43/94.

Gross Misconduct and Summary Dismissal

Gross misconduct is a single act of misconduct which is of such a serious nature that dismissal can be justified, even if no previous warnings have been given. Gross misconduct effectively destroys the trust and confidence between the employer and the employee, allowing the employer to justify terminating the contract immediately.

There is no official list of offences which represent gross misconduct but each employer may define what type of behaviour is to be regarded as gross misconduct. Different rules will be appropriate for different employers because of differing working environments and different business priorities and needs. It follows that it is important for every employer to ensure the rules regarding conduct are both clearly defined and fully communicated to all employees.

Examples of gross misconduct include (but are not restricted to):

(a) stealing from the company or from fellow workers;

(b) fraud or falsification of records;

(c) deliberate or negligent damage to company property or equipment;

(d) fighting or physical assault;

(e) gross negligence in carrying out duties;

(f) serious breach of safety regulations;

(g) insubordination or unreasonable refusal to obey a legitimate order;

(h) unauthorised use of computers;

(i) deliberate breach of confidentiality;

(j) drunkenness on company premises;

(k) harassment or bullying of another employee.

Dismissal following gross misconduct is known as summary dismissal. The term means dismissal without notice or pay in lieu of notice. Once implemented, summary dismissal brings employment to an end with immediate effect, with all pay and benefits under the contract terminating straight away. Gross misconduct on the part of the employee is the only circumstance which can justify the employer dismissing an employee without notice.

Summary dismissal may be justifiable even where the employee has had no previous warnings for similar offences and where there is no history of misconduct. Indeed the key feature of summary dismissal is that it may be implemented following a single act of serious misconduct.

In cases of gross misconduct/summary dismissal, the employer is still under an obligation to follow a correct procedure prior to dismissal, including the need to interview the employee, establish the full facts and allow a right of appeal. Failure to do so will render the dismissal unfair, regardless of the severity of the employee's misconduct.

Suspension from Work

In the event of an allegation of serious misconduct against an employee, it is usually advisable to suspend the person from work for a temporary period, in order to carry out a thorough investigation into the facts. Suspension is appropriate where the nature of the alleged offence (if proven) would make it inappropriate for the employee to continue to attend work or where the employer's trust and confidence in the employee has been placed in doubt. It follows that, whenever an act of gross misconduct is being investigated, suspension will be appropriate.

When suspending an employee, the manager should:

(a) tell the employee why they are being suspended and for what period of time;

(b) explain that suspension is being implemented in order to allow the employer time to investigate the alleged offence;

(c) ensure the employee knows that they have not been judged 'guilty';

(d) reassure the employee that there will be a full opportunity for them to explain their version of events in due course.

Normally this type of suspension from work must be on full pay, unless the employee's contract of employment contains a statement that the employer is entitled to suspend without pay in disciplinary circumstances. Suspension without pay could otherwise constitute a breach of contract. It could also lead an employment tribunal to conclude that the employer had already judged the employee 'guilty' before conducting any investigation or holding an interview, which in turn would prejudice the employer's chances of succeeding in defending a subsequent claim for unfair dismissal.

Dismissing an Employee for Behaviour Outside of Work

In certain circumstances, an employee may be fairly dismissed for behaviour which took place outside of work in the employee's own time. This would be particularly relevant if it came to light that the employee had committed a criminal offence.

The key criterion in assessing whether or not it is appropriate for the employer to take action against an employee in these circumstances, is whether, and to what extent, the employee's misdemeanour is in some way connected to their employment with the company. If there is no connection, then it is unlikely that a dismissal would be fair. A link to employment could occur in any of the following situations.

1. If the employee's out-of-work behaviour makes them unsuitable to do the job they are employed to do. One example of this was where a shop assistant was (fairly) dismissed following her arrest for shop-lifting in another retail store.

2. If the employer can demonstrate that they have lost trust and confidence in the employee's suitability to fulfil their responsibilities. An example was the (fair) dismissal of a manager for smoking cannabis in front of junior colleagues at a private function.

3. If the employee's conduct is of such a nature that it could damage the organisation's business interests or reputation (an example of this was where a senior employee, who was well-known in the local area, assaulted someone at a private function).

4. If other employees genuinely find it unacceptable to continue to work alongside the employee on account of their conduct.

If misconduct, for example drunkenness, takes place at a company function or company-sponsored training course, this may be regarded as sufficiently connected to the person's employment to justify disciplinary action or dismissal.

It can be seen, from the above, that misconduct committed outside of work does not automatically give a manager grounds to dismiss the employee. This is the case even where the employee's actions amount to criminal conduct. Similarly, a dismissal solely on the grounds that an employee is remanded in custody is unlikely to be sufficient grounds for dismissal on its own.

The best way for a manager to proceed in the event that information comes to light that an employee has committed a criminal offence outside of work, been remanded in custody or has simply behaved in an unbecoming manner is to:

(a) conduct a thorough investigation into the employee's alleged conduct (do not just rely on police investigations or reports);

(b) interview the employee to hear their version of events;

(c) assess all the circumstances of the particular case including the employee's length of service, position with the company, general background and status;

(d) ensure fair and reasonable procedures are followed before any decision is taken about whether to dismiss the employee;

(e) remember that the key issue for judging the fairness of a dismissal is whether there is a link between the employee's conduct outside of work and their position with the company.

AUTOMATICALLY UNFAIR DISMISSALS

Dismissal for certain specified reasons is automatically unfair in law. This means that, if the employee can show at an employment tribunal that the reason for their dismissal was one of the automatically unfair reasons, they will win their case irrespective of the surrounding circumstances or any excuses put forward by the employer.

There are currently ten categories of automatically unfair dismissals, as follows.

1. Where dismissal is on account of pregnancy or maternity leave (see Chapter 8).

2. Where a dismissal is connected with trade union membership or activities (see Chapter 13).

3. Where a dismissal is for a health and safety reason, e.g. because the employee has raised a complaint about safety at work, refused to work in conditions which they reasonably believe to be unsafe, or where an employee, who is a health and safety representative, is dismissed for carrying out their duties as a representative.

4. Where the reason for dismissal is connected with the transfer of an undertaking (see Chapter 12).

5. Where a dismissal is caused by the fact that the employee has, in good

faith, asserted a relevant statutory right. This protects employees who complain to their employer about an alleged breach of rights as well as those who are dismissed because they have taken, or plan to take, a case against their employer to an employment tribunal.

6. Where an employee is dismissed for enforcing their rights under the Working Time Regulations (see Chapter 5).

7. Where an opted-out shop or betting worker is dismissed for refusing to work on a Sunday (see Chapter 5).

8. Where the reason for the employee's dismissal is because they have a criminal conviction which is 'spent'. Under the provisions of the Rehabilitation of Offenders Act 1974, employers must (with some exceptions) disregard employees' spent convictions, i.e. those which have lapsed as a result of the passage of time.

9. Where an employee is dismissed on account of their filling the role of trustee of an occupational pension scheme.

10. Where an employee is dismissed because they have acted as an employee representative for consultation purposes or applied for election as employee representative.

In addition, a further category is to be added once the Public Interest Disclosure Act 1998 (known informally as the 'Whistleblowers Act') is implement, this is where the reason for dismissal is because the employee made a disclosure of information in good faith to the employer or to a relevant authority concerning a criminal offence, failure to comply with a legal obligation, miscarriage of justice, endangerment to any individual or damage to the environment perpetrated by the employer.

This Act is scheduled to be introduced in early 1999, but at the time of writing a precise date is not known.

For most automatically unfair dismissals, the employee is eligible to bring their case to an employment tribunal irrespective of their age or length of service. The only two exceptions to this (where the 2-year service qualification still applies) are dismissals on account of an employee's spent conviction and dismissals connected with a transfer of an undertaking.

GIVING EMPLOYEES A WRITTEN STATEMENT OF THE REASON FOR DISMISSAL

An employee who has been dismissed has the right to request a written statement giving the reason for their dismissal provided they have two or more years' continuous service. Where such a request is made, the employer must comply with it within fourteen days.

It is, in any event, sound practice to provide all employees with a written statement outlining the reason for their dismissal, regardless of length of service and whether or not a request is made. There is no prescribed format for a statement giving written reasons for dismissal but the reason given should always be clear and should be described as a subheading under one of the potentially fair reasons, *viz.* capability, conduct, redundancy, legal restriction or 'some other substantial reason'.

Naturally, the reason given for the employee's dismissal should be the true reason, because, if the employee takes a case to an employment tribunal for unfair dismissal, the statement may be used in evidence. Clearly, a tribunal will not be favourably impressed if the reason for dismissal given in the written statement conflicts with evidence produced at the tribunal hearing, or if the reason given is indecipherably vague.

REMEDIES AVAILABLE TO AN UNFAIRLY DISMISSED EMPLOYEE AT AN EMPLOYMENT TRIBUNAL

If a dismissed employee is successful in a claim for unfair dismissal at an employment tribunal, the tribunal may order one of the following remedies:

* reinstatement (see the next section);
* re-engagement (see the next section);
* compensation (see below);
* alternatively, the tribunal may simply make a declaration that the person was unfairly dismissed.

Reinstatement and Re-engagement

Reinstatement and re-engagement are similar but slightly different concepts. Reinstatement is re-employment (following dismissal) in the same job and on the same terms and conditions as before, whilst re-engagement represents re-employment with the same company on a new contract of employment, which must, nevertheless, be on terms and conditions which are not substantially less favourable than before. Normally, re-engagement will be considered only if reinstatement is not practicable or suitable (for example, if the tribunal takes the view that it would be inappropriate for the employee to have to work alongside the manager who dismissed them).

An employment tribunal will consider reinstatement (or re-engagement) only where the employee has specifically indicated that this is the remedy they are seeking. No tribunal will order reinstatement (or re-engagement) where the employee, who was dismissed, does not wish it. The employer may put up a defence that it is not reasonably practicable for them to take the employee back, and the tribunal will, before making a decision on whether to order reinstatement, consider whether this contention is justified.

If reinstatement (or re-engagement) is ordered by the tribunal, the employee will be entitled not only to re-employment, but also to (net) back pay and benefits to cover the period since the dismissal up to the date of re-employment. Deductions may be made from the amount of back pay equivalent to any income the employee has had in the meantime. If a pay rise has been instituted since the employee's dismissal, then both the back pay and the person's salary upon reinstatement must reflect the increase.

Once reinstated, the employee's total length of service must be calculated for all purposes as including the period of absence between dismissal and re-employment.

If, following a tribunal order for reinstatement or re-engagement, the company nevertheless refuses to take the employee back, the dismissed employee may apply to the tribunal for an additional award of compensation on top of the normal unfair dismissal compensation. Paradoxically, although tribunals can order re-employment, they do not have the power to enforce it.

Levels of Compensation for Unfair Dismissal

The majority of successful unfair dismissal claims result in an award of compensation rather than reinstatement or re-engagement. Awards of compensation for unfair dismissal are composed of two elements, a basic award and a compensatory award. In certain special cases, an additional or special award may also be made.

The basic award is calculated in accordance with a fixed formula which is identical to the formula used to calculate statutory redundancy pay. The amount awarded will depend on three elements: the employee's age, length of service and level of weekly pay. It should be noted that for the purposes of calculating a basic award, there is a ceiling on a 'week's pay' (£220 per week at the time of writing), and an overall maximum on the basic award of (at the time of writing) £6,600. Amounts are paid gross.

The formula looks like this.

Completed Years of Service	*Amount of Payment for Each Year*
Years of service up to age 21	½ week's pay
Years of service between ages 22–40 inclusive	1 week's pay
Years of service over age 41, up to age 64 inclusive	1½ week's pay

For employees who have reached age 64, the entitlement is reduced by one-twelfth in respect of each month they have remained in employment after that age. The effect of this is that the award becomes zero when the 65th birthday is reached.

The compensatory award, which is paid over and above the basic award, is not based on any formula but instead is an amount which the tribunal considers just and equitable under all the circumstances of the case. It is calculated in accordance with the employee's actual and projected net financial losses attributable to the dismissal. This may include losses up to the date of the tribunal hearing, and sometimes projected losses for a period into the future. The compensatory award does not, however, include an amount to compensate the employee for injury to feelings or loss of job satisfaction (unlike discrimination cases in which an element of compensation is usually awarded for injury to feelings). There is no punitive element in tribunal awards.

At the time of writing, the maximum on the compensatory award is £12,000, but the government has confirmed that this is to be raised to £50,000 once the Employment Relations Bill is implemented, since this represents a very substantial increase, employers may wish to consider any future dismissals very carefully before taking action!

CHAPTER EIGHTEEN

REDUNDANCY

DEFINITION OF REDUNDANCY

Redundancy is a form of dismissal occasioned by the employer's need to reduce the number of people employed in the business. The circumstances in which redundancy may arise are:

(a) where the employer has ceased trading or intends to cease trading;

(b) where the employer has closed down, or intends to close down, a particular business premises, because either that part of the business has ceased trading or because it has moved to other premises;

(c) where the employer's requirements for employees to carry out work of a particular kind have ceased or diminished (or are expected to cease or diminish). This may be the case in an overall sense or at one specific place of work.

The key criterion for redundancy is that the requirement for employees to perform work of a particular kind must have reduced. A range of circumstances could be at the root of the need for redundancies, such as:

(a) a downturn in trade or loss of a major contract;

(b) a reorganisation resulting in a more efficient use of manpower or in employees being able to take on a wider range of duties;

(c) a genuine need, based on business reasons, to make cutbacks for financial reasons;

(d) the introduction of new technology, with the result that fewer people than before are required to perform the same amount of work;

(e) the introduction of more efficient methods of work;

(f) a decision by management to replace employees by independent contractors or to 'outsource' a particular department or function.

Redundancy does not occur where the employer simply decides to reassign or rearrange the same quantity of work amongst the same number of employees.

It is important for managers to bear in mind that the need for redundancies will arise only where there is a reduction in the number of jobs of a particular kind and that the existence of a redundancy situation has nothing to do with a particular employee's competence to do the job, conduct, health or any other individual characteristic. It is not unknown for managers seeking an easy option to 'make an employee redundant' on the grounds that the person is a poor performer. This may at first seem kinder to the employee, who may in theory be able to save face by being labelled 'redundant' rather than 'fired'. It is not, however, in the employer's interests to put the wrong label on a dismissal. This is because, when an employee takes a claim for unfair dismissal to a tribunal, the onus is on the employer first to prove the reason for the dismissal and if the reason put forward is not the true reason, a finding of unfair dismissal will inevitably follow.

Following genuine redundancies, there is no obligation on the employer to offer redundant employees re-employment if, for example, there is an unexpected upturn in the business a month or two after the dismissal was effective. This contrasts with the employer's obligation to offer any suitable alternative work which occurs during the periods of notice of those affected by redundancy (see later in this chapter).

VOLUNTEERS FOR REDUNDANCY

Where the need for redundancies has arisen, the employer may elect to seek volunteers for redundancy. This has the advantage of reducing or avoiding the need to make compulsory redundancies with the associated trauma for the employees affected. It is not without difficulties for the employer, however, for example:

(a) the 'wrong' people may come forward to volunteer, in other words those whom the manager would prefer to retain;

(b) similarly, those who the employer would prefer to leave may not volunteer;

(c) there may be a preponderance of volunteers from one area of the company and none from another area;

(d) if employees who have volunteered are not accepted, this may cause disappointment, the perception of unfairness or even resentment.

It is important, if volunteers are being sought, to make it clear at the outset that management will retain the right to either accept or refuse an employee's candidacy for redundancy. In taking this approach, some of the above problems can be tempered.

Provided there is a genuine redundancy situation to begin with, employees who volunteer (and are accepted) for redundancy have the same rights in law as those who are selected for redundancy by the employer. Individuals who are made redundant as a result of volunteering are regarded in law as having been dismissed, rather than as having resigned. Volunteers consequently have the same statutory rights, including the right to statutory redundancy pay, as those who are selected for redundancy by the employer.

It is important to bear in mind that the above principle applies only where there is a genuine redundancy situation in the first place. An employee, who volunteers to leave the company in other circumstances, will be deemed to have resigned, even where the employer and employee together agree to call the termination a redundancy.

NOTIFICATION PROCEDURES

The company must notify the Secretary of State of proposed redundancies where the number of employees to be made potentially redundant is twenty or more. If the employer proposes to make 100 or more employees at one establishment redundant within a period of 90 days (or less), they must give the Secretary of State at least 90 days' notice of the proposed redundancies. Where the employer proposes to make twenty or more (but less than 100) redundant within 90 days, the period of notice required is not less than 30 days. These periods of notice must have elapsed before the first dismissal for redundancy takes effect. Failure to provide proper notification is a criminal offence.

THE REQUIREMENT TO CONSULT
WORKERS' REPRESENTATIVES

One of the most important duties applying to employers who are contemplating redundancies is the duty to inform and consult workers' representatives about their redundancy proposals. This duty arises when the employer proposes to dismiss twenty or more employees on the grounds of redundancy within a period of 90 days.

At the time of writing, however, there is a proposal to remove the threshold of twenty, thus imposing the requirement on all employers to consult representatives of the workforce about forthcoming redundancies, irrespective of the numbers of employees potentially affected.

Specifically, employers are obliged to consult either the representatives of a recognised trade union (if there is one) or else representatives elected for the purpose of redundancy consultation by the employees who may be affected by the redundancy programme. Thus, both unionised and non-unionised workplaces are affected by this requirement.

Specific time-scales are laid down in law for redundancy consultation which mirror those applicable to the requirement to provide official notification of impending redundancies outlined in the previous section. There is an overriding obligation to consult 'in good time', over and above which there must be at least:

(a) a 30-day period of consultation where twenty or more employees are to be made redundant at one establishment within a 90-day period; or

(b) a 90-day period of consultation where 100 or more employees at one establishment are likely to be affected.

An important point to note is that there can be no redundancy dismissals prior to the end of the consultation period (see also the section on 'Protective Awards' below). It should be noted that these consultation periods are minimum periods.

Differences of opinion have occurred over the years about the meaning of the phrase 'at one establishment' which is critical to the employer's duty to consult workers' representatives. The European Court of Justice has held that the term 'establishment' must be taken to mean the unit to which the redundant workers are assigned to carry out their duties. Whether or not there is a separate management team at the establishment is irrelevant. Any attempt on the part of an unscrupulous employer to divide an 'establishment' up into several smaller units for the purposes of avoiding redundancy consultation is likely to have detrimental consequences for that employer.

Elected Representatives

Currently the law does not specify how representatives should be elected, so long as it is the employees, and not the employer, who assume responsibility for the elections. It is acceptable for representatives who have been elected for another purpose to be utilised for redundancy consultation, for example those appointed to a staff council. There is no requirement for permanent representatives, but instead the employer may seek representatives when the need for redundancy dismissals arises.

Elected representatives and candidates for election are protected in law from dismissal, or action short of dismissal, on any grounds associated with the fact they have been appointed, or seek appointment, as employee representatives. Representatives also have the right to reasonable time off work to fulfil their responsibilities with regard to redundancy consultations and such time off must be granted with pay.

Additionally, the employer must provide the representatives with accommodation and other facilities which they require to fulfil their duties and permit them to have access to the employees they represent.

The Purpose of Consultation

The consultation with workers' representatives must be genuine and should begin 'in good time' and when proposals are at the formative stage. Where the employer consults after already having made firm decisions about how many people are to be made redundant, and how they are to be selected, the 'consultation' is not consultation at all but would instead fall under the heading of 'informing'. Informing and consulting are not the same thing!

If an employer conducts a sham exercise and merely pretends to consult in order to be seen to comply with the law, this is likely to lead to claims of unfair dismissal on the grounds of procedural irregularities from those eventually selected. Representatives must be provided with adequate information and given adequate time to respond. The employer, in turn, must give full and fair consideration to the representatives' response.

Information provided to the representatives should cover:

(a) the reasons for the proposals;

(b) the numbers and descriptions of employees who may be dismissed for redundancy;

(c) the total numbers of employees of the relevant descriptions employed at the establishment in question;

(d) the proposed method of selecting the employees who may be dismissed;

(e) the proposed method of carrying out the dismissals and the time period over which they will be carried out;

(f) the proposed method of calculating any redundancy payments which may be made over and above statutory redundancy pay.

The employer must provide this information in writing to the employees' representatives so that the representatives, in turn, are enabled to come forward with constructive proposals.

The nature of the consultation is laid down in law and must cover ways of:

(a) avoiding dismissals; and

(b) reducing the number of employees to be dismissed; and

(c) mitigating the consequences of the dismissals;

Furthermore the consultation must be undertaken with a view to reaching agreement with the representatives.

Protective Awards

A protective award is an amount of money awarded by an employment tribunal to an individual who has been adversely affected by their employer's failure to consult properly. A claim for a protective award can be made only by the employees' representatives and not by the employees themselves.

The amount of a protective award will depend on what the tribunal considers just and equitable in all the circumstances of the case, taking into account the number of days by which the consultation fell short of the statutory requirement and potentially including a penal element. The maximum payable (where the employer has failed to carry out any consultation at all) is in line with the consultation periods themselves, namely 90 days' pay where there have been 100 or more redundancies at one establishment or 30 days' pay where the number of redundancies is twenty or more (but fewer than 100). The time period over which the protective award is calculated is known as the protected period.

SELECTION PROCEDURES

During the process of consulting employee representatives about proposed redundancies, the employer must address the issue of the methods to be used to select individuals for redundancy. The first step is to identify the 'pool for selection' which will be the total group of employees from whom individuals will be selected. Unless there is an existing agreement or customary arrangement specifying a particular pool for selection, the employer will have considerable flexibility in determining what the pool should be. There is, however, an obligation on the employer to act reasonably and out of genuine motives. An employer would have to have an objective and justifiable reason, for example if they decided to exclude a particular group of employees from the selection pool, where those excluded performed the same or similar work to those who were nominated as part of the pool.

Case Study

The employer excluded a group of craftsmen from the pool for selection for redundancy. The craftsmen in question all had short service but were multi-skilled having recently been trained in the complete range of skills required by the company. The actual pool for selection which was identified by the employer was a pool of long-serving mechanical and electrical engineers. The selection criteria applied was that of 'last-in, first-out' (LIFO).

When challenged at tribunal, the tribunal judged that the multi-skilled craftsmen should have been included in the pool for selection, as they were able to undertake the same work as those in the selected pool. Because both groups did similar work, it was unreasonable of the employer to have excluded the group of craftsmen.

British Steel plc v. Robertson and Others [1994] E.A.T. 60/94.

Criteria for Selection

Having identified the pool for selection, the employer's next responsibility is to establish, in conjunction with the employee representatives, what criteria for selection will be applied and whether there will be only one criterion or several. In the event that a range of criteria are to be used, the employer must also determine how each will be weighted.

Whatever criteria are chosen, they must be objective and reasonable. Employers should take care to avoid criteria which:

(a) are subjective in the sense that they depend on the personal opinion of the manager doing the selection;

(b) cannot be backed up by data such as performance appraisal ratings, attendance records, documents showing length of service, etc;

(c) rely on only one manager's assessment of employees;

(d) are vague;

(e) cannot be applied reliably or reasonably;

(f) may have a disproportionately adverse impact on women (for example a policy to select part-timers for redundancy in preference to full-timers, in a company where the majority of the part-time workforce is female and the majority of the full-time workforce male);

(g) may have a disproportionately adverse effect on a minority racial group.

Examples of criteria which have been found unfair include:

(a) 'retention of employees who, in the manager's opinion, would keep the company viable' (ruled to be entirely subjective and unreasonable);

(b) 'to retain personnel best suited for the needs of the business under the new operating conditions' (judged to be unfair because the criteria were subjective and no records were referred to in making the selections);

(c) 'cost savings – sales people who generated least business and cost most in terms of overheads' (held to be unfair on the grounds of lack of objectivity and because of the employer's failure to conduct any real appraisal of the relevant employees).

Common criteria for selection may include one or more of the following.

1. **Length of service (last-in, first-out or LIFO).** This method of selection is easy to apply objectively, and used to be the most common method practised. Its popularity has declined in recent years, mainly because it gives employers no flexibility to retain those with the most suitable skills for the needs of the business. However, it can still provide a useful element

within a list of criteria and is often used as a last-stop, i.e. if all other factors are equal, length of service will be the determining factor.

2. **Capability and skill in performing the job.** It makes sense for employers to adopt an approach which will enable them to retain those employees who possess the skills and knowledge perceived as being in line with the future aims of the company. It is important, however, that these skills and knowledge are clearly defined and that they can be assessed objectively, rather than their assessment being left to the whims and notions of a particular manager.

3. **Job performance/results.** If an employee is selected for redundancy on the grounds of inadequate job performance, and the evidence is that the poor performance has not previously been drawn to the person's attention or recorded in an appraisal report, the employer would have great difficulty in convincing an employment tribunal of the objectivity of the selection. Matters would be even worse if the employer, having dismissed the employee, had provided a written reference to a prospective employer stating that the person was capable and competent in the job!

4. **Qualifications and training.** These criteria have the advantage of being capable of objective definition but may not necessarily be important to the company.

5. **Experience in particular type of work.** This is usually linked to length of service but where an employee has recently moved to a different area of work, this criterion may have an unfair adverse impact on that person.

6. **Flexibility/adaptability.** This criterion can cause difficulties for an employer because it risks being subjective. Consideration should be given as to how employees' flexibility can be measured and whether any records exist to back up managers' views on the matter.

7. **Attitude to work.** Attitude is notoriously difficult to define or prove. One tribunal judged that 'attitude to work' as a criterion for selection for redundancy was 'dangerously ambiguous' (*Graham v. ABF Ltd* [1986] I.R.L.R. 90).

8. **Disciplinary record.** Provided records are available, it would be legitimate to use them as part of the criteria for selection for redundancy. The overall test of reasonableness would, however, still have to be applied, which would effectively mean that a disciplinary warning relating to an incident many years earlier should not be included.

9. **Attendance records.** If using this criterion, the employer should exclude any absences on pregnancy-related conditions or maternity leave from their calculations, because this would be deemed to be discriminatory against the employee on the grounds of sex. Care should also be taken to

consider whether an employee's absences are due to a disability as defined in the Disability Discrimination Act, in which case selection on this basis could be discriminatory against that person.

The employer may opt to use several criteria and use a points system whereby the various factors are weighted and points allocated against each criterion to each employee. The points are then added up and those with the lowest scores are selected for redundancy. This can provide a structured method of redundancy selection.

It is automatically unfair in law for an employer to select employees for redundancy for any of the reasons listed below. Additionally, in these cases, an employee who is made redundant may bring a claim for unfair dismissal to tribunal irrespective of their length of service.

1. Pregnancy or maternity leave.

2. Trade union membership or non-union membership.

3. Carrying out health and safety activities.

4. Fulfilling the duties of an employee representative, or standing as a candidate as an employee representative (for collective redundancy consultation or consultation connected with the transfer of an undertaking).

5. Refusal of a shop or betting worker to work on a Sunday.

6. Fulfilling the duties as a pension scheme trustee.

7. Asserting a statutory right.

Additionally, redundancy selection which is connected with the individual's sex, marital status, race, ethnic origin or disability would be discriminatory and would, in all likelihood, render the redundancy dismissal unfair.

As well as ensuring that the criteria for selection for redundancy are objective and reasonable, they must be applied reasonably, fairly and consistently. It could happen that the criteria themselves are reasonable but the method of applying them unfair or inconsistent. There is little point in establishing criteria and then applying inconsistent methods of selection in practice, as digressing from the agreed criteria would render the dismissals of those affected unfair and discrepant application would have a similar effect. Equally, if there is evidence that a manager has applied a particular criterion unfairly to an individual, for example by allocating low marks for attendance to an employee who in fact had a good attendance record, then this too would render a redundancy dismissal unfair.

Individual Consultation

Although there is presently no statutory obligation to consult where fewer than twenty employees are to be made redundant, this does not afford employers the option to completely ignore the issue of consultation when only a handful of redundancies is proposed. There is still an obligation, as with all forms of dismissal, to act fairly and reasonably and a failure to consult individuals is likely to render an eventual dismissal unfair on procedural grounds.

Case Study

The employer wished, due to a need to reduce overheads, to make four delivery van drivers' jobs redundant and replace them with two van salespersons. Only one of the existing drivers was considered suitable for the new job. The other three were called into the office, told they were redundant and immediately driven home. One of the employees claimed unfair dismissal on the basis that there had been no consultation, warning or opportunity for him to be considered for alternative employment.

The case reached the House of Lords, which ruled that the lack of procedure, as regards the manner of carrying out the dismissals, made the redundancies unfair. This principle would apply except in extreme cases where consultation would clearly be utterly futile.

Polkey v. A E Dayton Services Ltd [1988] I.C.R. 142.

The *Polkey* case was very important because it firmly established the precedent that any flaw in the procedure used to carry out a redundancy would render the dismissal unfair. Furthermore, this principle applies to all forms of dismissal and not only redundancies.

Apart from the desire to avoid unfair dismissals, there are three key reasons why it is important to consult people individually about forthcoming redundancies.

1. To afford the employee the chance to put forward representations as to why the company should not select them for redundancy.

2. To allow the employee the opportunity to put forward any factors which may have adversely affected job performance, conduct or attendance at work, where these are being used as criteria for selection for redundancy. For example an employee may have been bullied by a colleague, thus causing poor work output or poor attendance may have been due to temporary family problems. The manager responsible for redundancy selection should take any such mitigating factors into account before making final selections.

3. To create the opportunity to discuss with the employee any alternative vacancies which may exist within the organisation (see the section 'Employees' Right to be Offered Suitable Alternative Employment', below.

> ### Case Study
>
> The employer had sent out a memorandum to all employees informing them that redundancies would have to be made, and setting out the criteria for selection. Subsequently, an employee received a letter from her employer informing her that she had been selected for redundancy and inviting her to come forward to discuss any matters arising from the letter. Following the termination of her employment, the employee claimed unfair dismissal.
>
> The EAT held that the letter did not amount to consultation with the employee and this absence of consultation constituted a key procedural flaw. Thus the employee succeeded in her claim.
>
> *Rowell v. Hubbard Group Services Ltd* [1995] I.R.L.R. 195.

In an earlier redundancy case (*R v. British Coal Corporation and Secretary of State for Trade and Industry ex parte Price and Others* [1994] I.R.L.R. 72), the judgment included guidance on consultation as follows:

> [Consultation] involves giving the body consulted a fair and proper opportunity to understand fully the matters about which it is being consulted and to express its views on those subjects, with the consultor thereafter considering those views properly and genuinely.

Although this statement was made in the context of collective redundancies, the principle is equally relevant to the need to consult individuals about forthcoming redundancies.

Where employees are selected for redundancy by means of a points system, i.e. having points allocated to them against a range of criteria, the manager who has allocated the points should be prepared to reveal the employee's 'score' directly to them and to discuss the reasons for it in advance of selections being finalised. The employee has no right to see other employees' scores, but a failure to explain to an individual the reasoning behind their selection could in theory render the whole process open to corruption and render the dismissal unfair.

Bumping

An employer may wish to adopt a policy of 'bumping' in a redundancy exercise. Bumping occurs where job A is redundant but instead of selecting employee A for redundancy, the employer moves employee A to job B with the result that employee B is made redundant. Thus, bumping is a kind of transferred redundancy which occurs when the employer has elected to apply the redundancy selection criteria to a wider pool of employees than the group in which the need for redundancies has arisen.

Provided the employer has in the first instance clearly identified their policy and approach towards redundancy, and identified a pool for selection which is fair, a policy of bumping is not unlawful. Its reasonableness depends, of course, just as much on the manner in which it is put into practice, and, if required to defend a case of unfair dismissal following a bumped redundancy dismissal, the employer would need to be able to show that they had acted objectively, fairly and reasonably in making their selections.

The problem with bumping is that it can be argued that redundancy is not the true reason for dismissal. Because redundancy occurs where the need for work of a particular kind has ceased or diminished, this is inconsistent with the notion of another employee being drafted in to perform the 'redundant' employee's job. In particular, managers who are contemplating bumped redundancies should carefully examine their own motives against the stated selection criteria. If a redundancy dismissal is challenged at a tribunal, the tribunal will scrutinise the real reason for dismissing an employee whose job continued after the dismissal. If, for example, the employee was selected for a bumped redundancy on the grounds of poor job performance, the tribunal may rule that the true reason for dismissal was poor job performance and not redundancy. This would have two implications:

(a) that the employee would have no entitlement to a statutory redundancy payment, although the employer may still opt to award an ex gratia payment on termination;

(b) the employer may lose a case of unfair dismissal on the basis of their failure to establish a fair reason for the dismissal.

If, therefore, a dismissed employee brings a case to tribunal in these circumstances, it is a wise precaution for the employer to 'plead in the alternative', i.e. provide more than one reason for dismissal when setting out the defence.

EMPLOYEES' RIGHT TO BE OFFERED SUITABLE ALTERNATIVE EMPLOYMENT

Once redundancy selection has been carried out and notice of termination given, managers should make genuine efforts to establish whether any suitable alternative employment exists within the organisation for those selected.

Employers should not only consider vacancies within their own company, but should also look to see whether there may be suitable vacancies in any associated companies. There is no obligation, however, to create a job for an otherwise redundant employee. If a suitable vacancy exists it should be offered to the redundant employee before their period of notice expires and the new job must start either immediately or else within four weeks of the original job terminating. If alternative employment is offered and accepted in this way, the individual is not entitled to a statutory redundancy payment.

Failure to offer alternative employment, where it exists, would convert an otherwise fair redundancy into an unfair dismissal. The onus is on the employer to take positive steps to identify any alternative vacancies, rather than expecting the employee to go on a hunting expedition to seek them out.

When is Alternative Employment Suitable?

An offer of alternative employment, in the context of redundancy, means work which the employee can reasonably be expected to do in relation to their level of seniority and skills and which is on terms and conditions not substantially less favourable than the previous job.

In assessing whether or not a particular offer of alternative employment was suitable, employment tribunals would consider a range of possible factors such as:

(a) level of pay;

(b) the working hours or shift pattern if these were different from the employee's original hours;

(c) any reduction in responsibility or status;

(d) the location of the new job;

(e) the working environment.

If in doubt about whether a job is suitable for a particular employee, the manager should consult the employee in question in order to put the opportunity to them and seek their views. In many cases, the employee can judge better than the manager whether the job is suitable for them in all the circumstances.

Even if an alternative job offer is on terms which are less favourable than the previous job, e.g. a lower rate of pay, an employee whose job is redundant may prefer this option to unemployment. It follows that the manager should not make the decision as to whether an alternative post is suitable for a particular employee on an arbitrary basis, as to do so could lead to claims of unfair treatment. Instead the manager should discuss the option directly with the employee.

The employee's personal circumstances will, inevitably, have an effect on their perception as to whether or not a particular job is suitable. For example, if an alternative position is located at a different workplace from the employee's original job, its suitability from the employee's point of view would depend on where the employee lived in relation to the new workplace (compared to the distance between their home and the old workplace). If hours of work are different, one employee's family responsibilities may preclude them from accepting the new job, whereas another employee may find the new hours suitable.

If, however, an alternative offer is clearly suitable – i.e. there is no marked difference between the original job and the new job in the terms and conditions or level of work – then an employee who refuses the offer will lose their right to a redundancy payment. However, they will retain the right to claim unfair dismissal subject to having a minimum of two years' continuous service.

If, on the other hand, the alternative employment is unsuitable, or where the employee's refusal of it is reasonable under all the circumstances, then the employee will retain their right to a statutory redundancy payment.

Trial Period in the New Job

Where the employee has been offered, and has accepted, an alternative job which differs from their old job, they have the automatic right in law to a 4-week trial period. This would be the case unless the differences between the original job and the new job were trivial or insignificant. The purpose of the trial period is for both parties to assess whether or not the job is in reality suitable for the employee. Such trial periods are mandatory unless the new job is on the same contractual terms (barring trivial differences) to the old.

If the job turns out to be suitable for the employee, there is no obligation on the employer to make a redundancy payment. Rather curiously, however, although there is no right to redundancy pay in these circumstances, the employee retains the right to claim unfair dismissal on account of the original job being terminated. This is because the unfair dismissal provisions are separate from the statutory provisions governing redundancy payments.

If during or at the end of the trial period, either the employer or the employee concludes that the job is not in fact a suitable alternative, the position reverts back to that of redundancy. The termination date in these circumstances is the date on which the original job ended rather than the date of expiry of the trial period and the reason for termination is still redundancy. Unless the employee acted unreasonably in deciding that the job was unsuitable, they would retain their right to a redundancy payment.

A trial period can be for a longer period than four weeks where there is a need for extensive retraining of the employee. In this case, the agreement for the extended trial period must be in writing and must specify its duration.

There is no reason why there cannot be more than one trial period and any number of trial periods in different jobs may, in theory, be put in place. If, despite these efforts, all the alternative posts prove unsuitable for the employee, the person is still deemed to have been dismissed on account of redundancy on the date their original contract came to an end.

TIME OFF FOR REDUNDANT EMPLOYEES
TO SEEK NEW WORK

There is a provision in the Employment Rights Act 1996 which entitles employees, who are under notice of redundancy, to take reasonable time off work to look for new employment or to make arrangements for training. Technically this right is available only to employees who have two or more years' continuous service, however, managers may feel it is appropriate to grant all employees under notice of redundancy this concession.

Where the employee has two or more years' service, the time off must be paid. No guidance is available in law as to how much time off is 'reasonable', but there is a provision in law that that the maximum amount of pay which the employee is entitled to receive for time off in this context is 40 per cent of one week's pay (i.e. two days' pay). This provision does not mean that further time off should not be granted but rather that, when it is granted, the employer is not obliged to continue to pay the employee.

The purposes for which employees should be granted time off include a wide range of reasons:

(a) attendance at a job interview;

(b) visit to a job centre;

(c) participation in a job club;

(d) arrangements for CV writing;

(e) visiting a college or other institution with a view to making arrangements for training;

(f) travel time for any of the above purposes.

If an employer unreasonably refuses to allow the employee time off for any of these purposes, or refuses to pay the employee for time off taken (up to two days), the employee may complain to an employment tribunal, which may award compensation of up to a maximum of two days' pay.

REDUNDANCY PAY

When an employee's job becomes redundant, the employer is obliged to pay statutory redundancy pay, which is calculated according to a fixed formula. Over and above statutory redundancy pay, employers may wish to make an ex gratia termination payment which they are free to do if they wish.

Eligibility for Statutory Redundancy Pay

Redundant employees are entitled to be paid statutory redundancy pay provided they have a minimum of two years' continuous service and are over the age of eighteen. Both full-time and part-time employees have this right. Furthermore, as mentioned earlier, volunteers for redundancy have the same statutory entitlement to redundancy pay as those selected by the employer.

Certain categories of people are ineligible for redundancy pay, including the following:

(a) employees working outside the UK (including those working in the Republic of Ireland). Additionally, if an employee has spent time working for the employer overseas, this time does not count for the purposes of adding up the number of years' qualifying service for redundancy pay purposes;

(b) employees who are over the company's normal retirement age or, if no normal retirement age exists, aged 65 or over;

(c) people employed on a fixed-term contract for two years or more which expires without renewal, where the contract contains a valid waiver clause in respect of statutory redundancy pay (see 'Fixed-term Contracts', Chapter 1);

(d) apprentices whose service comes to an end as a result of their apprenticeship contract expiring (whether or not the employer offers permanent employment afterwards).

Other exclusions are domestic servants, share fishermen/women and certain Crown servants.

Calculating Statutory Redundancy Pay

The formula for statutory redundancy payments is based on three factors; the employee's:

(a) age;

(b) length of continuous service;

(c) weekly earnings.

For the purposes of calculating redundancy pay, there is a ceiling on a 'week's pay' which is currently set at £220 per week. There is also an overall ceiling of £6,600. These amounts are reviewed by the government from time to time.

The formula for calculating statutory redundancy pay looks like this.

Employee's length of service (only complete years count)	Amount of payment for each year of completed service
Years of service between ages 18 and 21 inclusive	½ week's pay
Years of service between ages 22 and 40 inclusive	1 week's pay
Years of service over age 41, up to age 64 inclusive	1½ week's pay

Where an employee has reached the age of 64, their entitlement to statutory redundancy pay is reduced by one-twelfth in respect of each month they have remained in employment after that age. This has the effect that redundancy payments are scaled down to zero during the year the employee is approaching the age of 65. Statutory redundancy payments are paid gross and are tax free.

Employers are obliged to give redundant employees a written statement of how their payment is calculated.

Ex gratia Payments

Employers who wish to give redundant employees a financial settlement in excess of the amount required under statute may do so and this will not be subject to income tax provided the amount paid (including statutory redundancy pay) does not exceed £30,000 – and provided it is genuinely an ex gratia payment and not a sum due to the employee under the terms of their contract of employment.

Sums paid in excess of £30,000 are taxable at the normal rates, as are payments made in accordance with a term in the employee's contract of employment.

The employer should provide employees with clear information in writing covering the breakdown of their final payment, i.e. what amounts are attributable to normal wages, outstanding holiday pay, notice pay, statutory redundancy pay and any ex gratia payment.

CONCLUSION

Having gained a fundamental understanding of the key areas of employment law, the application of its key principles is largely a matter of plain common sense. If managers treat their employees in a fair and reasonable fashion in matters such as honouring contractual terms, allowing flexibility in working hours, monitoring sickness absence in a consistent way, giving access to equal opportunities, taking a positive attitude towards maternity and parental rights and handling discipline fairly, then they are less likely to be hit by claims to employment tribunals.

Fair and reasonable treatment of employees produces the additional benefits of improved morale, motivation and enhanced team spirit amongst workers. Conversely those who are forced into unwelcome changes to their contractual terms, coerced into working long hours, discriminated against, threatened with dismissal or in any way penalised for asserting their statutory rights, will hardly feel encouraged or empowered to perform their job to the best of their ability. Nor will such treatment enhance loyalty, working relationships or individual and overall productivity.

Employment law makes sense. Use it wisely and apply it consistently and fairly in order to get the best out of the company's most important asset – its workers.

INDEX

Blackhall Guide to Health and Safety in the UK

Jeremy Stranks

The last decade has seen considerable development in the field of occupational safety, health and welfare in the UK. There has also been a large amount of EC law in this area, which has to be implemented, and employers who fail to comply with the law face severe penalties.

The Safety, Health and Welfare at Work Regulations in 1993 brought in a new management-oriented approach to health and safety at work, placing the onus of ensuring compliance firmly on the management. As a result, all companies are now having to think about establishing effective health and safety procedures, and are, therefore, in need of guidance on how to go about it.

This book, written specifically for British companies by health and safety law expert Jeremy Stranks, considers both the legal aspects of health and safety at work, and also provides a blue-print for best practice in the area. It is written in clear, accessible language, and points made are backed up by examples and checklists. It will be of immense benefit to all companies who want to negotiate their way round this potentially hazardous minefield.

The author:
JEREMY STRANKS is a leading authority on health and safety at work, having written and lectured extensively on the subject. His recent books include *One Stop Health and Safety* (ICSA Publishing) and *A Manager's Guide to Health and Safety* (5th edn, Kogan Page).

180 pages
1-901657-40-X pbk: £13.99, 1998

Blackhall Guide to Applied Recruitment and Selection
Aidan Coakley

We often hear recruiters and employers confessing to being horrified at the prospect of having to recruit an employee for their organisation at an interview.

Applied Recruitment and Selection puts forward a series of globally applicable guidelines that can be tailored to suit the reader's own organisational needs. The book looks at the whole recruitment process as being a continuous series of interacting events, which will form a continuity of impressions leading to a more effective recruitment decision. It suggests that an interview should be looked on as a means of "discovery", from which both interviewer and interviewee can learn valuable lessons.

The book is packed with practical examples and case studies, and is written in a no-nonsense, accessible style. Areas covered include:

- the job and job environment analysis;
- establishing selection criteria;
- advertising and candidate selection;
- styles and types of interview;
- candidate evaluation;
- psychological and psychometric tests;
- remuneration;
- elementary induction;
- the barriers to effective recruitment.

The author:
AIDAN COAKLEY is an experienced recruitment consultant, based in Cork.

The above books can be purchased at any good bookshop or direct from:
BLACKHALL PUBLISHING
26 Eustace Street
Dublin 2.
Telephone: +44 (0)1-677-3242; Fax: +44 (0)1-677-3243;
e-mail: blackhall@tinet.ie